60 03

D1577346

DATE DUE FOR RETURN

UNIVERSITY LIBRARY

2 JUN 2006

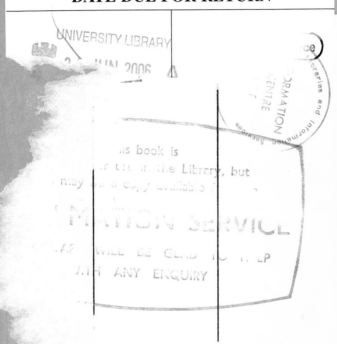

his book is
for use in the Library, but
may be a copy available

FORMATION SERVICE

WILL BE GLAD TO HELP

WITH ANY ENQUIRY

THE INDUSTRIAL ARCHAEOLOGY OF THE BRITISH ISLES
General Editor : Keith Falconer

Leicestershire Libraries and
INFORMATION CENTRE
CST

The Industrial Archaeology of Scotland

1   The Lowlands and Borders

1 Water-bucket pumping engine, Wanlockhead (see p. 105).

The Industrial Archaeology of Scotland

1 The Lowlands and Borders

JOHN R. HUME

B.T. Batsford Ltd · *London*

FOR MY WIFE

First published 1976
© John R. Hume, 1976

ISBN 0 7134 3234 9

Filmset by Servis Filmsetting Ltd, Manchester
Printed in Great Britain by
Butler & Tanner Ltd, Frome, Somerset
for the publishers
B.T. Batsford Ltd
4 Fitzhardinge Street, London W1H 0AH

6003723281

609.411 -7 JUL 1978 129

LEICESTERSHIRE LIBRARIES
AND INFORMATION SERVICE

DO NOT NOTIFY STSS

Contents

The illustrations

Preface

The gazetteer is arranged by county, subdivided into parishes, with further subdivision, where appropriate. Though the administrative areas are now regions and districts, these tend to be insufficiently precise for the location of sites in rural areas. This arrangement also allows direct and easy reference to the Statistical Accounts of Scotland (first published in the 1790s, second in the 1830s and '40s, and third in the 1940s and '50s) which are the best approximation the country has to a standard range of county reference books.

The illustrations have been chosen with an eye both to the typical and to the outstanding, and are intended to be representative of the industries of the counties to which they refer.

In compiling this gazetteer the author has inevitably been faced by problems of selection and compression. The aim has been to list as many sites as reasonably possible so as to encourage detailed study of their rapidly dwindling number. Throughout, the emphasis has been on sites where there are complete or substantial remains: many interesting locations have thus been omitted. Sites have been included largely on the basis of personal observation, though a few of the more remote have been mentioned when there is reliable information that they are extant. Observations have been made over a long period, but only sites known to have been in existence after 1971 have been included. Every effort has been made to keep pace with demolitions and alterations, but inevitably by the time the book is published some material will have disappeared. The author will be most grateful for further information on any of the sites mentioned – it must be stressed that the gazetteer is an outline guide only, and the inclusion of a site does not imply that it has been fully recorded.

One final point: many of the sites listed are not normally open to the public, and some are in the grounds or gardens of private houses. A courteous enquiry will usually result in permission to view but 'barging in' will result in hostility to you – and to others who come after you.

Acknowledgements

It would indeed be difficult to compile a gazetteer of this nature without assistance, and though the author has visited the great majority of the sites listed, he is greatly indebted to many people whose work he has used as a guide, and who have passed on information freely. David Walker, Frank Worsdall, Michael Moss, John Butt, David Sinclair and Ian Donnachie have been particularly helpful and the following present and former undergraduate and postgraduate students in the Department of History, University of Strathclyde working under John Butt and myself have provided information: Sinclair Calder, Donald Clark, Eamon Hyde, Doreen Lamont, Alison Nawrocka, Walter Stephen and Chris Whatley. The following have also helped: Sylvia Clark, Leslie Fraser, Graham Gilmour, William Harvey, Colin Johnston, Bruce Lenman, William Lind, Charlotte Lythe, Daniel Mackay, Kenneth Mackay, William Mackie, Dorothy Marshall, David Masterton, William Nimmo, Trevor Rees, John Robertson, Basil Skinner, Alan Stoyel, John Strawthorn, Thomas Welsh and James Wood, members of undergraduate and extra-mural classes, of the Scottish Society for Industrial Archaeology, and the Scottish Society for the Preservation of Historical Machinery. The author is also most grateful to the many farmers, industrialists and others who have given permission for photography on their premises, and to British Railways, the National Coal Board and the Board of Northern Lighthouses for information.

Debts of a different kind are owed to the University of Strathclyde, and to Professor S.G.E. Lythe in particular, for their support, financial and moral, of the field work on which the gazetteer is based. The Carnegie Trust for the Universities of Scotland most generously gave grants for photography and travel. Miss Elizabeth Clements, Mrs Ishbel Sheridan, and Miss Catherine Summerhill typed the manuscript. John Shaw Dunn kindly read the manuscript before typing, and made other helpful comments. Lastly, and by no means conventionally, the author is grateful for support from his wife throughout the preparation of this book, especially in the last stages, when he became more than usually disorganized.

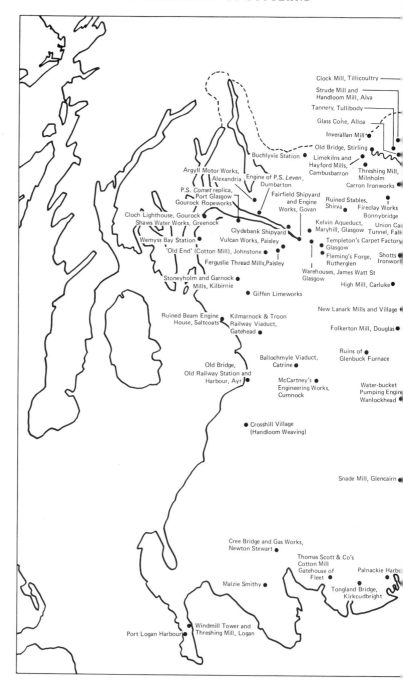

Clock Mill, Tillicoultry
Strude Mill and Handloom Mill, Alva
Tannery, Tullibody
Glass Cone, Alloa
Inverallan Mill
Old Bridge, Stirling
Buchlyvie Station
Limekilns and Hayford Mills, Cambusbarron
Threshing Mill, Milnholm
Carron Ironworks
Argyll Motor Works, Alexandria
Engine of P.S. Leven, Dumbarton
P.S. Comet replica, Port Glasgow
Gourock Ropeworks
Fairfield Shipyard and Engine Works, Govan
Ruined Stables, Shirva
Fireclay Works, Bonnybridge
Cloch Lighthouse, Gourock
Shaws Water Works, Greenock
Kelvin Aqueduct, Maryhill, Glasgow
Union Canal Tunnel, Fall
Clydebank Shipyard
Wemyss Bay Station
Vulcan Works, Paisley
Templeton's Carpet Factory, Glasgow
'Old End' (Cotton Mill), Johnstone
Fleming's Forge, Rutherglen
Shotts Ironworks
Ferguslie Thread Mills, Paisley
Warehouses, James Watt St Glasgow
Stoneyholm and Garnock Mills, Kilbirnie
High Mill, Carluke
Giffen Limeworks
New Lanark Mills and Village
Ruined Beam Engine House, Saltcoats
Kilmarnock & Troon Railway Viaduct, Gatehead
Folkerton Mill, Douglas
Ballochmyle Viaduct, Catrine
Ruins of Glenbuck Furnace
Old Bridge, Old Railway Station and Harbour, Ayr
McCartney's Engineering Works, Cumnock
Water-bucket Pumping Engine Wanlockhead
Crosshill Village (Handloom Weaving)
Snade Mill, Glencairn
Cree Bridge and Gas Works, Newton Stewart
Thomas Scott & Co's Cotton Mill Gatehouse of Fleet
Palnackie Harbour
Malzie Smithy
Tongland Bridge, Kirkcudbright
Windmill Tower and Threshing Mill, Logan
Port Logan Harbour

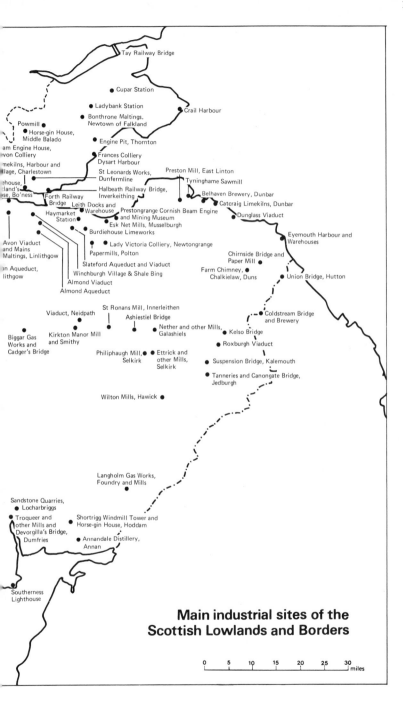

Tay Railway Bridge

Cupar Station

Ladybank Station

Bonthrone Maltings, Newtown of Falkland

Crail Harbour

Powmill

Horse-gin House, Middle Balado

am Engine House, von Colliery

Engine Pit, Thornton

Frances Colliery Dysart Harbour

mekilns, Harbour and lage, Charlestown

St Leonards Works, Dunfermline

Preston Mill, East Linton

house, land's se, Bo'ness

Halbeath Railway Bridge, Inverkeithing

Tyninghame Sawmill

Belhaven Brewery, Dunbar

Forth Railway Bridge

Leith Docks and Warehouse

Catcraig Limekilns, Dunbar

Haymarket Station

Prestongrange Cornish Beam Engine and Mining Museum

Dunglass Viaduct

Esk Net Mills, Musselburgh

Burdiehouse Limeworks

Eyemouth Harbour and Warehouses

Avon Viaduct and Mains Maltings, Linlithgow

Lady Victoria Colliery, Newtongrange

Papermills, Polton

Chirnside Bridge and Paper Mill

n Aqueduct, lithgow

Slateford Aqueduct and Viaduct

Farm Chimney, Chalkielaw, Duns

Winchburgh Village & Shale Bing

Union Bridge, Hutton

Almond Viaduct

Almond Aqueduct

St Ronans Mill, Innerleithen

Viaduct, Neidpath

Ashiestiel Bridge

Coldstream Bridge and Brewery

Biggar Gas Works and Cadger's Bridge

Kirkton Manor Mill and Smithy

Nether and other Mills, Galashiels

Kelso Bridge

Roxburgh Viaduct

Philiphaugh Mill, Selkirk

Ettrick and other Mills, Selkirk

Suspension Bridge, Kalemouth

Tanneries and Canongate Bridge, Jedburgh

Wilton Mills, Hawick

Langholm Gas Works, Foundry and Mills

Sandstone Quarries, Locharbriggs

Troqueer and other Mills and Devorgilla's Bridge, Dumfries

Shortrigg Windmill Tower and Horse-gin House, Hoddam

Annandale Distillery, Annan

Southerness Lighthouse

Main industrial sites of the Scottish Lowlands and Borders

0   5   10   15   20   25   30 miles

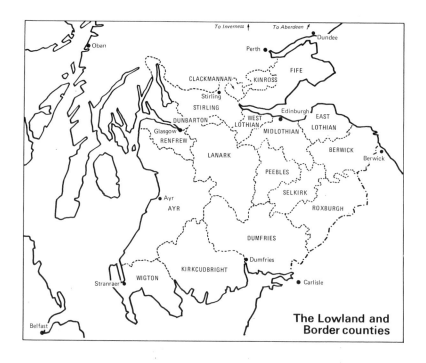

The Lowland and
Border counties

Introduction

The Lowlands of Scotland and the Border counties have an unusually varied industrial history. All manner of textiles, pottery, glass, a wide range of chemicals, heavy and light engineering products, coal, iron, copper, lead, lime, beer, whisky, flour, oatmeal and a host of other items flowed from the mills, mines and workshops of this area. Not only had the west of Scotland a good claim to be the 'workshop of the British Empire', but the woollen and hosiery areas of Stirlingshire, Clackmannanshire and the Borders became renowned all over the world for high-quality produce. Even before the Industrial Revolution, there were well-developed trade routes, and many small-scale mining, manufacturing and processing units.

From about 1760 onwards, as the pace of industrialization increased in Britain, Lowland Scotland, with its rich resources of ironstone and coal, developed rapidly, and in certain industries, such as cotton spinning and iron smelting, assumed an importance out of proportion to its size. This expansion was, as elsewhere, accompanied by agricultural improvement and by concentration of industry in towns. The coming of the railways opened up new areas for industrial activity and allowed towns hitherto handicapped by the high cost of fuel such as the Border woollen towns, to develop large-scale manufacturing enterprizes.

In the later nineteenth century some of the industries went into relative decline, but their place was taken by continued expansion of existing specializations, and by the introduction of new products, such as sewing machines, bicycles, motor cars and steel roofs and frames for buildings. Expansion and contraction were not, of course, continuous processes: the periodic booms and slumps with which we are familiar were even more pronounced in Victorian times, and they conditioned the attitudes of manufacturers to investment in new factories. One consequence was the adaptive re-use of suitable old buildings for new machinery and new processes, which has resulted in the survival of many of the buildings included in this gazetteer.

Though in some respects the industrial buildings and machinery of the region are part of the greater British, or even of the European cultural heritage, Scottish traditions of vernacular building adapted in many instances to early industrial buildings are distinctive, and many of the generalizations applicable to England do not apply to Scotland. For example the 'weaver's window' of the handloom worker's cottage in England is virtually unknown in Scotland, where weavers' cottages were much simpler and smaller (see plate 5). It therefore seems appropriate in this introduction to draw together some of the more important groups of sites mentioned in the gazetteer, rather than to explore the economic and social changes which had their physical expressions in them.

GRAIN MILLS

Perhaps the most numerous processing plants in Scotland – even today when their function is being steadily concentrated in a few large factories – by far the greatest number were small water-powered units, and produced oatmeal for men and beasts. Oatmeal milling also became to some extent centralized in large mills, usually urban, and a few water-powered examples survive, or have only recently gone out of use, such as Saucel Mills, Paisley, and Edington Mill,

2   Folkerton Mill, Douglas, Lanarkshire (see p. 162). A typical, though unusually complete, small lowland meal mill.

Berwickshire. Changing animal-feeding practices have led to the use of ground imported peas and maize in 'compound feeding stuffs' and most of the surviving country mills – Dripps Mill, Lanarkshire is an example – make such products. Water-powered flour mills, confined to wheat-growing or importing areas, were usually larger than meal mills, and succumbed to competition from roller mills from the 1870s and 1880's onwards. The roller mills were all in large towns and were until the early years of this century, normally steam-powered, sometimes with an ancillary water turbine. Related in technique were the making of pease meal for human consumption – which involved roasting peas in a heated pan (girdle) with mechanical stirring – and the preparation of pot barley by removing the husk from the grain using an edge-runner type of mill. All the older Scottish mills are rubble-built, usually with ashlar in the area of the wheel, and have layouts varying from simple rectangles to Ls (perhaps most commonly), Ts, Us and Xs. The majority are two storey and attic or three storey in height, with the gear cupboard and discharge chutes on the ground floor, stones on the first floor, and hoppers in the third floor or attic. The proportion of available space occupied by the machinery is usually small. Oatmeal mills have, or had, kilns, which in the main consist of brick or stone funnels, expanding upward, in which a coke fire at the base produced a large volume of warm air. The grain to be dried (or roasted) was spread on cast-iron perforated plates or on woven-wire grids, supported by iron bars. The moist air escaped through a ventilator. Ventilator design exhibited marked regional variations. The pyramidal roof with terminal ventilator was more common in the east of Scotland. In the south west, kilns usually had unobtrusive roof-ridge ventilators, as, for example, at Glencairn Mill, Kilmarnock, Ayrshire.

The commonest layout of mill gearing had an upright shaft carrying a bevel wheel, meshing with a comparable one on the wheel axle (pit wheel), and a large spur wheel. Drive to the stones was from pinions, meshing with the spur wheel, which could be put into and out of gear by a screw jack. The 'normal' mill had three pairs of stones, but many smaller mills had two pairs, and a few only one. In the mid nineteenth century, the main upright drive shaft was in some instances replaced by a horizontal shaft, geared to the wheel axle, carrying a series of bevel gears. Each pair of stones had its own drive. This arrangement gives a row of stones instead of a cluster, with more working space, but is relatively uncommon (Motherwell Mill, Lanarkshire). Apart from the stones drive, power was normally supplied to a sack hoist, which could be controlled from each floor by a friction clutch, and in many cases a power take-off was provided for seed dressing, threshing or some other purpose. Another variant was the use of belt drive from the main shaft to the stones, found in, for example, Pretts Mill, Sandilands, Lanarkshire.

Waterwheels vary widely in type and construction. The only all-wooden wheels (except for axle) known to the author are in Lindean Mill, near Selkirk, but a common type has wooden spokes, with iron axle and rings, and wooden buckets. A few wheels, like that at Carnwath Mill, Lanarkshire, have wooden axles. The type of wheel employed depends to a large extent on geographical considerations – the low-breast paddle wheel, for example, is, or was, common on the slow-flowing rivers of south-west Scotland (see plate 27). Surprisingly, however, this type is also found in the north east in situations where there is a sufficient head of water for an overshot or high-breast wheel. In these cases a wood or stone chute is provided to convert the potential energy of the water into kinetic energy before it hits the paddles. Some of these 'start and awe' wheels have only a single cast-iron ring; an isolated southern example of the type is at Southdean Mill, Roxburghshire. The great majority of wheels are between 10ft and 16ft (3·95 and 4·88m) in diameter, and between 2ft and 5ft (0·61 and 1·52m) in width. Though most are straightforward in design there are a few wheels of the suspended type, with tension spokes. Turbines are relatively rare; the few that do exist are mainly of the Francis type (but see plate 65).

Windmills were relatively uncommon in Scotland and none now have sails. Donnachie and Stewart listed the sites known in 1964, and a handful more have since been identified mainly in the north and east (see volume 2). The majority of mills appear to have been of the tower variety, with the peculiar 'vaulted-tower' type a Scottish variant (see plate 70). They were not all grain mills, as some drove pumps, threshing machines, or even, in one case, a cider press (Cannee, Kirkcudbrightshire).

Steam was used as an auxiliary source of power in both wind and water mills. At High Mill, Carluke (a windmill), the condenser and some shafting for a mid nineteenth-century engine can be seen, but elsewhere all plant has been scrapped. The largest steam-powered mills were the late nineteenth-century roller flour mills such as Regent and Scotstoun Mills, Glasgow, and Leith Flour Mills, Edinburgh, though their predecessors, with numerous pairs of grindstones, could also be sizeable – Kingston Mills, Glasgow, for example. Oil engines were also used to drive some small mills, usually as an aid to water power.

Other substantial grain-using industries in Scotland are brewing and distilling. As in England, domestic brewing began to decline in the seventeenth century, and by the end of the eighteenth century, most towns had their own breweries. Few of these were operating by the end of the nineteenth century, and now only two small town breweries survive – in Dunbar, East Lothian, and in Alloa, Clackmannanshire. Alloa, Edinburgh and Glasgow are now the centres of the industry. It is difficult to generalize about the construction and layout of Scottish breweries, but most seem to have been built round a courtyard, with a three- or four-storey brewhouse, normally with louvred ventilators on the upper floor, where the coolers were housed; frequently there is a range of maltings, with kiln; and stables and offices. As town-centre breweries grew in scale, so malting was in many instances removed to other sites, as in Edinburgh and Alloa. Good examples of early, mid and late nineteenth-century breweries are Belhaven, Dunbar (plate 3); Argyle, St Andrews; and Thistle, Alloa.

3   The Belhaven Brewery, Dunbar, East Lothian (see p. 116). The malting kilns here are unusually fine. The small scale of the brewery hints at its early date.

Distilling has much in common with brewing as a process, but its location tends to be different. Although distilleries are sometimes situated in town and cities, malt-whisky distilleries are frequently located in country districts – a consequence partly of their origins in illicit distillation, and partly of the need for cooling water. Most distilleries, until recent years, had their own maltings, often with the pyramidal-roofed kilns, hallmarks of the traditional distillery. In fact the ornate ventilators on such kilns are usually late nineteenth or early twentieth century in origin (see plates 26 and 36). The still-houses in the 'lowland' distilleries are not particularly distinctive.

The bonded stores, in which the whisky is matured are another noticeable feature of distilleries. These vary in height from one to seven storeys, the taller ones being in the urban distilleries such as Port Dundas, Glasgow, with its enormous output of grain whisky. The best examples of relatively unaltered distilleries are in the north of Scotland (see volume 2).

TEXTILES

The earliest substantial remains of the textile industry date from the late eighteenth century, but there are a few fragments from earlier periods, such as the ruins of waulk (fulling) and lint (scutching) mills. Waulk mills hammered woollen cloth under water with fuller's earth (a natural soap) to close up its texture, while lint mills were used to remove the woody particles from stem flax to prepare it for heckling (combing) prior to spinning. Parts of some of these mills have probably been incorporated in dwellinghouses, farm steadings and other buildings, but definite attribution is rarely possible. Handloom weavers' cottages of eighteenth-century or earlier date may also survive unidentified, but most derive from the late eighteenth or nineteenth centuries.

The oldest 'modern' textile mills are cotton-spinning mills of the 1780s, built to house Arkwright water frames, the earliest survivor being the 'Old End', Johnstone, Renfrewshire (1782), followed by a number of others built before 1790, including Gateside Mill, Neilston, Renfrewshire (plate 4); No 1 Mill, New Lanark; and the Bell Mill, Stanley, Perthshire. In each case, the structure is five or six storeys high, with the main wooden beams stretching from wall to wall (strengthened or replaced later in most cases). In later, wider, cotton mills, there were generally supporting columns, arranged in one or more rows, though in most cases wooden beams and floors were retained. No early 'fireproof' cotton mills survive, but the late-

Victorian brick cotton mills, such as No 1 Spinning Mill, Ferguslie, Paisley and the Glasgow Cotton Spinners' Mills in Dalmarnock, Glasgow, are 'fireproof' and impressively large. There was no marked increase in the number of storeys in cotton-spinning mills but the width, height of flats, and proportion of window area to wall tended to increase.

Many mid nineteenth-century, cotton-spinning mills incorporated power-loom-weaving sections. The first purely power-loom-weaving factories seem to have been multistorey – a classic example survives in Graham Square, Glasgow. From about 1850, however, single-storey, 'north-light' sheds were built for weaving, and this type remained standard until cotton weaving declined after 1900. Most cotton-weaving factories were in the Glasgow area, but there are scattered examples elsewhere, in particular in Strathaven, Lanarkshire, and the Irvine Valley, Ayrshire. From the earlier hand-loom industry, weavers' cottages survive in large numbers, for example, in Crosshill and Kirkmichael, Ayrshire, and Stonehouse, Lanarkshire, and with detached loomshops at Kilbarchan, Renfrewshire.

4   Gateside Cotton Mill, Neilston, Renfrewshire (see p. 217). A good though plain example of eighteenth century cotton mill construction, one of a series of mills intensively using the power of the Levern Water.

Linen manufacture, developed in the eighteenth century through the Board of Trustees for Manufactures, was widely diffused as a handcraft, with the fine branch of the trade in the west of Scotland and coarser products made in the east, particularly in Fife and Angus and Aberdeen. Good examples of hand-loom weavers' cottages survive in Dairsie, Fife, and Kilbarchan, Renfrewshire. Linen spinning was mechanized from the late 1780s. Most of the surviving early mills are in the north and east (see volume 2), though fragments of two mills of the 1830s still exist in Kemback, Fife. Garnock Mill, Kilbirnie, Ayrshire, is probably the oldest surviving linen-thread mill, now overshadowed by the neighbouring, later, Stoneyholm Mill (see plate 17). In the later nineteenth century, fine-linen manufacture became concentrated in Dunfermline, where some superb mills survive to show the effects of competition on industrial architecture. Coarser products were, and are, made in Kirkcaldy, and in several of the smaller Fife towns. From the 1830s, however, jute displaced linen for very coarse cloths, starting in Dundee, and spreading through its hinterland (see volume 2).

5   Wilton Mills, Hawick, Roxburghshire (see p. 231). Typical in scale, though not in details, of the Hawick textile mills.

WOOLLENS

There have been three significant branches of the woollen industry in Scotland – hosiery, wool and worsted cloth, and carpets. The hosiery industry (making knitted garments of all kinds) was organized in relatively small units until the introduction of power-driven knitting frames in the 1860s. An interesting example of a hand-frame shop survives at Denholm, Roxburghshire. The largest concentration of old-established hosiery works is in Hawick (plate 5), but it is difficult to generalize about design, though many have single-storey workshops complementing taller blocks. Several large Hawick works date from the period just before the First World War, when new construction was rare in the Scottish textile industry. Hosiery works are now scattered throughout the country, but few are old established, an exception being Elder's works in Strathaven, Lanarkshire.

Associated with hosiery, cloth and carpet making, are wool preparation and spinning. Small carding mills (preparing carded wool for spinners) appear to predate power spinning, and some were associated with grain, saw and other water-powered milling sites. A fairly complete carding mill building survives at Bridge of Urr, Kirkcudbrightshire (see plate 41). Large wool-spinning mills seem to have developed first in the Borders, and in Galashiels in particular (see plate 58), and operated at first in connection with hand-loom weaving. Examples of late eighteenth- or early nineteenth-century buildings are to be found in Innerleithen, Peeblesshire; Tillicoultry and Alva, Clackmannanshire; Twynholm, Wigtonshire; and Causewayhead, Stirlingshire. The bulk of the surviving spinning mills are of mid to late nineteenth-century date. Particularly fine examples are to be found in Selkirk (see plate 60), Galashiels and Hawick, and there are also good specimens in Tillicoultry, Alloa (worsted spinning for knitting wools), and Clackmannan. The construction and layout of woollen- and worsted-spinning mills differs little from contemporary cotton mills. Water power was normal until the mid nineteenth century, though auxiliary steam power was common; most of the later mills were entirely steam-powered.

The introduction of power weaving into the woollen and worsted industries in Scotland was slow, and indeed is not yet complete, as hand looms still operate in Lewis, and elsewhere. These are mainly of modern construction. Concentration of hand looms in factories was, however, a feature of the woollen industry in the Borders and in Alva, Clackmannanshire, where several examples survive. The integration of weaving with spinning was common from the mid nineteenth century, and if a typical border woollen mill can be said to have existed in the late nineteenth century, it was one where spinning was carried on in a three- or four-storey building and looms were situated in single-storey, north-light sheds. Sometimes looms were housed in multistorey blocks, and sometimes spinning machinery was installed in north-light sheds, as in Philiphaugh Mill, Selkirk. Outstanding in scale are Netherdale Mill, Galashiels; Ettrick Mill, Selkirk; Nithsdale Mill and Troqueer Mill, Dumfries; and Hayford Mills, Cambusbarron (see plate 64).

Carpet weaving was a handcraft until the mid nineteenth century, though sometimes carried on in factories. The greatest carpet firms in Scotland were certainly James Templeton and Sons, Glasgow, and BMK, Kilmarnock, but there have been several other firms, a handful of which still survive. Most of the BMK works are modern, but some of their older mills survive beside the Irvine Water in Kilmarnock. Templeton's still own the most flamboyant Victorian factory in Scotland, the so-called 'Doge's Palace' facing Glasgow Green.

IRON AND STEEL

Remains of early iron-smelting works are scanty, and are confined in the main to slag heaps, both of the pre-blast-furnace, bloomery industry (not included in this volume), and of the post-1800 industry. The principal structures are the furnaces and associated buildings at Bonawe and Furnace, Argyllshire (see volume 2), while the blast furnaces at Clyde Iron Works, Lanarkshire, are of interest as the first modern examples of the type in Scotland. The only other sites with remains of immediate interest are Glenbuck, Ayrshire; Shotts, Lanarkshire (plate 6); and Lochgelly, Fife. The steel industry, being later, has some buildings and plant of the late nineteenth to the early twentieth century still in use, as at Lanarkshire Steel Works, Flemington, Lanarkshire; Parkhead Forge, Glasgow; and Glengarnock Steel Works, Ayrshire. The structures in all these cases are typical of the big steel-framed, single-storey sheds built in large numbers at that period.

Iron foundries can be divided, as far as structure goes, into two main groups: those making light castings, which can be manipulated by hand or by light crane, and those making heavy castings. The former, found mainly in the Falkirk and Bonnybridge district, tend to have low single-storey moulding shops, rather like weaving sheds, while the latter resemble engineering shops. A typical heavy foundry of the mid nineteenth century had the cranes fixed, with their jibs

6 Engine-house and cooling-water tower, Shotts, Lanarkshire (see p. 179). The former housed the blowing engine for the blast furnaces, which stood in a row along the 'bank' to the right. The brick tower was one of two used to give adequate pressure to the supply of water to the tuyers (blast air nozzles) of the furnace. Shotts Ironworks stopped smelting in 1947.

describing intersecting arcs, thus covering most of the floor area, but most surviving foundries of this type now have more modern mechanical handling plant. Good examples of mid nineteenth-century foundry buildings are Titchfield Foundry, Kilmarnock (now part of Caledonia Works); Vulcan Foundry, Paisley; and Cranston-hill Foundry, Glasgow. The cupolas (melting furnaces) in several foundries are of a fair age, and several solid-bottom cupolas of late nineteenth-century date were in use in the early 1970s.

Engineering shops reflect in their construction the size of products and machinery they were designed to house and the constructional materials available at the time. The earliest surviving engineering shops appear to be early nineteenth century and were typically of more than one storey, with lighter machines housed on the upper floors (see plate 16). This basic type continued to be built throughout the century, often with a central bay or well with galleries. A complete example of the solid-floor type is the oldest range at Caledonia Works, Kilmarnock, Ayrshire, and galleried buildings include the former engine works at the Fairfield Shipbuilding Yard, Govan,

7 One bay of the Fairfield Engine Works, Glasgow (see p. 165). The finest surviving engineering works interior in Scotland, and perhaps in Britain. Note the galleries, which formerly housed light machinery.

Glasgow (plate 7), and the oldest part of Mavor and Coulson's works in Broad Street, Glasgow. The links in design between the older examples of the type and contemporary textile mills are obvious to even casual inspection. As size and weight of machines grew, new techniques were adopted, notably the casting of tall iron columns (1860s, 1870s) to support high roofs, crane rails, and, sometimes (as at Fairfield), galleries. The use of cast-iron columns in place of continuous or arched brick or stone walls made multi-bay workshops more flexible. Examples of arched brick construction are Vulcan Works, Paisley, Renfrewshire, and the 1870s part of Eglinton Engine Works, Glasgow. From the mid 1880s, Sir William Arrol and Co and other manufacturers introduced steel-framed engineering shops with columns, roof trusses and girder spans made of riveted rolled-steel sections. Clad cheaply in corrugated galvanized steel, or more expensively in brick, structures of this type were standard until recent years, when more sophisticated welded-steel and reinforced-concrete designs were adopted. Several examples of steel-framed shops are noted in the gazetteer, including the machine shops at Parkhead Forge, Glasgow, and workshops at Clydebank, Dunbartonshire.

CHEMICALS

Of the eighteenth- and nineteenth-century chemical-manufacturing industry, there are few substantial remains, but related industries have left some interesting survivals – for example, sugar refineries in Glasgow, Port Glasgow, and Greenock, Renfrewshire, and the surviving saltworks building in Prestonpans, East Lothian. Of the chemical-using industries, the most widely diffused have been bleaching and dyeing, and a handful of eighteenth- and nineteenth-century bleachworks are still working, though using different techniques. Examples are Avonbank, Lanarkshire, and Netherplace, Mearns, Renfrewshire (see also volume 2). Avonbank still has its beetling shed of 1839, with drying loft and bellcote. Beetling is a method of finishing cotton and linen cloth by hammering with wooden hammers. It produces a smooth, dust-repellent surface with something of the appearance of watered silk. Calico printing, a specialist branch of dyeing, has left survivals in the Vale of Leven, Dunbartonshire – notably in Bonhill parish.

Of other industries involving chemical change – apart from metallurgy – tanning (plate 8) and the various branches of the ceramics manufacture were particularly widely diffused. In the late eighteenth and early nineteenth centuries, most towns had tanneries to supply local shoemakers, saddlers and machine-makers. Examples survive in Gatehouse-of-Fleet, Ayr, and Falkirk. Larger, centralized tanneries grew up during the last century, eliminating many of the smaller units. Most of these have in turn disappeared, but particularly fine examples are to be seen in Bridge of Weir, Renfrewshire, and Tullibody, Clackmannanshire (see plate 23). The Bridge of Weir tanneries still operate, but most other surviving tannery buildings are converted to other uses.

Of the ceramics industries, the most refined, pottery, has left few remains, the most notable certainly being the bottle kilns at Portobello Pottery, Midlothian, though the flint-mill ruins at North Woodside, Glasgow, and the buildings of the Eagle Pottery, Glasgow, are of interest. Flint, calcined and ground to a white powder, is an ingredient both of the body of pottery, and of some glazes. The related clay tobacco-pipe trade has left a particularly substantial monument in Bain Street, Glasgow, and there is a reconstruction of a pipe-maker's workshop in the Huntly House Museum, Edinburgh. Scotland has long been famous for sanitary earthenware, and though

8   Tannery, Jedburgh, Roxburghshire (see p. 232). The louvred upper flats for drying hides after tanning are typical, but are also found in breweries.

most plant is modern, two bottle kilns survive at Longpark Pottery, Kilmarnock. Of the other branches of the trade, the making of 'composition' bricks from the shale raised as waste at collieries is the most important. All such brickworks use rectangular kilns of the Hoffman regenerative type; the oldest probably date from the early years of this century, but most are modern. Other brick-making apparatus includes pan mills, with revolving pans, and brick-moulding machines, some of which seem to be fairly old. Tile field drains, fired at a lower temperature than bricks, to ensure porosity, are made in multi-vented kilns of a type still in existence at Auchenheath and Law, Lanarkshire, and, in reduced form, near Kilmarnock, Ayrshire and at Terally, Wigtownshire. A third type of kiln, circular in plan with a domed roof, was formerly found in sanitary-pottery works, in firebrick works and in works making glazed stoneware, but is now rare: examples survive at Ochiltree Tileworks, Ayrshire, and at Law, Lanarkshire.

The ceramics industries have obvious links with mining and quarrying. Disused quarries exist all over Scotland, where stone was the material of choice for building construction until the mid to late nineteenth century (see also volume 2). Many such quarries were worked for specific purposes, such as those at Portpatrick for harbour works and others – one at New Lanark, for instance – were used intermittently for house and factory building. The great commercial quarries were those which supplied stone of such high quality that it could stand heavy charges for freight, and were located, in the main, conveniently for water or rail transport. Examples include the granite quarries at Dalbeattie, Kirkcudbrightshire, and the red-sandstone quarries of Ayrshire and Dumfriesshire (see plate 29). Metal mining, apart from the mining of ironstone, from the coal measures in the central rift valley, was rarely largescale, perhaps the biggest concentration being the Leadhills–Wanlockhead group of lead mines on the Lanarkshire–Dumfriesshire border (see frontispiece). The Glasgow Spelaeological Society, the Leadhills and Wanlockhead Mines Research Group and the Glasgow University Summer School in Industrial Archaeology are all working on this area. The Clackmannanshire Field Studies Society has recently completed a study of mining in the Ochils. Limestone mines and quarries have also been studied by Edinburgh University Adult Students and by the Glasgow Spelaeological Society. The former group has devised a system of classification of limekilns which is worth studying (see Skinner, *Limekilns*). The design of limekilns varied with the scale of operation.

The main use of lime in the eighteenth and nineteenth centuries was as a fertilizer, an antidote to the acid soils prevalent in Scotland. Secondary, but significant, uses were in mortar for building and in chemicals and metallurgy. Small farm kilns, or their remains, are to be found in north Ayrshire, though most lowland kilns were commercial in scale (see also volume 2).

Larger kilns, often built by landowners, are to be found in areas such as the Lothians, Ayrshire, Fife and Lanarkshire, where limestone and coal were found close together, or where coal, mixed with the limestone for burning, could be transported by sea, as at Dunure, Ayrshire, or by rail, as at Carham, Roxburghshire. These large kilns may be free standing, with one to four draw holes, or arranged in banks. The most striking ranges are at Cambusbarron, Stirlingshire, and Charlestown, Fife. Those in the east are commonly more elaborate in layout than in the west, where the four-draw kiln, with access to the fourth draw from a tunnel at the rear, is virtually unknown. The last limekiln to operate in Scotland was at Giffen, Ayrshire (see plate 15). Apart from shaft kilns, 'clamp' kilns were sometimes used. These were U-plan rubble, earth or brick enclosures. Examples survive at Barjarg, Dumfriesshire, and Balgrochan, Campsie, Stirlingshire. When possible, limestone was quarried, but sometimes mining had to be resorted to, as, for instance, at Lannielane, Ayrshire, and Newbigging, Fife.

MINING

By far the most significant branch of mining in Scotland, as elsewhere in Great Britain, has been coal mining, but apart from spoil heaps or 'bings' remains of abandoned collieries are disappointingly scanty. Among those collieries still in production, however, examples of buildings and equipment obsolete as far as new construction is concerned may still be seen. Most interesting are probably the steam winding engines at Highhouse, Ayrshire, Cardowan, Lanarkshire, and Lady Victoria, Midlothian (see plate 49), but 'traditional' headframes and surface buildings of other types may be found at several of the older pits (see plate 38). Some are noticed in the gazetteer, including Valleyfield, Blairhall and Comrie, Fife. A characteristic of many pit-head buildings is the use of steel framing with brick infilling. Of remnants of abandoned mines, the most important are certainly the Cornish pumping engine at Prestongrange, East Lothian, now the centre of a developing museum; the slightly older engine house and beam at Devon Colliery, Clackmannanshire; the

9 Three-draw limekiln, Burdiehouse Limeworks, Edinburgh (see p. 184). A
beautifully-built kiln of unusual design, though of a typical configuration.

remains of an engine pit at Thornton, Fife (see plate 39); and the remains on Preston Island, Fife. Abandoned shafts can be found, notably those discovered by A. I. Bowman at Culross, Fife.

The once significant shale-oil industry has vanished almost without trace, apart from enormous heaps of spent shale, found mainly in the counties of Mid and West Lothian (see plate 68). The form of most of these bings differs from that of the typical coal bing in that, because the quantities of material being dumped were very large, it was most economical to form a flat-topped tip. An interesting exception is a group of conical bings near Addiewell in West Lothian, with the tipping inclines radiating from the site of the works.

ROADS AND BRIDGES

Transport improvement, of course, underpinned much of the economic development of Scotland, though much road and canal construction and harbour building was inspired by military and administrative rather than commercial considerations (see volume 2). Major road bridges were comparatively rare before the eighteenth century, and because of their importance they were, on the whole, well maintained. Fine examples are the Old Bridge, Stirling, Devorgilla's Bridge, Dumfries, and the Auld Brig, Ayr (see also volume 2). These owe their survival to a sense of their historical importance, as do some of the smaller medieval and early modern bridges, such as the Auld Brig o' Doon, Alloway, Ayrshire, and Canongate Bridge, Jedburgh, Roxburghshire (see also volume 2). Characteristics of these bridges, the oldest of which date from the fourteenth century, are segmental or semicircular arches, massive triangular cutwaters in the case of multi-span bridges and, frequently, ribbed arches. The workmanship is generally of a high standard. A typical late seventeenth century bridge, not markedly different from its predecessors, is Clydesholm Bridge, Kirkfieldbank, Lanarkshire.

Many eighteenth-century bridges continued in the same tradition, but from mid century leading designers, such as John Smeaton, with his bridges at Coldstream and Perth, began to build lighter bridges with flatter arches. The process of lightening and flattening was continued in the work of Thomas Telford, John Rennie and their successors. Telford introduced the hollow arch and hollow pier as a means of reducing weight and cost, as for example in Cartland Crags, Lanark, Dean Bridge, Edinburgh, and Lothian Bridge, Cranston, Midlothian. Rennie produced assured designs with minimal obstruction of the river channel, as at Kelso (plate 10), on the Cree at Newton

Stewart, Wigtonshire, and on the Ken near New Galloway. Robert Stevenson was a disciple of Rennie, the latter's influence being clear in the North Water Bridge near Marykirk, Kincardine (see volume 2). Smaller bridges followed the trends set by the great designers, though for many purposes plain single-span rubble bridges were perfectly adequate. Where the stone was suitable, as in the Border counties, quite large spans were rubble-built, the longest being Ashiestiel Bridge, Selkirkshire (see plate 61).

New materials were used in bridge construction from *c* 1810. Telford introduced cast iron in his Craigellachie and Bonar bridges (see volume 2), and the material was used throughout the nineteenth century for small bridges like that at Cambus Distillery, Clackmannanshire, for medium-sized examples like Partick and Eldon Street bridges, Glasgow. In major bridges of the later nineteenth century, such as the North Bridge, Edinburgh and the Albert Bridge over the Clyde at Glasgow, cast-iron was used for the outer girders only, the main weight of the carriageway and traffic being carried on wrought iron or steel girders of arch form. Another way to use iron was in

10 Kelso Bridge, Roxburghshire (see p. 233). One of John Rennie's most beautiful bridges.

suspension chains or cables; here Captain Samuel Brown, of the Royal Navy, was the Scottish pioneer. His greatest work is probably the Union Bridge, Hutton, Berwickshire, which, like several smaller bridges, such as those at Kalemouth, near Jedburgh (see plate 56), and a footbridge at Melrose, has a wooden deck and chain links forged from iron bar (see also volume 2). Typical suspension bridges of the mid nineteenth century have links made from iron plate, as patented by Brown and used by Telford in Wales: specimens include a bridge at Dumfries and South Portland Street Bridge, Glasgow (see also volume 2). Other types of iron bridge are also to be found, of which probably the most attractive is the lenticular (lens-shaped) truss found in a footbridge at Roxburgh viaduct, but the most important is the lattice- or plate-girder bridge, relatively rare in iron but fairly common in steel (Walkerburn, Peeblesshire, and Dalmarnock Bridge, Glasgow). There are many other types of steel bridge to be found in Scotland, including suspension, cantilever [Dalginross Bridge, Comrie, Perthshire (see volume 2)], and bowstring girder (Bonhill, Dunbartonshire).

Concrete bridges in Scotland date in the main from the 1920s, and in the interwar period took a profusion of forms (see volume 2). In the early 1930s design had stabilized to some extent, and concrete 'arch' bridges were more or less standard. Sometimes designers covered the 'bones' of such bridges in masonry, as in the continuous-beam King George V Bridge, Glasgow and St Michael's Bridge, Dumfries.

Apart from bridges and road alignments, which are often unchanged from the eighteenth century and earlier, tollhouses, mileposts and stones and signposts are also of interest. Tollhouses vary widely in style of construction, but little in size, being mostly two-roomed, single-storey cottages (see plate 43). The neatest type is probably Telford's design with a semicircular projecting bay in the centre of the frontage, found on the Glasgow–Carlisle and associated roads, for example at Lanark Racecourse. Plain two-roomed rectangular cottages, sometimes with recesses for toll boards, are also common. Two-storey tollhouses are rare. Mileposts and stones and signposts have not been mentioned in the gazetteer, but are still common: Fife has a particularly good collection (see W. M. Stephen, 'Milestones and Wayside Markers in Fife', *PSAS*, 1967–8, 6, 170).

CANALS

Scotland, largely on account of its geography, never possessed a canal

network comparable with that of the English midlands. Of its six
major canals, three were 'broad' barge canals – the Monkland,
Edinburgh & Glasgow Union, and the Glasgow, Paisley & Ardrossan
– and three 'ship' canals – the Forth & Clyde, the Crinan and the
Caledonian. The two last named are still operational (see volume 2);
the others have been abandoned. The Monkland and the Glasgow,
Paisley & Ardrossan have almost completely disappeared, while the
other two have had bridges replaced by culverts and are partly infilled.
Standard overbridges on the Glasgow, Paisley & Ardrossan and the
Union canals were stone-arched. Two of the former survive in the
grounds of Ferguslie Mills, Paisley, and most of the attractive Union
canal bridges are still intact (see plate 66). Overbridges on the ship
canals are all of the bascule and swing type – mainly swing on the
Crinan and the Caledonian and bascule on the Forth & Clyde. A
handful of original wood and cast-iron bascule bridges survive on the
western section of the Forth and Clyde. Most of the moving bridges
on all three canals were replaced during road improvement in the
1920s and 1930s, when several electrically operated bascule bridges

11   Almond Aqueduct, Union Canal, West Lothian (see p. 259). The smallest, but
the most picturesque, of the major aqueducts on the Union Canal. The others are
similar in style.

were built on the Forth & Clyde. Aqueducts range from small tunnel-like structures on the Forth & Clyde (Bonnybridge, Stirlingshire), Union (near Ratho, Midlothian) and Caledonian (see volume 2), through moderately-sized, single-span ones, as at Linlithgow, West Lothian (Union), Kirkintilloch, Dunbartonshire (Forth & Clyde), to the major river crossings. There are three important aqueducts on the Union Canal, at Slateford, Edinburgh, and over the rivers Almond (plate 11) and Avon, West Lothian, all with iron troughs for the channel, supported on hollow masonry arches. The other significant aqueduct is on the Forth & Clyde, over the Kelvin in Glasgow. This was the largest viaduct in Britain when completed in 1790, and is of massive construction with the channel in a puddled clay bed.

Locks on the Forth & Clyde and Crinan canals (see also volume 2) are similar in construction, with stone chambers and wooden gates with balance beams. Most of the Forth & Clyde lock gates have been cut down, but complete examples survive at Wyndford and Bowling, Dunbartonshire. The most remarkable flight of locks on the lowland canals is at Maryhill, Glasgow (five locks).

Other canal structures of interest are stables, of which there was a standard Forth & Clyde type, found, for example, at Glasgow Bridge, Kirkintilloch, and Lambhill, Glasgow (see plate 31). There is a range of stables and houses on the Union Canal at Woodcockdale, West Lothian.

DOCKS AND HARBOURS

The indented coastline of Scotland has many natural harbours, giving shelter to fishing and trading vessels. Some of these are no more than inlets in rock cliffs with shores suitable for beaching small craft (see volume 2). Inlets of this type could be improved by quaying the sides for use by larger vessels, as at Staxigoe, Caithness (see volume 2), or by construction of more elaborate works forming an artificial harbour. Where no natural harbour existed, or where an inlet was inadequately protected from heavy seas, protective works were undertaken at least as early as the seventeenth century. Most of the surviving harbour works, however, date from the eighteenth and nineteenth centuries.

Harbours were built in that period to create or improve the fishing industry and provide better facilities for coastal and international shipping. Many harbours in fact served both purposes. It would be misleading to trace an evolutionary pattern of harbour design, but harbours can be classified according to type. The simplest is the quay on a river bank or inlet, such as at Glencaple, Dumfriesshire or Kirkcudbright, sometimes extended by creating a basin for additional berths, rather than for protection, as at Wigtown, and Kingholm Quay, Dumfriesshire.

Where some protection from a sea is required, a projecting pier can be used in its own right, as at Limekilns, Fife, or in the typical ferry pier (North and South Queensferry, Fife). More protection is afforded by angling the head of a pier, thus forming a rudimentary basin (Ballantrae, Ayrshire). The next stage is the addition of another pier to give a narrow entrance, which helps protect the interior of the basin from heavy seas, as, for example, at Cockenzie, East Lothian. If the basin is large, it may be subdivided by piers without altering the basic arrangement. When the harbour is exposed to heavy seas a stilling basin is often incorporated. This is a basin facing the harbour entrance, with a sloping end on which waves dissipate themselves. The entrance to the inner basin is in one side of the stilling basin, for example in the Old Harbour, Dunbar, East Lothian. These types are all tidal, as are several important dock systems, including Glasgow, Aberdeen and Dundee (see volume 2), but most docks in Scotland are 'wet docks' with gates to maintain the level of water in the dock at or near the high-water mark. These vary widely in size, from tiny docks such as that at Dysart, Fife, through moderately sized single basins, as at Kirkcaldy, Fife, to large dock complexes such as Leith, Grangemouth and Methil.

Constructional methods and materials depended in part on locality, but mainly on period. Early works were executed in rubble, the best in roughly squared blocks assembled without mortar, as at St Andrews, Fife. Local stone seems to have been generally used, except when works were required to resist very severe seas. Then granite or some other hard stone might be used. Granite was also used for copestones in dock construction to resist wear, as in the Glasgow and Greenock docks. Concrete was used for foundations in Queen's Dock, Glasgow, in the 1870s, and mass concrete was widely used for new harbour construction and for repairs and extensions from the 1880s, for instance at Buckie, Banffshire (see volume 2). Timber was also used for quay faces and sometimes for piers, as in the case of Clyde Estuary steamer piers, and at Methil, Fife. Of harbour fittings, perhaps the most interesting are cranes and other lifting apparatus. Steam cranes are now only found at Leith Docks, where the last hydraulic crane also survives (see plate 46). Coal drops are now extinct except for a group at Methil. An early electric crane exists at

Leith (Victoria Dock) and a few electric cranes from the interwar period can still be found, for instance at Irvine, Ayrshire. Hand-cranes may occasionally be found, both of the fixed-post type (see volume 2), and of the mobile type, as at Kirkcaldy, Fife (see also volume 2).

LIGHTHOUSES

These prominent navigational aids are well-represented round Scotland's rocky coast. A selection of mainland lights is included in this volume (see also volume 2). Early examples include Southerness, Kirkcudbrightshire. Apart from the Clyde lighthouses, which were administered by the Clyde Lighthouses Trust (see plate 52), now by the Clyde Port Authority, Scottish lighthouses are the responsibility of the Board of Northern Lighthouses. This body has been served by a remarkable family of engineers, responsible for the design of all the Board's lights since 1798. Robert Stevenson was the first, followed by his son, grandson and great-grandson. One of his grandsons was Robert Louis Stevenson, the novelist. It is not surprising, therefore, to find a degree of standardization of design in the main Scottish lights, with plain tapering circular towers, often on semicircular bases, and single storey, flat-roofed keepers' cottages as common features. Classical details are sometimes found in early nineteenth-century construction but become vestigial later on. The standard material for lighthouse construction is stone, but there are a few brick towers, notably the now disused south light at Portpatrick. The un-manned navigation lights associated with harbours are often unconventional in design – for example the cast-iron towers at Port Glasgow, Renfrewshire and Aberdeen (see volume 2) and the tiny leading light at Portpatrick on an ordinary cast-iron lamp-post. The disused light towers at Dunure, Ayrshire and Port Logan, Wigtownshire (plate 12), are interesting survivals.

RAILWAYS

Though the active railway network is a fraction of its former size, it is still possible to see examples of stations, bridges and viaducts, representative of all phases of railway development in Scotland. The first railway in Scotland was the Tranent–Cockenzie wagonway, East Lothian, part of whose trackbed still survives as do sections of the routes of other horse-hauled wood or iron colliery lines, such as the Fordell, Halbeath and Elgin railways in Fife and the Alloa Railway in Clackmannanshire. Overbridges survive from these lines at Alloa (two) and Inverkeithing (see plate 52). The first Scottish public railway was the Kilmarnock & Troon, a plateway later converted to an edge railway, and still in use. A four-span viaduct bypassed in conversion still exists – just – near Gatehead, Ayrshire. Relics of the Lanarkshire coal railways of the 1820s are now sadly reduced. Railways of the 1830s are better represented, for example by the stations at Renfrew (Fulbar Street) and Carnoustie, Angus (see volume 2). Newtyle Station, Angus, is arguably the most interesting of the period. The group of 'trunk' lines promoted in the late 1830s opened a new era in Scotland and the best of these railways, the Edinburgh & Glasgow, can stand comparison in the quality of its engineering with English railways of the period, with its superb viaducts – notably at Linlithgow and near Ratho – its handsome over- and underbridges, including a skew underbridge at Linlithgow, and its pleasing stations, including the original Edinburgh terminus at Haymarket with its early cast-iron-framed train shed. The Glasgow, Paisley, Kilmarnock & Ayr and the Glasgow, Paisley & Greenock lines also have important surviving relics, such as part of Paisley (Gilmour Street) Station, stations at Ayr and Irvine, and the viaduct at Irvine. As in

12 Port Logan Harbour, Wigtonshire (see p. 268). Part of this once-impressive work survives, fortunately including this attractive light-tower.

England, the 'railway mania' schemes that materialized were very variable in the quality of their engineering and in the amount of money available for station building. Notable works of that period are the unparalleled Ballochmyle Viaduct, Mauchline, Ayrshire; the North British Railways viaducts at Dunglass, Berwickshire and Roxburgh (see plate 57); and the cast-iron viaduct at Uddingston on the Caledonian Railway. Interesting stations of the 1840s are to be found on the Caledonian at Lockerbie and Midcalder, on the Scottish Central and other railways to Aberdeen (see volume 2) and on the Edinburgh & Hawick Railway at Melrose. It is, on the whole, the minor station buildings that survive from this period, the main stations either were not built at that time, or, as at Perth, Dumfries and Kilmarnock, have been submerged and altered in later developments. The major exception is the Edinburgh & Northern Railway in Fife, whose terminus at Burntisland and major intermediate stations at Cupar and Ladybank (plate 13) are particularly fine, as indeed are the remaining minor stations on the line. Cupar is particularly interesting as an example of a mid nineteenth-century station

13   Down-platform building, Ladybank Station, Fife (see p. 129). One of the superb stations of the Edinburgh, Perth & Dundee Railway, who economized on earthworks, but spent money on buildings.

layout, complete with two-storey goods shed and staithes (rare in Scotland) for coal traffic. At Ladybank the carriage and wagon works of the company are still in railway use.

In the 1850s, new construction was on a more modest scale, the main activity being in the north east, where the Inverness & Nairn, Inverness & Aberdeen Junction and Great North of Scotland railways formed the first link with the Highland capital in 1856 (see volume 2). Other railways opened in the 1850s included the Forth & Clyde Junction Railway, with extant stations at Buchylvie (see plate 62), Balfron and Kippen, Stirlingshire and Drymen, Dunbartonshire, and other 'cheap railways' (see A. J. Robertson, *Transport History*, 1974, 7, 1) such as the Perth & Dunkeld Railway, whose station at Dunkeld, Perthshire, is one of the finest of the period (see volume 2).

A feature of the 1860s was the extension of railways in the Highlands, with the construction of the Inverness & Perth Junction Railway and the beginning of its extension north to Wick and Thurso (see volume 2). The railways built in the Borders in the 1860s have all been abandoned, but some beautiful viaducts, such as that at Leaderfoot near Melrose Roxburghshire, survive and also the most attractive skew viaducts over the Lyne and Tweed on the Broughton–Peebles line.

Apart from further extension of the Highland Railway's sphere of influence by completion of the lines to Wick and Thurso and to Strome Ferry (see volume 2), the main development in the 1870s was the re-organization of the Glasgow termini of the Caledonian, Glasgow & South Western and North British Railways. The original arched overall roofs of St Enoch and Queen Street stations are still extant, as is the ridged roof of the first part of Central Station. All are impressive reminders of the scale of railway investment in the 1870s. Another interesting Glasgow survival is College Passenger Station with its cast-iron columns and girders, a classic train shed. Another pleasing viaduct of this period is at Stewarton, Ayrshire. The most daring engineering achievement of the 1870s was undoubtedly the first Tay Bridge, partly blown down in 1879. Some of the girders were incorporated in its replacement, and the stumps of its piers are still visible. Other girders were re-used in a road bridge at Caputh, Perthshire (see volume 2).

Penetration of new territory continued in the 1880s with the opening of the Callander & Oban Railway, with its handsome wooden station buildings, most notable at Oban (see volume 2), but the characteristic of the decade was consolidation, with the construction of suburban lines round Glasgow and Edinburgh, such as the Cathcart District and Glasgow City & District, the commencement of strategic lines, like the Lanarkshire & Ayrshire Railway, and the Portsoy–Elgin railway via Buckie (see volume 2). Characteristic of many of these lines was the construction of wooden station buildings – in place of stone – and the increasing use of metal in bridge construction. The Tay Bridge was replaced in this decade, and most of the Forth Bridge erected: the former was wrought iron, the latter steel.

The 1890s saw the start of another round of terminal improvement, a consequence of rising traffic. Waverley Station, Edinburgh, was rebuilt into its present form, and St Enoch Station was enlarged. Further major projects completed were the Glasgow Central Railway; the West Highland Railway from Craigendoran, Dunbartonshire to Fort William, Inverness-shire; and the Highland Railway's direct Aviemore–Inverness line (see volume 2). All were built to compete with existing or proposed lines, and were both expensive and difficult to build. The first two involved extensive tunnelling and the two latter were built over rugged terrain, with many bridges. An unusual line of this decade was the Glasgow District subway, a circular underground line, still in operation, though converted from cable to electric operation in 1934. Stations rebuilt at this time included Bridge Street, Glasgow, and Paisley (Gilmour Street).

The first decade of this century saw the mileage of Scottish railways reach its greatest extent. Many of the new lines built ran through sparsely populated country, and several of them came under the Light Railways Act of 1896. These included the Leadhills & Wanlockhead; Dornoch, Wick & Lybster (see volume 2). Gifford & Garvald; and Cairn Valley railways – all worked by main-line companies. Some of their tiny wooden stations survive, as at Saltoun, East Lothian (see also volume 2). A substantial viaduct with concrete arch rings still stands on the Leadhills line. Steel was the material chosen for several spectacular bridges on Caledonian Railway-sponsored lines in central Lanarkshire, and in Appin, Argyllshire (see volume 2). The viaduct at Millheugh, Lanarkshire, is reputedly the tallest in Scotland. Substantial station rebuilding took place between 1900 and 1914, the largest single project being the extension of Glasgow (Central), involving a major new bridge over the Clyde. Other important work was carried out at Glasgow (St Enoch), Wemyss Bay and Leith (Central) stations.

The typical station building until the 1880s incorporated at least one dwellinghouse, usually in an upper storey, and had somewhat rudimentary provision for passengers. Awnings, often in the angle between the main body and a wing, were frequently incorporated. Small wooden huts were usually provided on the opposite platform. In the 1880s, wooden station buildings were developed incorporating waiting rooms, booking office, staff rooms, toilet facilities and stores, without living accommodation. The motive for the change was partly a desire for economy and partly the need to provide detached accommodation for the agent. Station rebuilding seems to have begun on a large scale in the 1880s, and many buildings were replaced up to 1914. Others were improved by adding offices, often wooden, and by installing new awnings, often of iron- or steel-framed glazed construction.

One reason that new railways were not built in any numbers after c 1905 was the success of the electric tram. Horse and steam trams had been introduced into Scotland in the 1870s and cable trams were used in Edinburgh, but the introduction of electric traction reduced costs, and hence fares, and extended the economic range of operation. All the Scottish cities, and many of the larger towns, had electric tramways, and though these are extinct, several depots survive – in Edinburgh and Glasgow – and power stations in Glasgow, Kirkcaldy and Edinburgh (cable).

Ayrshire

Ayrshire was once noted for its mineral resources, which were second only to those of Lanarkshire. In the north of the county, engineering, chemicals and ceramics manufacture are legacies of the mineral wealth of the area. Kilmarnock is the dominant industrial town, with carpet weaving and shoemaking complementing engineering and ceramics. Irvine and Ayr are less important industrially. The southern and eastern districts are predominantly agricultural, the small towns supporting that base, as well as a modest fishing industry. Lime-working was widely dispersed through the county. Apart from the railway through Kilmarnock to the south, communications are mainly of local importance.

ARDROSSAN

ARDROSSAN

The town, NS2342, laid out in 1806, PETER NICHOLSON, architect, for the Earl of Eglinton. Much remains of the original town, built in connection with the dock development, including rows of 2-storey dwelling houses, and the Eglinton Arms Hotel, with stables at the rear. Along the South Bay are villas built to create a 'select watering-place', also by Eglinton.

Ardrossan Harbour, NS2242, built 1806 on, by the 12th and 13th Earls of Eglinton. A natural harbour, greatly improved. Until recently there were 3 basins, one locked, but the latter is now being filled in. Between 1886 and 1891, the Eglinton Dock, an outer basin, and a new breakwater were constructed by the Ardrossan Harbour Company. The machinery is now virtually all modern.

Ardrossan Shipyard, NS224419, late 19th–early 20th century. Some buildings remain here, including a 3-storey, 6-by-4-bay flat-roofed office block and a 13-bay brick and corrugated-iron workshop shed, both derelict.

Ardrossan (Montgomerie Pier) Station, NS225423, opened 1890 by the Lanarkshire & Ayrshire Railway. A 2-platform terminal station, with a 15-bay iron-framed wooden-clad building, originally with a glazed overall roof supported on lattice girders. Closed 1966, but still intact in 1974.

Ardrossan (Town) Station, NS231421, rebuilt *c* 1890 by the Glasgow & South Western Railway. Formerly a 6-platform through and terminal station, with a bay platform at the north end. The main offices are on the up platform, in a 1- and 2-storey ashlar building.

Custom House, NS228420, early 19th century. A 2-storey rubble building, with a 3-bay bowed frontage.

Hydraulic power station, NS227420, built *c* 1892. A tall 1-storey, 3-by-3-bay, red-brick building, with a lower single-storey block and a 3-storey accumulator tower in the style of a campanile.

Saltcoats Harbour, NS246408, reconstructed 1914. Formed by 2 natural headlands, improved by the construction of a rubble L-plan pier, 17th century and later, extended in concrete by 1914. The width of the quays is a pointer to the harbour's use for coal shipment rather than for fishing.

Saltcoats Station, NS248413, rebuilt 1894 by the Glasgow & South Western Railway. A 2-platform through station, with the main office on the up platform, in a 2-storey, 3-by-3-bay Renaissance building, with a single-storey wing. The down-platform building is a long single-storey structure in similar style, with a bracketted awning and glazed side screens. The platforms are linked by a lattice-girder footbridge.

Ruin of beam-engine house, Saltcoats, NS257414, reputedly built 1719 (plate 14). Most of 1 gable wall and parts of the other 3 walls of a sandstone-rubble engine house. Supposed to have been the site of the second Newcomen engine in Scotland. The masonry of the gable suggests that the house has been occupied by a rotative engine at some time.

AUCHINLECK

Auchinleck Station, NS549219, opened 1848 by the Glasgow, Paisley, Kilmarnock & Ayr Railway. A 2-platform through station, with the main offices on the up side in a 2-storey pinned rubble building on an L plan, incorporating a dwellinghouse.

Glenmuir Limeworks, NS631208, late 18th to early 19th century. A long open-cast working, with a block of kilns set into the side. One is 2 draw, and the other, with a single-draw arch, has two pairs of draw holes, perhaps indicating an oval kiln. The masonry is of unusually high quality.

Highhouse Colliery, Auchinleck, NS549217, late 19th century. A 2-shaft pit, with steel-framed corrugated-iron-clad surface buildings.

14 Ruin of beam-engine house, Saltcoats

There is still (1974) a steam winding engine on one shaft, built *c* 1896 by Grant, Ritchie & Co Ltd, Kilmarnock, with 2 horizontal cylinders 20in diameter by 4ft stroke (0·50 by 1·22m) and a drum 10ft diameter by 6ft 7in wide (3·05 by 2·01m). The engine has Stephenson's link valve gear, operating slide valves, and reversing is by hand. The headframe for the steam engine shaft is of unusual design, and was wooden until *c* 1968.

Lugar Ironworks and Village, NS590213, rebuilt *c* 1866 by the Eglinton Iron Company. The main part of the ironworks is the site of modern National Coal Board workshops, but the laboratory block and another single-storey rubble building survive. In the village, built to serve the works, the square, an L-plan row of foremen's cottages, with the church (1867) formerly a foundry (1840s) at one end still exist. All the older rows of workers' housing have gone, apart from walls now forming boundaries, but some brick rows built in the 1920s survive, as do the houses of the works' manager and underground manager, school, schoolhouse and institute (1892). The school and institute are now hosiery works.

Bello Mill, Lugar, NS597205, 18th century and later. A small rectangular rubble building, repaired in brick, with a corrugated-iron roof. There is a 6-spoke, low-breast paddle-wheel, with iron axle and rings, and wooden spokes and paddles, about 3 ft wide by 10ft diameter (0·91 by 3·05m) driving 1 pair of stones and, through belts, an oat bruiser. Disused, but substantially intact. The mill house, now rebuilt, was the birthplace of William Murdoch, pioneer of gas lighting.

Viaduct, Lugar, NS599214, opened 1872 by the Glasgow & South Western Railway. A tall 7-span masonry viaduct with segmental arches.

AYR

Alloway Mill, NS324187, early 19th century. A large 2- and 3-storey rubble building, on an X plan, with the kiln at one end of one of the long arms of the X. In the centre of the building is an 8-spoke, wood-and-iron paddle-wheel, still usable, which formerly drove 4 pairs of stones through individual bevel gears. Now a store.

Auld Brig o'Doon, Alloway, NS332178, 15th century, repaired 1832. A slender segmental-arched bridge, with a dressed-stone arch ring and rubble spandrels and wing walls. Now a footbridge only. Made famous by Robert Burns's poem 'Tam o' Shanter'.

New Bridge, Alloway, NS332179, built 1816. A single-segmental

arch, with dressed-stone arch ring and coursed-rubble spandrels.
Dutch Mills, Alloway, NS334177, early 19th century. A 2-storey
rubble building on an L plan, with a ruinous wing. At the rear are a
detached kiln and a square-section brick chimney. Now an ice
factory.
Railway Bridge, Alloway, NS321180, opened 1906 by the Maidens
& Dunure Light Railway. A 4-span masonry bridge with 2 large
central spans.

AYR

Ayr Harbour, NS333228. Quays on both banks of the river Ayr,
with a mid 19th-century breakwater projecting from the south bank.
Also on the south side was a slip dock (now disused). On the north
side is an enclosed basin, formerly gated, built 1874–8. The south
quay is used largely by fishing vessels, and the north quay and basin
are designed for coal export, with modern coaling cranes and a coal
drop. There is an attractive 2-storey harbourmaster's office with a
corner pepperpot turret.
Lighthouses, Ayr Harbour, NS333227 and NS333228, mid 19th
century. The larger of the two, now inland, is a 5-storey circular
tower, with a corbelled machicolated parapet and a circular lantern
with rectangular panes and a domed top. Adjoining the base is a
small single-storey keeper's cottage. The other lighthouse is an
unmanned circular iron tower on a concrete base with a conical cap.
Warehouses, Ayr Harbour, NS335223, early 19th century. A range
of 4 rubble-built warehouses, on the south quay of Ayr Harbour.
These are (east to west): 2 storey, 5 bay; 3 storey and attic, 7 bay;
4 storey and attic, 7 bay; and 3 storey, 13 bay. Probably contemporary, but detached, is a 3-storey and attic, 2-by-8-bay store, at
NS336222, with a projecting hoist.
Ayr Station, NS340214, rebuilt 1886. A 2-platform through station,
with 2 bay platforms at the north end. The up-platform offices are in
part of the ground floor of the 4-storey, red-sandstone hotel, and the
down-platform offices in a 1-storey, 15-bay sandstone block. There
were formerly extensive glazed awnings on cast-iron columns with
cast-iron roof trusses, but these have been cut back.
New Bridge, NS338222, built 1878–9. A 5-span bridge with dressed-
sandstone arch rings, sandstone-rubble spandrels, and granite
parapets. The cutwaters are rounded and above each, on the parapet,
is a cast-iron lamp standard.
Old Bridge of Ayr, NS339221, built 1470–1525, extensively repaired

1910. A 4-span rubble bridge, with 3 segmental arches and a pointed arch, built of dressed stone throughout. There are massive triangular cutwaters. Now a footbridge.

Harbour Branch Bridge, NS337223, built 1899 by the Glasgow & South Western Railway. A 5-span steel bridge on a curve, with riveted parallel truss spans supported on pairs of circular stone piers, one of which has been replaced in brick.

Turner's Bridge, NS341219, built 1900, presented by Mr Turner to the citizens of Ayr. A 5-span steel footbridge, with arches on masonry piers with vertical H-section members supporting the deck, which has lattice railings.

Brewery, NS340219, late 18th to early 19th century. A group of 2- and 3-storey rubble buildings, of which the largest is a 3-storey, 5-bay block with an elliptical-arched cart entry. Now a plumber's store.

Limekiln, NS355212, early 19th century. A massive 3-draw kiln, with segmental-arched drawholes. Now preserved in a public park.

Old Railway Station, NS337223, built 1840 for the Glasgow, Paisley, Kilmarnock & Ayr Railway. A 2-storey sandstone building in 'Elizabethan' style, with carved bargeboards. An opening was made through the building when the Ayr Harbour Branch was constructed in 1899. There is also a small single-storey lodge on a T plan and a group of single-storey rubble buildings, probably the original workshops of the GPK & A.

Railway viaduct, NS342217, completed 1856 for the Glasgow & Belfast Union Railway and rebuilt c 1878. A 4-span masonry structure, with segmental arches and rounded cutwaters.

Worsted mills, NS340217, built 1878 for James Templeton & Co. A 3-storey, 18-bay, yellow-brick building with various ancillary buildings. The complex includes 2 circular-section chimneys.

Tannery, NS341217, mid 19th century. A 3-storey, 7-bay rubble building with the louvred ventilators in the top floor. Adjacent to this structure is a much-altered, 3-storey and attic rubble building. Now disused.

Brewery, Newton-on-Ayr, NS339224, early 19th century and later. A group of 1- and 2-storey harled rubble buildings, with a 3-storey, 12-bay, brick office block. Now an aerated-water works.

Carpet factory, Newton-on-Ayr, NS344229, mid 19th century. A large group of single-storey, red-brick, north-light weaving sheds with a small castellated clock tower. Closed 1974.

Tannery, Newton-on-Ayr, NS343230, late 19th or early 20th century. A large single-storey, 8-bay, red-brick block of north-light sheds with a decorative frontage. This has large semicircular windows and a central 'feature'. At the rear are a 9-bay drying shed with louvred ventilators on the upper floor, and a large circular-section chimney. Disused.

Victoria Mills, Newton-on-Ayr, NS336225, 1870s and later. A 3-storey and attic, 7 bay, red-and-white-brick building, with a 4-storey, 2-bay kiln block. Adjacent is a 4-storey and attic, 6-by-9-bay, red-brick seed store. The mills are now also used for storage.

BALLANTRAE

Ballantrae Bridge, NX087823, built 1770. A 2-span bridge, with arch rings of dressed stone and rubble spandrels and wing walls. The arches are segmental, and there are triangular cutwaters extending upwards to form refuges. In the south abutment is a small segmental arch at a higher level, probably for a mill lade. At the north end is a single-storey cottage, probably a tollhouse.

Ballantrae Harbour, NX082831, improved c 1860. A sandstone pier on an L plan with a protective wall on the outer limb of the L. The outer face of the pier has a pronounced batter. There are single-storey wood and rubble gear stores, and nearby a range of 12 single-storey and attic fishermen's cottages and a similar block of 2 houses.

Ballantrae Windmill, NX091833, late 17th or early 18th century. A well-preserved rubble, 'vaulted-tower' mill.

BEITH

Barr Mill (linen thread), Barrmill, NS368513, mid 19th century. The main block is a 3-storey, 2-by-10-bay rubble structure, cut down from a taller building and now with a flat roof. Other buildings on the site include a 2-storey, 7-bay block, and a 2-storey, 3-by-5-bay block with segmental-arched windows. Now occupied by a firm of fertilizer manufacturers.

Giffen Mill, Baroill, NS369514, early 19th century. A 3-storey, 4-bay rubble building on a rectangular plan, now gutted and used as a store.

Caledonian Cabinet Works, Beith, NS345533, founded 1879 by Matthew Pollock. A complex of 2- and 3-storey, red-brick and red-and-white-brick buildings dominated by a 6-storey tower. The street frontage consists of two 3-storey blocks, one 5-bay, with a stone-faced ground floor and red-and-white-brick upper floors, and the other 4 bay. Now largely disused.

Janefield Cabinet and Chair Works, Beith, NS348544, founded *c* 1883 by Stevenson, Higgins and Co. A 2-storey and attic, red-brick block on an L plan, now a foundry.

Joinery, Beith, NS348541, mid 19th century. A 2-storey, 2-by-4-bay, red-brick building, with small-paned windows and an outside wooden stair. There is also a small wooden timber store.

Coldstream Mill, NS385544, early 19th century. A 2-storey rubble building on an L plan, with a small single-storey rubble extension and a larger wood and corrugated-iron one. There is an 8-spoke wood and iron overshot wheel, about 3ft 6in wide by 20ft diameter (1·06 by 6·10m). Still occasionally used.

Smithy, Gateside, NS363536, mid 19th century. A single-storey rubble building, with 2 square-section, red-brick chimney stacks. Still in use.

Giffen Limeworks, NS364507, mid to late 19th century and later (plate 15). Probably the last traditional limekilns to work in Scotland, closed in 1972. A bank of 2 single-draw rubble kilns, reinforced with buttresses, and with old rails, and heightened in brick. Covered conveyors link the segmental-arched draw holes with a wood-framed, corrugated-iron crushing and bagging mill.

Giffenmill Viaduct, NS367511, opened 1903 by the Lanarkshire & Ayrshire Railway. A 7-span viaduct, with semicircular concrete arches, now disused.

Gree Viaduct, NS399513, opened 1903 by the Lanarkshire & Ayrshire Railway. An 11-span concrete viaduct, with semicircular arches, now disused.

Lyonshields Limekilns, NS374538, early 19th century. A bank of 2 single-draw limekilns, rubble-built, with roughly elliptical-arched drawholes.

Mill of Beith, NS366559, late 18th to early 19th century. A small rectangular rubble building with an offset square kiln. The lower part of the wheel gable is faced with ashlar. The wheel was mid breast, about 3ft wide by 16ft diameter (0·91 by 4·88m), and was fed from a rough dam on top of a dyke which forms a high natural waterfall. Now gutted and disused.

COLMONELL

Kinclaer Viaduct, NX202912, opened 1877 by the Girvan & Portpatrick Railway. A handsome 10-span viaduct on a curve, with semicircular arches. The arch rings are of dressed stone, with coursed-rubble piers and random rubble spandrels.

15 Giffen Limeworks, with one kiln in centre, the other on the right.

Pinwherry Station, NX194873, opened 1877 by the Girvan & Portpatrick Railway. Formerly a single-platform through station. The 2-storey rubble platform building, containing offices and a dwellinghouse, survives, as does the signal box, of standard Glasgow & South Western pattern. The platform edge has been removed. The station building at Pinmore (NX203920) is similar, but brick-built.

COYLTON

Millmannoch, NS432187, rebuilt early 20th century. A 2- and 3-storey stone building on an L plan, extended in brick. The stone portion is dated 1788. The machinery, consisting of 3 pairs of stones and an oat bruiser, was originally driven by an overshot wheel, now removed, more recently by a turbine, still in position, and now, occasionally, by a tractor.

CUMNOCK

Bank Viaduct, NS574205, opened 1850 by the Glasgow, Paisley, Kilmarnock & Ayr Railway. A very fine tall 13-span masonry viaduct, with semicircular arches.

McCartney's Engineering Works, NS571200, mid 19th century (plate 16). An interesting 2-storey and attic, 3-by-11-bay rubble block, typical of the mid 19th-century, west of Scotland engineering works. Made agricultural machinery, now a joinery works.

Viaduct, NS573195, opened 1872 by the Glasgow & South-Western Railway. A 13-span masonry viaduct, with segmental arches, now used as a footbridge.

DAILLY

Craighead Lime Works, NS234014, early 19th century and later. An extensive works, with 3 kilns: 2 conventional 3-draw, rubble, with brick-lined shafts; and 1 curious 3-draw kiln, with 2 draw holes in the front and 1 at the side. This has brick voussoirs in a rubble kiln body. In all 3 kilns some patching has been done in brick. There are corrugated-iron processing buildings, which were in 1969 pulverizing limestone. Behind the works is a large quarry, now disused.

Aird Bridge, Kilkerran, NS293033, built 1779. A handsome segmental-arched, single-span bridge, with vermiculated voussoirs and ashlar spandrels and wing walls. There are quatrefoil recesses in the spandrels. Drumgirnan Bridge, NS306042, is similar.

Killochan Station, NS223007, opened 1860 by the Maybole and Girvan Railway, probably rebuilt c 1900. Formerly a 2-platform through station, with the main offices on the down platform in a 2-storey, red-brick block with 1-storey wings. Similar to Cassillis Station.

Lannielane Limeworks, NS313018, late 18th to early 19th century. A bank of 2 single-draw limekilns, with the indications of opencast working, and of the mining of a seam of limestone about 3ft (0·91m) thick, dipping steeply. The mine workings are now flooded.

DALMELLINGTON

Dalmellington Ironworks, Waterside, NS442083, opened 1848 by the Dalmellington Iron Co. The much-reduced remains of a typical mid 19th-century iron-smelting works. The most notable surviving structure is the Italianate blowing-engine house, with round-headed windows, dated 1847, now part of a brickworks. The single-storey ashlar locomotive repair workshops, probably contemporary, are still in use. The slag-hill, though reduced by recent excavation, is still a landmark. (See David L. Smith, *The Dalmellington Iron Company*, David & Charles, 1967.)

16 McCartney's Engineering Works, Cumnock.

DALRY

DALRY

Bridgend Woollen Mills, NS297494, late 19th century. A 3-storey, 15-bay, yellow-brick block, with a central 3-bay tower on the south side. The brickwork is panelled, giving a pleasing effect. There is a neat 2-storey stone office block, and a range of single-storey weaving sheds. Now in multiple occupation, and part disused.

Carsehead Bridge, NS301497, early 19th century. A graceful 3-span bridge, with the main span flanked by smaller flood-relief spans. The arch ring of the main arch is of dressed stone, the rest is of coursed rubble. The arches are segmental.

Dalry Station, NS297492, opened 1840 by the Glasgow, Paisley, Kilmarnock & Ayr Railway, and rebuilt c 1905. A 4-platform through station, with the booking office in a 2-storey, 2-bay, brick and sandstone building on the up side, linked to the platforms by a covered footbridge with ramps instead of stairs. The waiting rooms are on the platforms, in single-storey wooden buildings, with steel-framed glazed awnings cantilevered out. The goods shed, a large wooden structure, also survives.

Base of water tank, NS298483, built c 1843 by the Glasgow, Paisley, Kilmarnock & Ayr Railway. A small rectangular dressed-stone building with panelled walls and a hipped roof. All that remains of Dalry Junction Station, closed 1849.

Clay mine, NS290477, early 20th century. An 'ingaun' e'e' mine, linked with the Douglas Firebrick Co's factory by a narrow-gauge, double-track rope-worked incline. One of the few remaining examples of this mode of operation.

Auchengree Foundry, Glengarnock, NS327524, founded c 1860 by Robert Kerr. A small single-storey rubble building, with arched entrances, which was formerly the foundry, and a later 2-storey and attic, 9-bay building, which had a pattern shop in the first floor and pattern stores in the attic. The ground floor houses a machine shop, and the foundry is now used for machinery. The roof structure of the foundry was obviously designed for post cranes. There is a large derrick crane in the yard, with steel frame and cast-iron crab.

Glengarnock Station, NS322527, opened c 1845 by the Glasgow, Paisley, Kilmarnock & Ayr Railway. A 2-platform through station, with main offices on the up platform in a 2-storey rubble building incorporating a dwellinghouse. A platform awning has been added. On the down platform is a small wooden shelter. The platforms are linked by a lattice-girder footbridge.

Limekilns, Hourat, early to mid 19th century. At NS286541, a massive single-draw kiln with wide segmental draw arch flanked by buttresses. At the rear is a large disused quarry. At NS293534 a pair of single-draw kilns, with segmental-arched draw holes. Both have stone linings, partly collapsed.

DALRYMPLE

Burnton Viaduct, NS372153, opened 1856 by the Ayr & Dalmellington Railway. A handsome 16-span masonry viaduct, with semicircular arches.

Purclewan Mill, NS379158, early 19th century. A 2-storey and attic rubble building, on an L plan, with adjacent single-storey block, probably built as a granary. The mill is now gutted and used as a store.

DARVEL
DARVEL

Darvel Bleachworks, NS565372, built 1903 for James Clelland & Co. A 2-storey, 4-by-11-bay, red-and-white-brick building with a tall chimney. Disused for many years.

Lace factory, NS564377, built 1896 for John Aird & Co. A 2-storey and attic, 4-by-9-bay, cement-rendered front building.

Lace factory, NS563373, built from 1876 for Alexander Morton. An extensive group of yellow-brick, single-storey weaving sheds with 2-storey office block and decorative tower.

Lace factory, NS571376, built 1899 for Morton, Aird & Co. A 2-storey and attic, 3-by-7-bay, yellow-brick front block, with single-storey weaving sheds at the rear.

Lace and madras factory, NS562376, built from 1886 for Alexander Jamieson & Co. An extensive group of buildings, the oldest being a 3-storey, 7-bay block of madras loom shops, followed by 3-storey, 2-by-17-bay buildings. A typical 2-storey, 8-bay, lace-loom block and some single-storey sheds complete the complex.

Lace and muslin factory, NS569375, built from 1877 for Stirling Bros & Co. Behind a 20th-century frontage is a neat 6-bay range of north-light weaving sheds with a circular-section brick chimney.

Loudounhill Viaduct, NS602373, opened 1905 by the Strathaven & Darvel Railway. A 13-span brick viaduct, with semicircular arches.

DREGHORN

Bourtreehill Brickworks, NS387399, late 19th century. The sadly reduced remains of a large brickworks with associated clay pit. The

two 16-chamber kilns, brick-moulding sheds and some other buildings survive, but the steam winding engine (A. BARCLAY, SONS & CO
LTD) and wooden headgear were demolished c 1970.
Cunninghamhead Mill, NS373422, early 19th century. A handsome 3-storey rubble building on an L plan, with a single-storey
rubble block nearby. Now gutted and being converted to a house.
Montgomeryfield Brickworks, NS348376, late 19th to early 20th
century. A large disused works, with 4 long Hoffman kilns, and 3 tall
square-section chimneys.

DUNDONALD

Lave Sawmill, NS377368, mid 19th century. A 1-storey and attic,
rubble and brick building, with a wooden lean-to addition. The
sawbench has been removed, but the skeleton of a 6-spoke, low-breast
paddle-wheel with iron axle and wooden rings and spokes survives,
as does a complex system of gearing and belt pulleys.
Tollhouse, Gatehead, NS377355, late 18th to early 19th century. A
single-storey building with prominent quoins. Now disused.
Troon Harbour, NS311310, built 1808 on, for coal shipment, by the
3rd Duke of Portland. Formed by a natural headland, improved by
the construction of a west pier, a long east pier and by quaying the
east side of the headland. The basin thus formed is subdivided by 2
piers into inner and outer basins, and there are 2 dry docks, now
owned by the Ailsa Shipbuilding Co. Now used for shipbuilding and
breaking, and by small craft. Interesting features are an attractive
range of single-storey cottages and the 'Ballast Bank', composed of
earth and shingle ballast from sailing colliers, and acting as a shield
from the prevailing wind.
Troon Station, NS326309, rebuilt 1892 by the Glasgow & South
Western Railway, architect JAMES MILLER. A 2-platform through
station, with striking platform buildings with harled finish and
imitation wood framing. There are steel-framed awnings, linked,
with an open centre section, and the platforms are linked by a covered
footbridge.
Shipbuilding Yard, Troon, NS310313, late 19th century. A much-
modernized group of structures, with 2 dry docks. The engine-works
building, a red-brick structure, is probably original.

DUNLOP

Dunlop Station, NS409493, opened 1873 by the Glasgow, Barrhead
& Kilmarnock Joint Railway. A 2-platform through station, with the

main offices on the down platform, in a single-storey stone building. On the up platform is a neat wooden shelter on a brick base. There is a substantial stone goods shed in the now disused goods yard.

Hapland Mill, NS411491, late 19th century. A group of 1- and 2-storey buildings, mostly of brick, with a square-section brick chimney. Now weaves carpet yarn for Kilmarnock.

Limekiln, NS394467, early 19th century. A rubble-built, single-draw kiln, with segmental-arched draw hole.

Viaduct, NS409492, opened 1873, by the Glasgow, Barrhead & Kilmarnock Joint Railway. A 4-span viaduct, with 3 small segmental arches over the river and a wider one over a road, slightly skewed. The arch rings are of dressed stone, rusticated on the outer faces, and the rest of the bridge is of rusticated coursed rubble.

Limekilns, Lugton, NS411528, early 19th century. A pair of single-draw limekilns, with segmental-arched draw holes. The upper part of the kilns has collapsed.

FENWICK

Waterside Woollen Mill, NS486435, early 19th century. A 3-storey, 8-bay rubble building, with a 3-storey, 3-bay dwellinghouse at one end. Later additions include another dwellinghouse and a 2-storey, 3-bay brick block.

GALSTON

Galston Bridge, NS502367, built 1839. A 3-span masonry bridge, with segmental arches.

Lace Mill, NS503367, late 19th century. A 2-storey, 16-bay brick main block, with a bay-fronted office at the west end and a taller 2-storey block at the east end. Now occupied by a firm of electrical engineers.

GIRVAN

GIRVAN

Bridge Mill, NX193989, early 19th century. A 4-storey, 3-bay whitewashed rubble main block, with a kiln and single-storey dwellinghouse and stores. Now a warehouse.

Girvan Harbour, NX183982, rebuilt 1869–70, and extended in 1881–3. A rivermouth harbour, with quays on the south bank, protected by a concrete breakwater with a small light-tower at the seaward end (1881–3). A relatively recent addition is an L-plan piled pier in the inner harbour, giving increased berthage. There was a

coal quay on the north bank, but this has been demolished.
Viaduct, NX190986, opened 1860 by the Maybole & Girvan Railway.
A 3-span viaduct, with dressed-stone archways and rubble spandrels
and wing walls.
Weavers' cottages, NX185971, early 19th century. Many of the
houses in the older parts of the town were weavers' cottages, some
with double windows and a few with triple windows. Some good
examples are at the end of Glendoune Street.

IRVINE

Tollhouse, Girdle Toll, NS341404, late 18th to early 19th century.
A single-storey, 3-bay harled building, with a 3-sided bay window.
Irvine Harbour, NS303380, late 19th century. A rivermouth
harbour, with the main quays (wood-piled) on the south bank. There
are 3 rail-mounted cranes, 2 by ALEXANDER CHAPLIN & CO, Glasgow,
and one by SMITH RODLEY. The harbour office and custom house are
small single-storey structures.
Irvine Station, NS316385, opened 1839, by the Glasgow, Paisley,
Kilmarnock & Ayr Railway. A 2-platform through station. The line
is on a viaduct, with the platform buildings entered from the railway
at first-floor level. The main offices are on the down side, in a handsome 2-storey, coursed-rubble building on an L plan, and there is a
smaller stone building of similar construction on the up platform.
Both platforms have awnings.
Queen's Bridge, NS313398, built c 1840 for the Glasgow, Paisley,
Kilmarnock & Ayr Railway. A 6-span masonry viaduct, with flat
segmental arches.

KILBIRNIE

Glengarnock Steelworks, NS324530, founded 1840, as an iron-
smelting works, but dates in its present form from 1916–18, when
reconstructed by David Colville & Sons. The steel-framed, open-
hearth melting shop and the rolling mill are substantially of that date,
though the furnaces and machinery have been renewed and enlarged.
The building of the Bessemer converter shop, built 1884, also
survives.

KILBIRNIE

Dennyholm Mill, NS315543, founded as a spinning mill by W. & J.
Knox, c 1830. A large complex of rubble buildings, now sadly
reduced. The main surviving range is now a 4-storey, 20-bay block,
used as a sawmill.

Garnock Mill, NS317543, built 1834 by Wilsons & Jamiesons for flax spinning. A 3-storey and attic, 3-by-8-bay rubble building, with jack-arch interior. The corners of the building are braced by iron-rod cross ties with external tieplates. There is also a 3-storey range at right angles to the main block.

Nether Mill, NS318538, mid 19th century. The ruins of a rectangular rubble building, with the framework of a suspended iron mid-breast wheel, 3ft wide by 18ft diameter (0·91 by 5·49m). The buckets and sole, now missing, appear to have been of sheet iron. Drive to the mill was by an internal gear ring. At the rear of the mill a large mill-pond, now drained, still exists.

Net works, NS317547, built 1883. A small group of single-storey rubble buildings, with a neat office block and a circular-section chimney. Now used as a builder's store.

Ropeworks, NS316549, late 19th century. A complex of red-brick buildings, of which the largest is a 2-storey, 6-bay building, with segmental-arched windows. There is a circular-section brick chimney.

Stoneyholm Mill, NS317545, built 1831 (plate 17). A very interesting complex. The oldest part is a 4-storey and attic, 8-bay block built as a cotton mill in 1831, with a similar 3-by-4-bay extension. Adjacent to the former is a beam-engine house, and adjacent to that a later horizontal-engine house. This old block, now used for storage, forms an E plan with a later building. The latter is a 3-storey and attic rubble structure, with a 9-bay pedimented frontage and 8-bay wings. Behind the E block is a 4-storey rubble block, a range of single-storey weaving sheds, and a 2-storey, 5-by-28-bay, yellow-brick, net-weaving factory, built in 2 portions. There is a very large red-brick, circular-section chimney. Still in use as a net and twine factory by W. & J. Knox, who bought the mills in 1864.

KILBRIDE

Fairlie High Station, NS210547, opened 1880 by the Glasgow & South Western Railway. A 2-platform through station with the main offices on the down platform in a single-storey wooden building. On the up platform is a small brick shelter. The platforms are linked by a lattice-girder footbridge.

Sea Mill, West Kilbride, NS202472, late 18th century. A 2-storey rubble building on an L plan with a small wood and iron wheel. The mill pond is in good condition, though no longer used.

West Kilbride Station, NS209485, opened 1878 by the Glasgow &

South Western Railway, and rebuilt *c* 1900. A 2-platform through station, with the main offices on the down platform, in a handsome single-storey, stone and harl building with a gabled porch and, on the platform side, a bracketted glazed awning. On the up platform is a small wooden shelter. The platforms are linked by a plate-girder covered footbridge.

KILMARNOCK

KILMARNOCK

Bishopfield Print Works, NS432383, early 19th century. A large group of 1-, 2-, 3- and 4-storey rubble and yellow-brick buildings, the largest of which are a 4-storey, 5-bay block, a 3-storey and attic, 2-by-5-bay building, and a 3-storey and attic, 8-bay structure, extended in brick from a 2-storey rubble building. Of the others, the most interesting is a 3-storey, 4-bay rubble building with louvred ventilators in top floor. Now occupied by the Townholm Spinning Co.

17 Stoneyholm Mill, Kilbirnie, Garnock Mill on right.

Caledonia Works, NS424382, built from 1847 by Andrew Barclay. The oldest part of this complex is probably the 2-storey and 2 attics, 16-by-4-bay rubble block in West Langlands Street, while the other 2-storey (now 1-storey internally), 18-by-6-bay rubble block which houses the light-machine shop cannot be much later. The 3 bays of erecting and heavy-machine shops and the 2-storey and attic, 2-by-5-bay, red-brick office date from *c* 1900, as does the single-storey, steel-framed boiler shop. A curious feature of the oldest block is a double dormer window in the upper attic at one end, which is reputed to have been used as an observatory by Andrew Barclay, who was an amateur instrument-maker of repute. Also included in the complex is the former Titchfield Foundry, a long single-storey rubble building, lit at 2 levels, with rubble and corrugated-iron additions.

Glencairn Mill, NS428366, early 19th century. A 3-storey and attic, 2-by-6-bay building, incorporating a kiln, with louvred roof-ridge ventilator, at one end. Now gutted and used as an Electricity Board store.

Engineering works, NS429368, founded on this site in 1871 by the Kennedy Patent Water Meter Co Ltd. A large complex of engineering shops, mainly modern, with a 19th-century office block, 2 storey by 22 bay.

Kilmarnock Bus Station, NS429381, built 1923. Probably the oldest surviving purpose-built bus station in Scotland. A large steel-roofed, single-storey building, with a red-sandstone Renaissance frontage with offices on the first floor. There are 4 bus platforms.

Kilmarnock Station, NS427383, opened 1843 by the Glasgow, Paisley, Kilmarnock & Ayr Railway, and rebuilt 1878. A 6-platform through and terminal station, with 2-bay platforms at the north end and one at the south. The main station building is on the down side, and is a 2-storey red-sandstone structure, with a tower, with a 20-bay glazed awning supported on cast-iron columns. The island platform (up side) had, until recently, a wooden shelter and awning. Incorporated in the down-side building, is the original 3-storey, 3-by-2-bay cream-sandstone station building.

Kilmarnock Standard Printing Works, NS426379, late 19th century. A 2-storey and attic, brick and sandstone building on a triangular site, with a 1-bay and 14-bay Renaissance frontages. The roof is mansarded.

Kilmarnock Viaduct, NS430382, opened 1848 by the Glasgow, Paisley, Kilmarnock & Ayr Railway. A 23-span viaduct, with dressed-stone arch rings and pier quoins, the remainder of the masonry being coursed rubble. The fifth arch from the north is a wide elliptical arch spanning a main road, the others being smaller and segmental.

Kilmarnock Works, NS422384, built from 1855 for the Glasgow & South Western Railway. The fragmentary remains of a once large complex consisting of a 2-bay wagon works, and a 2-storey office block with a clock tower.

Loanhead Mill, NS431372, late 19th century. A group of 2- and 3-storey, yellow-brick buildings, of which the most interesting is a 3-storey, 4-bay block, with a central gabled feature.

Bottle kilns, Longpark Pottery, NS427387, late 19th to early 20th century. Two bottle kilns, with square brick bases reinforced by rolled steel joists, a cylindrical section reinforced by steel bands, a tapering section, and a cap with alternate courses of red-and-white bricks.

New Mill, NS438372, early 19th century. A 3-storey and attic, 7-bay rubble building, with a large kiln, forming an L with the main range. Now gutted and used as a store.

Riverbank Print Works, NS434373, early 19th century. A 2-storey and attic, 2-by-8-bay, coursed-rubble building, with iron-framed windows.

Townhead Mills, NS432383, late 19th century. A group of buildings of various dates, including a 4-storey, 5-by-8-bay, red-and-white-brick building, with 3 semicircular light windows in the top floor, and a similar 6-bay block facing the river.

Townholm Works, NS433387, founded c 1844 by George Caldwell, but most famous from c 1877 in the hands of Grant, Ritchie & Co, engineers. A large single-storey, 26-bay, yellow-brick engineering shop now harled and used as a warehouse. This was lit at 2 levels by round-headed windows. To the north are the cut-down remains of a much older 2-storey rubble block.

Vulcan Foundry, NS424383, mid 19th century. A tall single-storey rubble building, 16 bays long, with a large arched doorway. At one end is a 2-storey, 3-bay office block. Now a wool store.

Bonded warehouses, NS428381, late 19th century. Three large bonded stores. One is a 3-storey, 14-by-4-bay, terra-cotta, brick-faced block, with red-sandstone dressings. The others, in French Renaissance style, are a 3-storey building, with rusticated grey-sandstone ground floor, with round-headed openings, and white-brick upper floors, with arcades on the first floor and pairs of pilasters in the second floor; and a similar, particularly fine, 4-storey block,

with a rounded end and frontages to 2 streets.
Brewery, NS422371, early 19th century. A group of 1- and 2-storey buildings round a courtyard, with a truncated pyramidal-roofed kiln. Now a skinworks.
Lace factory, Lawson Street, NS431372, founded *c* 1880 by W. E. & F. Dobson. A 4-storey, 7-by-4-bay corner block, with a bowed end, and a 3-storey, 9-bay building. The 4-storey section has a tall ground floor for the lace looms. Both buildings are yellow brick, with segmental-arched windows.
Printing works, Nelson Street, NS427379, late 19th century. A 2-storey and attic, 4-by-5-bay, red-brick building, with a Flemish gabled frontage and a smaller gable in similar style on the east side.
Seed store, Nelson Street, NS427377, late 19th century. A 2-storey and basement, 3-by-6-bay, yellow-brick building, with a Renaissance red-sandstone street frontage.
Seed store, Grange Street, NS425379, late 19th century. A 2-storey attic and basement, 5-by-9-bay Renaissance building.
Seed store, NS427388, late 19th century. A 2-storey and basement, 11-bay coursed-rubble building, with a single-storey engine and boiler house with a truncated chimney. Still contains some seed-dressing machinery.
Tile works, NS411369, late 19th to early 20th century. An L-plan range of pantiled single-storey drying sheds, with louvred sides, and a single multi-vented kiln. Now disused.
Shoe factory, NS427372, *c* 1908 and later. A group of 2-, 3- and 4-storey buildings, the block facing the street being 4-storey, 5-bay. The river frontage consists of 3-storey, 4-bay, 2-storey and attic, 17-bay, 3-storey, 15-bay, 3-storey, 10-bay and 4-storey, 14-bay buildings, all yellow brick, with a water tower.
Old Bridge, Riccarton, NS428365, 18th century. A 3-span, segmental-arched bridge, with dressed-stone arch rings, rubble spandrels, and triangular cutwaters. The central span is larger than the other two.

KILMAURS

Kilmaurs Mill, NS413413, early 19th century. A large 3-storey and attic, 6-bay rubble building, on a T plan, with a kiln with roof-ridge ventilator at one end. There was an internal overshot wheel, now removed. An unusual feature is a carved stone showing a millstone drive spider, a ring of rope, a bill for dressing millstones, and a grain shovel. Now disused.

Boot factory, NS408412, late 19th century. A 3-storey and attic brick block, with a 7-bay gabled frontage. Now a hosiery works.
Weaver's cottage, NS408412, early 19th century. A classic single-storey weaver's cottage with the characteristic double window.
Laigh Milton Mill, NS382373, early 19th century. A large 3-storey and attic, rubble building, on an L plan, with the remains of an 8-spoke, low-breast paddle-wheel, with cast-iron rings and axle, and wooden spokes and paddles, 5ft 6in wide by 16ft diameter (1·67 by 4·88m). Now disused.
Bridge, Gatehead, NS392362, mid 19th century. A 2-span bridge, with dressed-stone arch rings and coursed-rubble spandrels and wing walls. The arches are segmental, and the cutwaters are triangular.
Railway viaduct, Gatehead, NS383369, opened 1812 by the Kilmarnock and Troon Railway. A 4-span bridge, with dressed-stone arch rings and rubble spandrels and piers. The arches are segmental, and there are rounded cutwaters, extended up to form semicircular buttresses. In poor condition. The oldest railway viaduct in Scotland.

KILWINNING

Dalgarven Mill, NS297458, early 19th century. A 2- and 3-storey rubble building on a T plan, with a 2-storey dwellinghouse. There was a kiln at one end of the main range. Across the mill-race is a small brick building, probably once a boiler house, with a square-section brick chimney. A low-breast paddle-wheel about 3ft wide by 14ft diameter (0·91 by 4·27m), with wooden paddles and spokes and iron rings and axle, drives a sack hoist.
Sevenacres Mill, NS333443, early 19th century and later. A complex of buildings, mostly brick, but including a 2-storey and attic rubble range, with the skeleton of a high-breast, wood and iron wheel, about 12ft diameter by 3ft wide (3·66 by 0·91m).
Horse-gin house, East Balgray, NS360427, early 19th century. A very well preserved circular rubble structure, slate-roofed, with matching barn.

KIRKMICHAEL

Balgreggan Limeworks, NS347049, early 19th century. A fairly well-preserved, 2-draw limekiln, with segmental-arched draw holes side by side. There are rebates in the masonry for some form of wooden shelter. The probable site of the quarry is now thickly wooded.

Weavers' cottages, Crosshill, NS3206 (plate 18). The village was built from *c* 1808 specifically as a handloom-weaving village, and most of the older houses were at one time weavers' cottages. Almost all are single storey, harled, some with double windows, 1 with triple windows.

Aitkenhead Mill, NS349081, early 19th century. A 3-storey, 3-bay rubble building, now asbestos-roofed, with a 2-storey kiln at one end. The kiln has a large roof-ridge ventilator. The low-breast paddle-wheel has been removed and the gutted building is now a store.

KIRKOSWALD

Kilkerran Acid Works, NS303053, mid 19th century. A 2-bay rubble shed, now with asbestos roof, the remains of a pyroligneous acid works owned at one time by Stewart Turnbull & Co (Camlachie) Ltd. Now a store.

Kilkerran Station, NS297043, opened 1860 by the Maybole & Girvan Railway. Formerly a 2-platform through station, with the

18   Weaver's cottage, Crosshill.

main offices on the down platform. These were in a 1- and 2-storey rubble building, on an L plan, incorporating a dwellinghouse, with crow-stepped gables. The rubble goods shed also survives, as does the signal-box of typical Glasgow and South Western wooden pattern.

Hamilton Bridge, Kilkerran, NS309050, built 1825. A single segmental arch with dressed-stone arch ring and coursed-rubble spandrels.

Smithy, NS299042, early 19th century. A single-storey, 2-by-2-bay rubble building, still in use.

Maidens Harbour, NS210082, probably 18th century in origin. An irregular masonry pier, repaired in concrete, with a low concrete breakwater on the east (c 1950). At the landward end are 4 cast-iron pots in brick settings, with chimneys, used for boiling fishing nets in preservatives.

LARGS

Fairlie Slip Dock, NS209555, founded 1812. A group of wood, brick and corrugated-iron sheds, perhaps the most interesting being a 2-storey block with a large mould loft on the upper floor. Many celebrated late 19th-century yachts were built here.

Largs Harbour, NS201595, built 1834. An L-plan masonry pier, the head of which is used by passenger steamers. To the north are the remains of a ramped rubble ferry pier.

MAUCHLINE

Smithy, Crosshands, NS486307, early 19th century. A single-storey rubble building. Now disused.

Horse-gin house, Woodhead Farm, Crossroads, NS472343, early 16th century. A circular rubble building with a slate roof. Now used as a barn.

MAUCHLINE

Ballochmyle Creamery, NS496254, early 20th century. The main range is a 3-storey harled block on an L plan, with a small ventilating tower. A good example of early 20th-century factory building.

Ballochmyle Viaduct, NS508254, built 1846–8 for the Glasgow, Paisley, Kilmarnock & Ayr Railway. A splendid 7-arch viaduct with a central span 181ft long (55.2m). All the arches are semicircular, with dressed-stone arch rings and coursed-rubble piers and spandrels. Reckoned to be the longest masonry railway arch ever built.

Barskimming Bridge, NS490253, 18th century. A single segmental arch, 100ft (30·5m) span, with dressed-stone arch ring and spandrels and rubble wing-walls. Strengthened with tie rods.

Barskimming Mill, NS492253, rebuilt *c* 1893 by William Alexander. A complex group of 2-, 3- and 4-storey brick buildings, some with sandstone quoins. Now used as a small engineering works.

Howford Bridge, NS516253, late 18th century. A 2-span bridge, with dressed-stone arch rings and rubble spandrels. The arches are segmental, and the cutwaters triangular.

Mauchline Station, NS497265, opened 1848 by the Glasgow, Paisley, Kilmarnock & Ayr Railway and rebuilt *c* 1900. Formerly a 3-platform through station. The main offices, on the up platform, were in a long single-storey harled brick building on a sandstone base, with a glazed awning on cast-iron brackets. The island-platform shelter is of wooden construction, with an all round glazed awning on cast-iron brackets. There is a red-sandstone goods shed, and a single-storey agent's house on an L plan (probably 1847–8).

Victoria Box Works, NS498271, built in the late 18th century for Andrew Kay & Co, snuffbox manufacturers. A 2-storey, 10-bay, red-sandstone building, with windows in the upper floor close together. Now a store.

Mill at Haugh, NS498253, early 19th century. A 2-bay, 1- and 2-storey, red-sandstone building, rubble-built except for the wheel gable. Now gutted and used as a garage and store. The lade, which also served a long-defunct woollen mill, can be traced for several hundred yards upstream, partly in tunnel.

MAYBOLE

Threshing mill, Beoch, NS296146, late 19th century. A 2-storey and basement rubble building, part of a steading, with a 6-spoke, suspended overshot all-iron wheel, 12ft diameter (3·66m), which drove a threshing mill by J. & T. YOUNG of Ayr. The mill has now been removed, but the wheel survives.

Dunure Harbour, NS254160, built 1811. A small rectangular basin formed by 2 straight rubble piers with rounded ends. The landward sides are partly rock-cut. There is also a rubble breakwater to protect the entrance from northerly winds. At the seaward end of the longer pier is a small circular light-tower, much eroded. Other features are a series of wooden frames for net drying and a 2-storey range of fishermen's cottages on the south quay.

Dunure Mill, NS253148, late 18th century. An unusual 3-storey,

2-by-3-bay rubble building, with pairs of small round-headed windows and crow-stepped gables surmounted by crosses. At the east end is a kiln, and at the rear the ruins of a wheelhouse for a large overshot or high-breast wheel.

Limekilns, Dunure, NS254158, early 19th century. A bank of 2 large single-draw rubble kilns. The segmentally arched draw holes are used as stores, while a shop has been built on the kiln top.

Waulk Mill, Minishant, NS329143, late 18th century. A 2-storey and attic, 5-bay building, now harled. Used as the village hall.

Weavers' cottages, Minishant, NS330143, late 18th century. A range of five 2-roomed, single-storey rubble cottages, with harled fronts.

Maybole Station, NS298101, rebuilt 1880 by the Glasgow & South Western Railway. A 2-platform through station, with the main offices on the down platform. These are in a 2-storey, 4-bay rubble building, with a single-storey wood and rubble wing. On the up platform there is a large rubble and wood single-storey building with a glazed awning supported on cast-iron brackets. A lattice-girder footbridge links the platforms.

St Cuthbert's Boot & Shoe Factory, Maybole, NS303100, mid 19th century. The cut-down remains of a 3-storey rubble factory, with a 3-storey, 3-bay, red-brick building and a 3-storey, 12-bay, red-and-white-brick block. Lower down on this sloping island site is a 3-storey and attic, 12-by-9-bay, red-and-white-brick building on an L plan, and an older 3-storey and attic, 5-by-9-bay block with louvred ventilators on the top floor. Now used as stores.

Engineering works, Maybole, NS304103, mid 19th century. A complex of buildings including a 2-storey, 3-by-7-bay, rubble-front block.

MONKTON

Windmill, Monkton, NS362281, early 18th century. A well-preserved vaulted-tower windmill stump, with a conical roof.

MUIRKIRK

Glenbuck Furnace, NS750295, built c 1796, by John Rumney of Workington and others. The partly buried remains of a rubble structure, with portions of 3 walls, 1 with the head of a semicircular arch, visible. This may well be the furnace, though only careful excavation would confirm this supposition.

Muirkirk Ironworks, NS697268, founded 1786. The substantial

remains here were demolished by the National Coal Board in 1968.
McAdam Cairn, NS695256. A cemented rubble cairn, erected 1931, constructed out of stones from the ruins of the tar works constructed by Lord Dundonald in 1786 and managed by J. L. McAdam, the road engineer. The outlines of buildings can be discerned round the cairn.
Gas works, NS695270, mid 19th century. A small horizontal-retort works with brick buildings. One of the chimneys is heavily reinforced with steel strapping. There are atmospheric condensers, and a 2-lift guideless holder.
Tramway embankment, NS695265, c 1805. The well-defined remains of the embankment for the horse tramway which linked the tar kilns with the ironworks.

NEW CUMNOCK

Benston Limeworks, NS581159, early 19th century. The remains of two 3-draw limekilns, with brick-arched draw holes and rubble bodies.
Craigdullyeart Limeworks, NS663153, late 18th to early 19th century. An extensive quarry and mine, with a range of kilns consisting of a pair of single-draw kilns and a double-arched, single-draw kiln of earlier date. Nearby, at Hall of Mansfield (NS638150), is a 3-draw kiln.
New Cumnock Station, NS618142, opened 1850 by the Glasgow, Dumfries & Carlisle Railway and rebuilt c 1890. Formerly a 2-platform through station, with the main offices in a single-storey, 9-bay rubble building on the down platform, incorporating a dwellinghouse. This structure is similar to, but simpler than that at Crookston, Glasgow.

NEWMILNS & GREENHOLM

Annabank Factory, NS530370, built 1882 for Robert Muir. The first Irvine Valley lace factory of more than 1 storey, with the characteristic tall ground floor for the lace looms and lower upper floor for mending and making up. A 2-storey and attic, 4-by-16-bay, yellow-brick building, with single-storey weaving sheds. Now disused. To the east are Caledonia Factory, built 1886, a similar building, 23 bays long, and Vale Lace Works, built 1886 for Johnston Shields & Co, a complex of 1- and 2-storey buildings with a 2-storey and attic, 2-by-11-bay sandstone frontage.
Craigview Bridge, NS537373, early 19th century. An elegant single-

span, segmental-arched bridge, with dressed-stone arch ring and rubble spandrels and abutments.

Greenhead Mills, NS540373, built from 1877 for J. & J. Wilson. A group of single-storey sheds, with a handsome 5-bay enamelled-brick frontage, built in 1886, as part of a madras shed.

Irvinebank Powerloom Factory, NS532371, built 1877 for Morton, Cameron & Co, and rebuilt after a fire in 1923. A very handsome brick range, with a 3-storey, 6-bay main block and a 2-storey, 9-bay wing. Both have segmental low-relief arches along the ground floor and sandstone cornices. Now occupied by the Vesuvius Crucible Co.

Loudoun Mill, NS544371, late 18th to early 19th century and later. A 2- and 3-storey yellow-brick and rubble building, which formerly had a 10-spoke, wood and iron low-breast paddle-wheel about 3ft wide by 20ft diameter (0·91 by 6·10m). The yellow-brick extension is dated 1914.

Northbank Factory, NS531371, built 1905–6 for D. Ligat & Co, as a muslin factory and subsequently extended. The original block is 3 storeys high, flat-roofed, and the extension 2 storeys high, both yellow brick.

Pates (Patie's) Mill, NS532371, probably early 19th century in its present form. A 3-storey and attic rubble building on a T plan, now disused and gutted.

Riverbank Factory, NS528371, built 1897 for Goldie, Steel & Co. A 2-storey and attic, 3-by-10-bay office block with single-storey weaving sheds at the side and rear, and a circular-section chimney.

Lace factory, NS534372, built 1908 for Clelland & Co. A 2-storey, yellow-brick block on an L plan, with an older front block and single-storey ancillary buildings.

Lace factory, NS541373, built 1898 for Henderson, Morton, Inglis & Co, architect THOMAS B. TODD. A typical 2-storey and attic New-milns lace factory, 6-by-10-bay, of yellow brick with a sandstone frontage.

Lace factory, NS541373, built c 1915 for J. Muir & Co Ltd. A 2- and 3-storey, 6-by-8-bay block, with a 2-storey building to the north, both yellow brick.

Lace factory, NS544371, built 1904–5 for Pollock & Co, architect THOMAS B. TODD. A group of single-storey, red and yellow buildings, with a circular-section, red-brick chimney.

Smithy, NS542373, early 19th century. A single-storey, 3-bay rubble building, with a small roof-ridge ventilator. To the rear is a corrugated-iron extension.

OCHILTREE

Mill of Dyke, NS506215, mid 19th century. A small single-storey rubble building, with a 6-spoke, wood and iron low-breast paddle wheel, about 3ft wide by 12ft diameter (0·91 by 3·66m), driving a moving-table saw bench, a surfacer, and a drilling machine, by gearing and belt.

Ochiltree Mill, NS508215, early 19th century. A rectangular 3-storey rubble building, with a 1-storey wing at right angles. The main block incorporates a kiln with roof-ridge ventilator. Now gutted and used as a store.

Ochiltree Tile Works, NS517206, late 19th century. A typical drainage tile works, still in operation, with an L-plan range of louvred single-storey drying sheds and 2 kilns, 1 circular, with a square-section brick chimney.

Old Bridge, NS512214, early 19th century. A 2-span rubble bridge, with flat segmental arches, now bypassed.

PRESTWICK

Prestwick Station, NS349262, opened permanently 1846 by the Glasgow, Paisley, Kilmarnock & Ayr Railway and rebuilt c 1900. A 2-platform through station, with the main offices on the down platform. These are in an attractive single-storey, 9-bay building of red sandstone and harl finish. On the platform side is a bracketted awning. The platforms are linked by a covered footbridge, and on the up side is a small building with a glazed bracketted awning.

RICCARTON

HURLFORD

Blair Foundry, NS449367, founded 1864 by Andrew Strang, rebuilt 1904 and extended 1921. A large 2-bay steel-framed, corrugated-iron-clad foundry block, with a lean-to bay at the south end, and a 2-storey brick pattern shop and light-machine shop.

Riccarton Mill, NS446370, early 19th century. A large 2- and 3-storey rubble mill, extended in brick, on an L plan. The mill is now gutted, but had a large low-breast wheel. Unusual features are the ornamental openings in the gable of the main range facing the river. There is a substantial angled weir a short distance upstream.

Vulcan Foundry, NS458369, founded c 1890. A single-storey, 9-bay, brick moulding shop, with 2 rows of windows, with an extensive yard containing a derrick crane. At one side is a single-storey pattern shop and store. The cupola is modern.

Viaduct, NS447371, opened 1848 by the Glasgow, Paisley, Kilmarnock & Ayr Railway. A handsome 7-span viaduct, with semicircular arches. The arch rings are of dressed stone, and the spandrels and piers of coursed rubble.

ST QUIVOX

Privick Mill, Annbank, NS407223. A large 2- and 3-storey rubble building on an irregular plan, now gutted and used as a barn. The sites of 2 wheels can be seen, 1 at right angles to the wheel gable of the other.

Horse-gin house, Highfield, NS372244, early to mid 19th century. A circular rubble structure, slate-roofed, with large openings divided by cast-iron columns. Little altered.

SORN

Catrine Village, NS5225, founded 1787 by Sir Claud Alexander of Ballochmyle and David Dale. Though the splendid cotton mills, architecturally the finest in Scotland, have been demolished, most of the original 2-storey rubble housing survives, together with the weir, approach spans to the wheel-house, and the tail-race installed in 1827 for the great 50ft (15·24m) wheels built by William Fairbairn. The tail-race exit is at NS523261. Other interesting features are the remains of the brewery (NS529258) and of a former corn mill (NS526259) beside the exit of the original tail-race.

Dalgain Limeworks, NS573262, early 19th century. A bank of 2 single-draw limekilns, much overgrown and partly flooded. The kilns have semicircular draw arches, inner segmental arches and twin draw holes. There is a flooded quarry nearby, with the earthworks for a tramway leading to the kiln top.

SORN

Dalgain Mill, NS550268. A 1-storey and attic rubble building, now gutted and used as a village hall.

New Bridge, NS556264, late 19th century. A 2-span segmental arched bridge, with dressed-stone arch rings and coursed-rubble spandrels.

New Mill, NS558264, built c 1850 for Thomas Hendry, worsted spinner. A 1-storey and attic, 4-by-4-bay rubble building, cut down from a longer range, now part of a small farmstead. Probably ceased operation in 1901.

Old Bridge, NS550268, early 18th century. A 2-span bridge, with dressed-stone arch rings and rubble wing walls. The arches are nearly semicircular, and there are triangular cutwaters.

Horse-gin house, near Sorn, NS540269, early 19th century. An octagonal rubble building, with a slate roof, used as a store.

STAIR

Stair Bridge, NS437235, built 1745. A 3-span masonry bridge.
Tam o' Shanter & Water of Ayr Hone Works, NS436235. The main parts of this complex are on opposite banks of the river Ayr. On the north bank is the original whetstone works, a range of 2-storey rubble buildings, with later additions, including a water-turbine house, and on the south side is Dalmore Mill (1821) a 2-storey building on a T plan, with the axle only of a low-breast wheel. Near the latter is the mine from which some of the stone is extracted. This has a simple headgear made of rolled-steel joists, with wooden surface buildings. Nearby can be seen the circular-section brick chimney of a steam winder of an earlier period. The 2 parts of the complex are linked by a suspension footbridge with steel wire-rope cables and suspenders, steel-tube pylons and a wooden deck.

STEVENSTON

Stevenston Station, NS270413, rebuilt *c* 1900 by the Glasgow & South Western Railway. A 2-platform through station, with the main offices in a single-storey building on the up platform, of stone and harl, with wooden trimming and a bracketted steel-framed glazed awning. There is a wooden shelter on the down platform with an awning supported on cast-iron brackets. A lattice-girder footbridge links the platform, and supplements the level crossing at the west end of the station.

STEWARTON

Annick Water Viaduct, NS417455, opened 1873 by the Glasgow, Barrhead & Kilmarnock Joint Railway. A 10-span viaduct on a curve, with dressed-stone arch rings and rubble spandrels and piers. The arches are semicircular.
Nether Robertland Mill, NS424463, early 19th century. A 3-storey and attic, 3-by-10-bay rubble building, with small-paned windows on the ground floor. At the side is a small enginehouse with Gothic windows, and at the rear a circular-section brick chimney.

TARBOLTON

Enterkine Mill, NS418239, mid 19th century. A rectangular 2-storey building, now gutted and used as a barn. There appear to have been 2 wheels, both mid breast, supplied with water, through a cast-iron pipe, from a dam about 200yd (183m) upstream.

Horse-gin house, Tongue, NS432278, early 19th century. An octagonal rubble building, with a slate roof.

Berwickshire

Berwickshire is a rich agricultural county, with little large-scale industry at any time. Important road and rail links pass through it, with appropriate remains. The coastal villages were, and in some cases are, active fishing centres.

AYTON

Smithy, Ayton, NT925610, early 19th century. A small single-storey rubble building, with an asbestos roof. Immediately adjacent is a modern single-storey workshop.

Railway bridges, Ayton, NT922598 and 923598, built 1845 for the North British Railway. Two underbridges, the former with a segmental skew arch, carrying a plaque with the inscription 'North British Railway, Ayton Section, Robert Dodds, Contractor 1845'. The other has a semicircular arch. Both have dressed-stone arch rings and rubble spandrels and wing walls.

Burnmouth Harbour, NT958610, rebuilt 1879. A harbour of enclosure made by a substantial pier and a breakwater. Inside the harbour a straight pier projecting from the main pier and an L-plan pier projecting from the shore form an inner basin.

Burnmouth Station, NT954612, opened 1846 by the North British Railway. Probably the original station building for this former 2-platform through station is a single-storey, coursed-rubble building on a T plan, on the down side. This is now a dwellinghouse. Nearby is a skew overbridge, with dressed-stone segmental arch and rubble spandrels and wing walls.

Farm chimney, Whiterig, nr Ayton, NT920584, mid 19th century. A slender brick chimney with an ornamental cap, on a stone base, serving small rubble boiler and engine houses.

BUNKLE

Chirnside Paper Mill, NT853561, founded 1842. A much-altered complex, with the original frontages retained. These are 2-storey and attic, with two centre-gabled blocks, one 9, the other 13 bay, the latter flanked by 3-bay gabled wings. There is a large circular brick chimney (see plate 19).

Joinery, Preston, NT790573, probably mid 19th century. A single-storey, 3-bay rubble building. Nearby is a small sawmill, with the decayed remains of a waterwheel.

Smithy, Preston, NT790573, early 19th century. A neat single-storey rubble building, with a pantiled roof.

Houses, Cumledge Mills, NT790570, early to mid 19th century. The mills have been demolished, but the associated housing survives. There are 3 blocks of 4 two-storey houses, an irregular 1- and 2-storey block and a 2-storey block of 2 houses. The manager's house, a substantial 2-storey building, also still exists.

Preston Bridge, NT787568, built 1770. A handsome 3-span bridge, with dressed-stone arch rings and rubble spandrels and buttressed wing walls. The central segmental arch is larger than the other 2. There are a dentilated cornice and oculi in the spandrels between the arches.

CHIRNSIDE

Edington Mill, NT893549, mid 19th century. A 4-storey, 6-bay

19   Chirnside Bridge, with Chirnside Paper Mill behind.

rubble main block with a 2-bay kiln block, and a range of 2-storey workshops. There are 4 waterwheels, the principal ones being 6-spoke, 3-ring, low-breast wood and iron shrouded paddle-wheels, 6ft wide by 16ft diameter (1·83 by 4·88m) with rim drive. In the same house is a ruinous Poncelet wheel about 2 ft 6in wide by 6ft diameter (0·76 by 1·83m). In another house is a low-breast, wood and iron shrouded paddle-wheel 3ft wide by 13ft diameter (0·91 by 3·96m). Still in use, grinding oatmeal.

Smithy, Edington, NT896563, early 19th century. A small single-storey, 3-bay rubble building, with large small-paned windows and a pantiled roof. At the rear is a single-storey cottage. Now disused.

Tollhouse, Chirnside, NT853563, early 19th century. A 1-storey and attic rubble building, with a projecting central bay.

Chirnside Bridge, NT852562, mid-18th century (plate 19). A 3-span rubble bridge, with the 2 main spans segmental-arched. A smaller flood and access arch is semicircular. There are triangular cutwaters carried up to form pedestrian refuges. There is a dentilated cornice. Now bypassed.

COCKBURNSPATH

Bridge, Dunglass, NT771722, built 1932, engineers BLYTH & BLYTH. A reinforced-concrete bridge with a wide central span, with 5 arched ribs supporting smaller arches (5 on each side). There are smaller approach spans at both ends.

'New' Bridge, Dunglass, NT769721, early 19th century. A single-segmental rubble arch, with rusticated voussoirs and a castellated parapet.

Cove Harbour, Cockburnspath, NT785717, 18th century. Two piers, 1 straight, the other with an angled head, protecting a bay. There are ruins of 2-storey cottages on the angled-head pier. A tunnel through a headland provided access to the shore of the bay.

Smithy, Cockburnspath, NT774710, probably late 18th century. A low single-storey rubble building on an L plan, with a pantiled roof.

Sawmill, Cockburnspath, NT774710, probably late 18th century. A 2-storey rubble building with a part-wooden extension. Both have pantiled roofs.

Dunglass Viaduct, NT771721, opened 1846 by the North British Railway. A 6-span viaduct with a 135ft (41·1m) central span, flanked on 1 side by 2 smaller arches and on the other by 3. The arch rings, quoins on the piers, and the buttresses on either side of the main span are of ashlar, the rest of the masonwork being coursed rubble. The buttresses have incised linear ornament.

Cockburnspath Station, NT776717, opened 1846 by the North British Railway. A 2-platform through station. The main block is on the up platform. A single-storey rubble building on an H plan, with overhanging eaves.

COLDINGHAM

Railway bridge, Houndswood, NT853627, built *c* 1846 for the North British Railway. An example of a standard NBR type, with cast-iron arched side girders, and steel main girders, on rubble abutments.

St Abbs Harbour, NT920673, built 1833 and subsequently enlarged. A harbour of enclosure, with an L-plan pier and a straight pier enclosing a roughly rectangular basin. An inner basin is formed by 2 straight piers. Ancillary features include 2 net-boiling tubs.

Horse-gin house, Coldingham, NT905662, early 19th century. A hexagonal building, with rubble corner pillars. The roof is slated.

20   Brewery, Coldstream.

COLDSTREAM

Brewery, Coldstream, NT843396, probably late 18th and early 19th century (plate 20). The part-demolished remains of an attractive group of 1- and 2-storey rubble buildings round a courtyard. These consist of a 1-storey and attic stable block, a 2-storey, 6-bay brewhouse with louvred upper floor and roof-ridge ventilator, and a 2-storey and attic building, also with roof-ridge ventilator, and a range of 2-storey stores.

Corn store, Coldstream, NT843398, early and mid 19th century. A 3-storey, 6-bay rubble building and a more recent 3-storey, 3-bay, snecked-rubble block, both with hoists.

Coldstream Bridge and tollhouse, NT849401, built 1763–7, engineer JOHN SMEATON, widened 1962. A 7-span bridge, with dressed-stone arch rings and rubble spandrels, which are pierced between the main piers by flood relief holes (now blocked). The 5 main segmental spans are flanked by single semicircular flood arches. There is a dentilated cornice. The tollhouse is a 1-storey, 5-bay pantiled structure, with a lower single-storey extension.

CRANSHAWS

Smiddyhill Bridge, Cranshaws, NT696613, built 1887. A 2-span bridge, with dressed-stone arch rings, snecked-rubble spandrels and wing walls. The segmental arches are of unequal size. The cutwaters are rounded.

Ellemford Bridge, NT729600, built 1886 by the Berwickshire Road Trustees. A large 3-span bridge with dressed-stone arch rings, snecked-rubble spandrels and wing walls. There are rounded cutwaters.

DUNS

Duns Station, NT788532, opened 1849 by the North British Railway. Formerly a 2-platform through station. The buildings are largely intact, and consist of wooden platform shelters with awnings, that on the down platform containing the offices. The up-platform building shares a wall with a wooden goods shed. Nearby is a 3-storey, 7-bay rubble granary with a central hoist and a louvred roof ventilator. The wooden buildings are now occupied by a joiner and a blacksmith: the granary is still used as such.

Putton Mill, Duns, NT796519, early 19th century. A large rectangular 2-storey and attic rubble building with a partly detached square kiln. The kiln has a pyramidal pantiled roof with a marine-type ventilator. Now gutted and used as a barn and pigsty.

Duns Mill, NT784526, early 19th century. A small 2-storey and attic building, with single-storey wings at right angles. At the rear is an overshot 6-spoke iron wheel, 3ft 7in wide by 12ft 6in diameter (1·09 by 3·81m) with a 240-tooth gear ring round the rim. Probably drove a threshing mill, though the drive has been removed.

Farm chimneys, Brieryhill, Manderston, NT817541, Chalkielaw, NT803542 (plate 21), and Turtleton, NT815535, mid 19th century. All circular-section brick chimneys on square stone bases. That at Chalkielaw is attached to a 2-storey engine house, the others are single storey.

Smithy cottages, Crumstane, NT807537, late 19th century. Two ranges of 2-storey and attic farm workers' cottages, with steeply pitched roofs, dormer windows and gabled porches. At the end of one range is a smithy, in the same style, with a 1-storey extension at the rear.

EARLSTON

Rhymers Mill (old), Earlston, NT572383, rebuilt 1842 by C. & M. Whale. A 3-storey, 6-bay building embedded in modern single-storey structures. There is a bowed stair bay. Now part of an agricultural engineer's works.

Old Bridge, Earlston, NT571382, probably 18th century. A 2-span bridge with dressed-stone arch rings and rubble spandrels. There are tall triangular cutwaters.

Viaduct, Earlston, NT573381, built c 1865 for the Berwickshire Railway. A 3-span viaduct, with dressed-stone arch rings and rubble spandrels and curved wing walls. There are rounded cutwaters.

ECCLES

Bridge, Leitholm, NT787440, late 18th to early 19th century. A single-segmental rubble arch, with a dentilated cornice.

Farm chimney, Eccles Newton, NT777406, mid 19th century. A square-section chimney of rubble, with a relatively large engine and boiler house.

EDROM

Farm chimney, Broomdykes, NT879536, mid 19th century. A circular-section block chimney on a square stone base, attached to a single-storey engine house.

Tollhouse, NT839519, early 19th century. A single-storey, 2-by-3-

21   Farm chimney, Chalkielaw, Duns.

bay building, with round-headed windows. A gabled porch has been added.

Allanton Bridge, Allanton, NT865545, built 1851. A 2-span bridge, built entirely of dressed stone. The segmental arches have the masonry carried up along the line of the voussoirs to the level of the carriageway. There is a pilaster rising from the rounded cutwater, with pairs of pilasters on the abutments.

Blackadder Bridge, Allanton, NT864544, built 1851. An attractive 2-span bridge with elliptical arches. The arch rings are of dressed stone, as are the piers and the quoins of the wing walls. The rest of the masonry is square-dressed rubble. The cutwaters are pointed.

EYEMOUTH

Eyemouth Harbour, NT947642, formed 1768 by JOHN SMEATON, engineer, and rebuilt several times, most substantially in 1885–7, engineers THOMAS MEIK & SON. The harbour is basically the quayed mouth of the Eye, protected by 2 piers. At the inner end there are sluices to allow scouring of the basin to take place. The 1887 works are concrete, but earlier masonry can be seen in various places.

Bridge, Eyemouth, NT943647, late 18th century, engineer JOHN SMEATON. A single-span, segmental-arched rubble bridge, reinforced with old rails. A small semicircular arch has been added at the north end for a railway.

Warehouses, Eyemouth, NT947644, probably late 18th century. Two impressive rubble buildings, probably designed as granaries. One, facing the harbour, is a 4-storey, 8-bay block, the other, at the rear, is a 4-storey, 5-bay structure. There are also smaller 2- and 3-storey warehouses in the harbour area.

Eyemouth Mill, Eyemouth, NT941634, built 1849. A 2-storey, 4-bay rubble building, with a square kiln with a pyramidal asbestos roof with a square louvred vent. An awning has recently been added over the entrance.

FOGO

Bridge, Fogo, NT770492, rebuilt 1843. A single-segmental arch, with dressed-stone arch ring and rubble spandrels and wing walls. There is a dentilated cornice.

Cairns Mill, NT781495, early 19th century. A 2-storey and attic rubble building, with a lean-to sawmill extension at the rear. The kiln now has a marine-type ventilator. Machinery now all modern.

FOULDEN

Bridge over Whiteadder, Foulden, NT921546, erected 1837, engineer JAMES JARDINE, re-erected 1878, engineers D. & T. STEVENSON, contractors, Edinburgh. A 3-span bridge, with light iron-girder trusses on slender masonry piers.

Farm chimney, Foulden West Mains, NT911559, mid 19th century. A circular-section brick chimney on a square stone base attached to a small single-storey engine and boiler house.

GORDON

Windmill stump, Rumbletonlaw, NT676453, 18th century. The stump, 4 storeys high, of a tapering circular-section rubble tower windmill.

Gordon Mid Mill, NT660432, built 1781. A partly ruined 3-storey rubble building, now gutted.

Gordon Station, NT647437, opened 1863 by the Berwickshire Railway. Formerly a single-platform through station, the only surviving structures are the platform building, a 2-storey rubble structure with a single-storey wing, and a segmental-arched over-bridge.

Mack's Mill, Gordon, NT660448, probably late 18th century. A 3-storey, 3-bay rubble building, now gutted.

GREENLAW

Bridge, Greenlaw, NT709459, probably mid 19th century. A 2-span bridge, with flat-segmental dressed-stone arches. There are rounded cutwaters.

Castleloan Tollbar, Greenlaw, NT726456, built 1831. A single-storey coursed-rubble building with gabled porch and 2 bow windows.

HUTTON

Smithy, Hutton, NT908537, early 19th century. A single-storey, 4-bay rubble building, now in the garden of a private house.

Salmon fishery, Hutton, NT934512, early 19th century, and later. A small single-storey hut, with a wooden extension for gear storage, a vaulted ice-house, and wooden supports for net drying.

Union Suspension Bridge, and tollhouse, Hutton, NT934511, built 1820, engineer CAPTAIN S. BROWN, and strengthened 1902–3, engineer J. A. BEAN. The first large suspension bridge in Britain.

There are 3 sets of iron link chains on each side each consisting of pairs of links, with iron-rod suspenders to a light wood-truss deck. The pylons are monumental in design, of dressed stone. Unusually, the pylon on the south side is set back from the end of the truss, into a hillside. The 1902–3 strengthening consisted of adding a wire-rope cable on each side, with wire-rope suspenders to steel reinforcement at the sides of the original deck. There is a light wrought-iron railing of attractive design. The tollhouse is a plain 1-storey, 3-bay building.

LADYKIRK

Ladykirk–Norham Bridge, and tollhouse, NT890473, built 1885–7, engineers CODRINGTON & BRERETON. A 4-span bridge, with dressed-stone arch rings, coursed-rubble spandrels and wing walls. The central pier has a rounded cutwater carried up to form a pedestrian refuge; the other piers have triangular cutwaters. The arches are segmental. The tollhouse is a single-storey, 3-bay structure, with a central stone porch.

Tollhouse, Ladykirk, NT886473, early 19th century. A single-storey rubble building on an L plan, with a porch in the angle of the L. There is a small bay window in the gable facing the road.

LANGTON

Joinery, Gavinton, NT768521, probably early to mid 19th century. A 2-storey wood-framed rubble building on an L plan, with an external wooden stair to the upper floor.

LAUDER

Bridge, Newmills, NT526497, late 18th to early 19th century. A single-segmental rubble arch.

Smithy, Lauder, NT532475, early 19th century. A single-storey, 4-bay rubble building, still in use.

LEGERWOOD

Dod Mill, NT581480, late 18th to early 19th century and later. A small 2-storey rubble building, with a turbine house.

Bridgehaugh Mill, Galadean, NT558433, late 18th century. A single-storey and attic and a 3-storey rubble building on either side of a lade. The smaller block appears to have been a threshing mill. Both are now gutted and used as piggeries.

Bridge, Galadean, NT559431, early 19th century. A 2-span, segmental-arched bridge, with dressed-stone arch rings and rubble spandrels and curved wing walls.

Bridge, Galadean, NT559432, late 18th century. A single-segmental rubble arch.

MERTON

Mertoun Mill, Mertoun, NT610321, early 19th century. A 3-storey rubble building on an L plan, apparently gutted.

Farm chimney, Brotherstone, nr Smailholm, NT616354, mid 19th century. A circular-section brick chimney, with a small rubble engine and boiler house.

SWINTON

Bridge, Swintonmill, NT813461, late 18th to early 19th century. A neat little 3-span rubble bridge with an elliptical-arched main span flanked by semicircular arches.

Bridge, Swintonmill, NT810456, built 1904. A single-segmental arch bridge, with dressed-stone arch ring and part-ashlar, part-snecked rubble spandrels and wing walls.

WESTRUTHER

Horse-gin house, Westruther, NT633499, early to mid 19th century. A hexagonal rubble building, with a slate roof.

WHITSOME

Joinery, Whitesome, NT866507, early 19th century. A single-storey rubble building, with unusually large small-paned windows. The roof is pantiled.

Clackmannanshire

Clackmannanshire is Scotland's smallest county. It has a significant woollen industry, now much reduced, and had breweries, distilleries, a glassworks, and coal works of national importance. For its size, its industrial remains are unusually fine.

ALLOA

ALLOA

Alloa Glassworks, NS881923, founded *c* 1750 (plate 22). Most of the buildings and plant here are modern, but one of the 2 glass cones survives (*c* 1825), the last in Scotland. It is a conical brick structure on a stone base, and houses a modern glass furnace.

Alloa Mills (corn and flour), NS889928, early 19th century. A 4-storey building in 3 sections, two are 7 bay, the other 5, with 1- and 2-storey additions. The interior of 1 of the 7-bay sections is wood-framed, the others have steel beams and cast-iron columns, supporting wooden joists and floors. There is a datestone of 1735 built into the building. Now a grain store.

Carsebridge Distillery, NS898935, founded 1799 by John Bald. A large and much modernized group of buildings, incorporating some 19th-century stone buildings, including a 2-storey office block with an oriel window at first-floor level.

Kilncraigs Mills, NS888927, mid 19th century and later. An extensive group of multistorey mill buildings, the oldest of which dates back to the 1860s. This is a 5-storey and attic, 3-by-13-bay rubble building with a Palladian front. The Burnside Mill (*c* 1880–90) is a 5-storey, 13-bay block, with a belfry at 1 end and an 8-storey water-tower in the angle between it and a 4-storey and attic, 4-by-13-bay block. The contemporary West Mill is also 5 storeys high, 8 bays long, with a later 3-storey, 11-bay block, extended by 3 storeys in brick. A continuation of this range is the bow-fronted, 5-storey Waste House, also with 3 rubble storeys. The main offices are in a 5-storey, 3-by-13-bay Renaissance block. Originally the mills were powered by steam engines and one single-storey engine house survives. Power is now supplied by a generating station with 3 Belliss

22   Glass cone, Alloa Glassworks.

& Morcom steam turbines in a 2-by-4-bay brick house with round-headed windows. There is a wooden cooling tower of a now rare pattern. Most of the machinery is modern, and there are modern single-storey spinning sheds.

Thistle Brewery, NS888927, founded 1830 by James Maclay, rebuilt late 19th century. A neat complex consisting of a 2-storey and attic, 7-bay office block (1896), a 2-storey, 5-bay malt store, with a central hoist, a 4-storey, 2-by-8-bay brewhouse with a tower, and various single-storey buildings. There is a single mash tun, 2 oil-fired coppers, a hop-back, 10 wooden fermenting vats and ancillary equipment. One of 2 surviving active small Scottish breweries.

Maltings, NS882924, late 19th century. The last of the large Alloa maltings, a 5-storey and 2-attic, red-brick building, with 2 pyramidal-roofed kilns. Most of the original windows have been blocked up.

Wagonway Bridges, NS884927 and NS886929, opened 1768 by the Alloa Railway. These 2 bridges, both under main roads, are of rubble construction. The former has a semicircular arch, and has been lengthened in brick; the latter is segmental-arched.

Woollen Mill, NS889933, mid 19th century. A 3-storey, 6-by-15-bay rubble block, with an arched cart entry, similar in style to the main building at Devonvale Mill, Tillicoultry. Now disused.

Bridge, Bridge End, NS847952, 16th century, rebuilt 17th century. A 2-span masonry bridge, with ribbed segmental arches and triangular cutwaters. The western approach is walled, and is pierced by 3 widely spaced arches, 1 of which is ribbed. Bypassed by a late 19th-century, lattice-girder bridge with battlemented corner towers.

Cambus Distillery, NS854942, founded 1806 by John Moubray. A very large group of buildings, mainly modern. The most notable features are an early 19th-century, cast-iron arch bridge at NS853940, recently restored, and a masonry water-tower with cast-iron sectional tank, dated 1886.

Cambus Station, NS855943, opened 1852 by the Stirling & Dunfermline Railway. Formerly a 2-platform through station, with the main offices in a 2-storey masonry building on the up (Stirling) platform. This has been extended by a wooden shelter and there is a similar shelter on the down platform. There is an unusual iron-truss footbridge.

Devon Colliery engine house, NS898958, built 1865. A tall rectangular ashlar building, with a hipped roof. In the front wall is a large arched opening, partly timbered, through which worked the cast-iron beam of a Cornish pumping engine, built by NEILSON & CO,

Glasgow in 1865. The beam and part of the pump rod are all that survive of the engine.

Windmill, New Sauchie, NS897950, probably late 17th to early 18th century. Well-preserved stump, 2 storeys high, of a vaulted tower windmill. Has been used as a dovecote, and has been fitted with a castellated parapet.

Tannery, Tullibody, NS863951, built *c* 1880 by John Tullis & Co (plate 23). The largest surviving tannery in Scotland. The main block is a 4-storey and attic, 18-by-27-bay, red-and-white-brick structure, on an L plan, with louvred ventilators in the top 2 floors. In the angle formed by these 2 ranges is a 5-bay range of 1-storey workshops, with prominent roof-ridge ventilators, and at the rear is a detached 4-storey boiler house, with a circular-section brick chimney. There is also a tall brick water-tower.

ALVA

ALVA

Burnbrae Works, Henry Street, NS885968, late 19th century. A

23   Tannery, Tullibody.

2-storey, 8-by-14-bay main block, a 2-storey, 2-by-5-bay office building, both red and white brick, and 4 bays of north-light sheds.
Braehead Mill (woollen), NS884974, mid 19th century. A 3-storey, 3-by-5-bay rubble building, entered at first-floor level. Now used as a store.
Coblecrook Mill, NS878969, early 19th century. A 3-storey and attic, 3-by-7-bay rubble building with a projecting semicircular stair tower, set among some modern structures.
Glentana Mills, NS878972, late 19th to early 20th century. A group of single-storey buildings, mainly brick, with a tall circular-section brick chimney. A small single-cylinder horizontal Corliss-valve engine by DOUGLAS & GRANT, Kirkcaldy, is still in use.
Ochilvale Mills, NS888969, late 19th century. A 2-storey, 2-by-30-bay, red-and-white-brick main block, with a 1-storey, 7-bay wing. There is a circular-section brick chimney, with a flared top.
Strude Mill, NS887975, possibly c 1820, but probably later (plate 24). The finest of the Hillfoots woollen mills, in a superb setting. A 6-storey and attic, 25-bay rubble building, with a pediment, sur-

24 Strude Mill, Alva.

mounted by a bellcote, over the 4 centre bays. At the base of these bays is an ornamented entrance, with an arched main door flanked by arched windows.

Woollen mills, Brook Street, NS884970, early to mid 19th century. From south to north: (1) a 2-storey and attic, 8-bay rubble building, with a 2-bay dwellinghouse at the south end, now a youth club (plate 25). At the rear is a 2-storey, 9-bay block, now disused. (2) a 2-storey and attic, 11-bay rubble mill, incorporating a dwellinghouse, now partly an electronics factory. (3) a 2-storey, 14-bay harled building with a pantiled roof. The windows are now bricked up and the building is used as a builder's store.

Woollen mill, Henry Street, NS884969, late 19th century. A 2-storey and attic, 4-by-12-bay main block, forming an L with a 2-storey, 7-bay building and a 1-storey, 5-bay range, all red and white brick. Now a hosiery works.

Woollen mill, NS884974, early 19th century. A 3-storey, 5-by-5-bay rubble block, with an external stair to the first floor.

Glenochil Distillery, Menstrie, NS858965, founded 1746. A large

25   Hand-loom woollen mill, Alva.

complex of buildings of various dates, including a 4-storey rubble range of maltings with 2 pyramidal-roofed kilns.

Woollen mill, Menstrie, NS848968, mid 19th century. A 2-storey, 5-by-12-bay rubble building with a clock tower, formerly part of a much larger complex. Now water-board offices.

CLACKMANNAN

Paton's Mill, NS913923, built 1875–6. A flat-roofed, 5-storey, 4-by-11-bay, red-brick building, with various ancillary buildings. There is a tall circular-section brick chimney. Still engaged in mule spinning.

Miners' houses, 1–20 Kennet, NS926910, late 18th century. A range of low single-storey, 2-room rubble cottages, mainly pantile-roofed.

Kennetpans Distillery, NS913890, late 18th century. A remarkable group of ruins of a once extensive complex. The main block was 3 storeys high, and there are lower buildings, now overgrown, ranged along a creek. The wooden piles of a large pier are clearly visible at low tide, and an artificial mound on the east bank of the creek may have been a dump for earth ballast.

Kilbagie Paper Mills, NN 928899, built as a distillery in the 18th century, rebuilt as a paper mill 1874 by J. A. Weir. A complex of buildings of various dates, dominated by a brick water-tower. Some of the masonry buildings probably date from the period when the complex was a distillery.

TILLICOULTRY

Clock Mill, NS914974, early 19th century. A 3-storey and attic, 3-by-9-bay rubble building, with a 2-storey, 2-by-2-bay dwelling-house on the north end. There is a clock in the south gable, which has a ball finial.

Devonpark Knitwear Factory, NS918963, built as a spinning mill, late 19th century. Two blocks of single-storey workshops, one 3-by-15-bay, the other 4-bay, with a central boiler house, former engine house and a circular-section chimney inscribed 'Glentilly Knitwear'.

Devonvale Mills, NS922965, mid to late 19th century. A complex of 1-, 2- and 3-storey buildings, the largest of which is a 3-storey, 6-by-16-bay, cement-rendered stone building, with, internally, 2 rows of columns supporting pairs of cross-beams, braced with wrought-iron tie rods and cast-iron straining posts. There is a neat 2-storey, 6-bay pedimented office block. Now disused.

Middleton Mills, NS914972, mid 19th century. A complex of rubble buildings, with a 3-storey and attic main range and a block of single-storey weaving sheds.

Paton's Woollen Mills, NS914969, early 19th century and later. A 3-storey and attic, 2-by-34-bay rubble main block (1836) and a 3-storey, 3-by-5-bay late 19th-century building.

Weavers' cottages, NS915974, late 18th to early 19th century. A pleasing pair of single-storey cottages, 1 with double window.

Dumfriesshire

Dumfriesshire is predominantly agricultural, with the county town the main manufacturing centre. The minor Sanquhar and Canonbie coalfields were the only mineral resources of note, apart from the lead veins at Wanlockhead and building stone near Dumfries. Annan was for a time an industrial town of some importance, and, with Dumfries, was a magnet for 'new industry' in the early years of this century. The major lines of communication between west central Scotland and England pass through the county.

ANNAN

Annandale Distillery, NY194683, founded 1830 by George Donald and rebuilt 1883 by J. S. Gardner (plate 26). Now disused, but remarkably well preserved, with a 3-storey main range on an L plan, incorporating maltings and pyramidal-roofed kiln. The complex is completed by a 2-bay range of bonded stores, and a free-standing circular brick chimney. At the rear are the proprietor's house and a farm which operated in connection with the distillery.
Brydekirk Bridge, NY187706, built 1817. A singularly graceful, 3-span bridge, with dressed-stone arch rings and coursed-rubble spandrels. There is a large central span flanked by smaller arches, all segmental, with triangular cutwaters.
Farm chimney, Howes, NY187670, mid 19th century. A neat square-section brick chimney rising from a 2-storey engine and boiler house.
Tollhouse, Mount Annan, NY202694, early 19th century. A plain but well constructed single-storey, 3-bay ashlar building, with a central chimney.

ANNAN

Annan Bridge, NY191666, built 1826, engineer ROBERT STEVENSON. A 3-span bridge, with dressed-stone arch rings and rubble spandrels. The arches are segmental and the spandrels rubble.
Annan Station, NY193662, opened 1848 by the Glasgow, Dumfries & Carlisle Railway. A 2-platform through station, with the main offices on the up platform in a handsome 2-storey ashlar block, in-

corporating a dwellinghouse, with an awning added later. The down-platform shelter is single storey, of wood and rubble construction. The platforms are linked by a lattice-girder footbridge. In the goods yard is a fine single-storey sandstone goods shed.

Welldale Mill, NY188661, mid 19th century. A 9-bay, 2-storey, rubble-front block, continued as 6 (formerly 8) houses, with a central ornamented entrance. To the rear are single-storey weaving sheds with wooden roofs on cast-iron columns, and a 3-storey, 6-bay block. Now a store.

Harbour, NY187660, early 19th century. The quayed east bank of the river Annan, with a series of warehouses along the quay walls, the largest of which are a 4-storey and attic, 5-bay rubble block, with a central hoist, and a 3-storey, 6-bay building. Now virtually disused.

Mill, NY190664, early 19th century. A 4-storey, 5-bay rubble building, and a 2- and 3-storey rubble block with a wheelpit for a mid- or low-breast wheel. Now an engineering works.

Railway viaducts, NY187663, opened 1848 by the Glasgow, Dumfries & Carlisle Railway. A 6-span viaduct over the river Annan, with

26 Annandale Distillery, Annan.

5 main arches, and a smaller approach arch on the east side, all segmental. The arch rings are of dressed stone and the spandrels of coursed rubble. To the east is a 4-span viaduct with 3 semicircular arches and a segmental arch over a road.

Boiler works, Newbie, NY183652, built 1898 on by Cochran & Co. A large group of single-storey workshops, of various dates. The original bays are wooden-framed, with Belfast roofs, and are wooden-clad: later additions are steel-framed. Two early Cochran boilers are preserved in the apprentice-training school.

Housing, Newbie, NY181651, built c 1898. A row of 20 four-roomed, 2-storey brick houses, and 2 blocks of 4 one-storey and attic rubble cottages, built in connection with Cochran's boiler works.

Suspension footbridge, Blacketlees, NY192686, built 1897 by P. & R. Fleming, Glasgow. A small structure, with steel tubular pylons, wire-rope suspension cables, steel-rod suspenders and a wooden deck.

CAERLAVEROCK

Glencaple Harbour, NX994687, rebuilt 1836–40. A large rubble pier, with 2 small single-storey, 19th-century warehouses on it, and the decayed remains of quays along the river bank. Now little used.

CANONBIE

Canonbie Bridge, NY395765, probably 18th century. A massive 3-span bridge, with segmental arches and triangular cutwaters. Steel footpaths have been cantilevered out from the sides.

Canonbie Mill (Hollows Mill), NY385783, probably early 19th century. A 3-storey and basement rubble building with single-storey additions. The 4 pairs of stones have been removed, but an internal low-breast wooden paddle-wheel about 4ft wide by 18ft diameter (1·2 by 5·5m) with steel-reinforced rings and cast-iron axle is still used to drive modern equipment for feeding-stuff preparation.

Tarras Tileworks, NY381809, early 19th century. A small works, with a single kiln and an L-shaped range of drying sheds. Closed in 1969 and used as a store.

Miners' Rows, Rowanburn, NY410772, late 19th century. A group of 3 ranges of single-storey cottages with associated coal stores and wash-houses. The colliery here closed in 1922.

Suspension bridge, Harelaw Slack, NY443785. A long narrow footbridge, about 160ft (49m) long, with wire-rope suspension cables, rod suspenders with cross bracing, and a light wood and steel deck.

Viaduct, Tarrasfoot, NY379810, opened 1864 by the Border Union Railway. A 12-span masonry structure, with semicircular arches, now disused.

CLOSEBURN

Barburgh Mill (woollen), NX901833, early 19th century. A 2-storey, 7-by-9-bay rubble building on an L plan, closed since 1950 and used as a store. Nearby is a single-storey smithy, disused.

Cample Mill, NX899942, early 19th century. A 2-storey and attic, 6-bay block, with 1- and 2-storey outbuildings. Now gutted and used as a store.

Viaduct, Cample, NX898941, opened 1850 by the Glasgow, Dumfries & Carlisle Railway. A 4-span masonry viaduct with segmental arches.

Limekilns, Closeburn, NX907913, late 18th century. A range of 3 single-draw kilns of rubble construction.

CUMMERTREES

Cummertrees Station, NY139665, opened 1848 by the Glasgow, Dumfries & Carlisle Railway. Formerly a 2-platform through station, with the main building on the down platform, a handsome single-storey ashlar building on a U plan with prominent eaves.

DRYFESDALE

Lockerbie Station, NY137818, opened 1848 by the Caledonian Railway. A 2-platform through station, formerly with a bay at the north end. The main offices are on the down platform, in a 1- and 2-storey rubble building, with crow-stepped gable, formerly with a large glazed awning. The up-platform building, which was similar in style, has been demolished. The platforms are linked by a truss footbridge with boarded sides.

Lockerbie Engine Shed, NY137818, opened c 1863 by the Caledonian Railway. A handsome 2-road, 8-bay rubble building, with a roof-ridge ventilator. There is a dressed-stone relieving arch above the door.

Sandbed Mill (woollen), NY129844, early 19th century. A 3-storey and attic rubble building, with single-storey wooden additions. Now converted to a sawmill.

Stullahill Bridge, NY106807, late 19th century. A 5-span bridge, with flat segmental arches. Arch rings and spandrels are rusticated.

DUMFRIES

Devorgilla's Bridge, NX969760, built 1432, east half rebuilt 1620, and 3 spans demolished 1794. A 6-span masonry bridge, with dressed-stone arch rings and rubble spandrels. There are prominent triangular cutwaters, the central ones carried up to form pedestrian refuges. The arches are semicircular. The westmost arch is reckoned to be original. Now a footbridge only.

Dumfries Mill (corn), NX970758, built *c* 1780, engineer ANDREW MEIKLE. A 3-storey, cut down from 5-storey, building on a T plan, with a 6-bay main range. There is a single-storey brick addition, probably on the site of the kiln. Now a store. The weir is a notable one.

Dumfries Station, NX977765, opened 1848 by the Glasgow, Dumfries & Carlisle Railway. A 4-platform through and terminal station, with the main offices on the down platform, in a 2-storey, coursed-rubble building with single-storey wings and a substantial steel-framed glazed awning, supported on cast-iron columns. A covered plate-girder footbridge links the platforms.

Kingholm Quay, NX975735, rebuilt *c* 1836–40. A quay running along the east bank of the Nith with a small, badly silted basin. This has red-brick, single-storey transit sheds. Nearby was an interesting 3-storey and attic, 4-bay warehouse, with 2-storey dwellinghouses adjoining, unfortunately rather tastelessly modernized. The basin is used by pleasure boats.

Tweed Mill, Kingholm Quay, NX975735, founded 1846 by Robert Scott and Sons. A 2-storey, 13-bay block, and a 3-storey, 4-bay extension, together with a detached, 3-storey, 4-bay building, all rubble-built. Now a potato store.

New Bridge, NX968762, built 1793, architect THOMAS BOYD, and widened 1893. A 4-span bridge, 245ft (74·7m) long, built of dressed stone, with segmental arches and rounded cutwaters, which are carried up to support bracketted iron footpaths.

Nithsdale Mills, NX976754, founded 1857 by Robert and Walter Scott, as a tweed factory. A massive 4-storey, 8-by-16-bay, red-brick Italianate block with sandstone dressings, with an equally impressive octagonal brick chimney. Now a wool store.

Rosefield Mill, NX974753, built 1886–94, for Charteries Spence and Co, architect ALAN CROMBIE. Two large 2-storey ranges of red-brick buildings, with single-storey workshops behind. The more ornate is a 3-by-22-bay block, with machicolated corner towers and a central device. The other is a 9-by-34-bay structure, with Italianate corner towers. Both have round-headed windows in the upper floors. There are 2 fine octagonal brick chimneys. Built as a tweed mill, now in multiple occupation.

St Michael's Bridge, NX973757, built 1927, engineer J. B. BRODIE. A 4-span, reinforced-concrete bridge, 233ft (70·0m) long, with 3 segmental arches and a smaller semicircular arch over a roadway. Faced with sandstone. There are triangular cutwaters.

Shortridge Laundry, NX967764, late 19th century. A 2-storey and attic, 2-by-6-bay main block, with 4 bays of single-storey shop with roof-ridge ventilators.

Troqueer Mills, NX973754, built 1866 by Walter Scott and Sons for tweed manufacture. A large block of single-storey weaving sheds with an ornate 12-bay river frontage. Now in multiple occupation.

Motor car factory, Heathhall, NX989791, built 1913 for the Arrol-Johnston Co Ltd. A large group of 3 storey reinforced-concrete flat-roofed buildings, now a rubber works.

Suspension footbridge, NX973757, built 1875, engineer J. WILLET. A light lattice-truss span, with flat-link chains and iron-rod sus-

27   Snade Mill, Glencairn.

penders. The pylons are of cast-iron, consisting of pairs of Doric columns with entablatures.

Windmill, NX968758, built 1798. A 4-storey tapered rubble tower, with pedimented doors and windows, and a circular corbelled cap, since 1834 part of Dumfries Burgh Museum.

DUNSCORE

Horse-gin houses, Merkland, NX902852, and Newton, NX873843, early 19th century. Circular rubble buildings, with slate roofs.

DURISDEER

Drumlanrig Bridge, NX860998, repaired 1860. A handsome 2-span ashlar bridge, with semicircular arches, triangular cutwaters, and unusual corbelled footpaths.

Bridge, Eliock Wood, NS834056, early 19th century. A 2-span bridge with dressed-stone arch rings and rubble spandrels. The arches, 1 of which is a flood arch, are segmental.

GLENCAIRN

Snade Mill, NX846871, late 18th to early 19th century (plate 27). A 2-storey rubble building on an L plan, with a 6-spoke, low-breast wood and iron paddle-wheel, 3ft 9in wide by 16ft diameter (1·14 by 4·88m). One pair of stones is still in position, and there is an unusual geared sluice-operating mechanism. Nearby is a modern suspension footbridge with steel-joist pylons, wire-rope cables and wooden deck.

GRETNA

Tollhouse, NY327671, c 1820. A Telford-type tollhouse, with bowed centre bay, now converted to a tearoom. Runaway marriages were celebrated here, as at the nearby smithy (NY327673), now almost unrecognizable as such.

HODDAM

Smithy, Hoddamcross, NY177736, early 19th century. A neat single-storey rubble building on an L plan with a 3-bay cottage adjoining, both harled.

Bridge, Meinbank, NY186728, late 18th to early 19th century. A single-segmental arch, with dressed-stone arch ring and rubble spandrels.

Windmill and horse-gin house, Shortrigg, NY162744, late 18th to early 19th century (plate 28). A unique combination of prime movers.

28 Windmill and horse-gin house, Shortrigg, Hoddam.

The windmill tower is 3 storeys high, tapering, with a slated conical cap, and the gin house is circular. Both are rubble-built.

HOLYWOOD

East Cluden Mills, NX942794, early 19th century. A 2-storey attic and basement block, now converted to a house, with two 8-spoke, low-breast paddle-wheels with iron axles and rings and wooden paddles and spokes, about 4ft wide by 16ft diameter (1·22 by 4·88m). The axles were originally wooden.

Bridge, Gribton, NX917797, mid 19th century. A 2-span bridge, with dressed-stone arch rings, and coursed-rubble spandrels and wing walls. The arches are segmental and the cutwaters rounded.

KEIR

Bridge, Auldgirth, NX912864, built c 1780. A handsome 3-span bridge, 200ft (61·0m) long, of dressed-stone construction, with segmental arches on narrow piers, with rounded cutwaters extended upwards to form unusual pedestrian refuges with curved heads. At the east end is a distinctive inn with Gothic windows.

Limekilns, Barjarg, NX884903, and clamp kilns, NX883902, founded 1788. A range of 3 single-draw rubble kilns, with segmental draw arches, each with 2 draw holes. One of the arches is smaller than the other 2. The clamp kilns, 2 in number, are set into a hillock, and appear as U-shaped depressions with scattered rubble visible.

Horse-gin house, Cairnhall, NX907860, early 19th century. A circular rubble structure with a slate roof.

Keir Mill, NX861931, built 1771. A rectangular 2- and 3-storey rubble building, part harled, with a square kiln vent. The wheel and machinery have been gutted, except for the wooden pit wheel.

Limekilns, Porterstown, NX 876912, late 18th century. A pair of single-draw rubble kilns, similar to those at Barjarg, but with buttresses, supporting the kiln fronts. The roadway/tramway linking the quarries to the kilns is clearly visible.

KIRKCONNEL

Viaduct, Crawick, NS775110, opened 1850 by the Glasgow, Dumfries & Carlisle Railway. A 6-span masonry viaduct, with semicircular arches.

Kirkconnel Station, NS734123, opened 1850 by the Glasgow, Dumfries & Carlisle Railway. A 2-platform through station, with the main offices on the down platform, in a small single-storey ashlar building. In the goods yard is a small (30cwt) wood-jib, hand-operated, rail-mounted crane.

Bridge, NS722123, late 18th century and later. A 3-span masonry bridge, with segmental arches and triangular cutwaters, widened by adding plate-girder spans supported by the cutwaters.

KIRKMAHOE

Mill, Dalswinton, NX948852, late 18th to early 19th century. A 2-storey and attic rubble building on an L plan, with an 8-spoke, high-breast, wood and iron bucket wheel, about 3ft wide by 14ft diameter (0·91 by 4·27m). Now disused.

Windmill, Duncow, NX974838, late 17th to early 18th century. The squat tapering rubble stump of a tower windmill.

Sandstone quarry, Locharbriggs, NX987813, mid 19th century and later (plate 29). A large red-sandstone quarry, now partly flooded, worked on a small scale, with several derrick cranes, both wood and steel. There are corrugated-iron saw sheds, and an interesting plant for making bricks from waste, with a narrow-gauge railway, at NX986814.

29 Sandstone quarry, Locharbriggs.

LANGHOLM

Bell's Mill, NY364842, late 19th century. A complex of rubble buildings, with a 3-storey and attic, 16-bay main block and single-storey sheds. There is a neat engine house with a cast-iron roof tank, and a tall circular-section brick chimney.

Langholm Gas works, NY364844, founded 1836 (plate 30). A group of white-washed rubble buildings, with a Belfast-roofed retort house containing 2 benches of 6 retorts, and a square-section brick chimney. The purifiers are under an open-sided shelter, supported on cast-iron columns. The main holder is of the 2-section, self-supporting type, made by HENRY BALFOUR AND CO, Leven, 1932, and there is a small regulating holder used in conjunction with a rubber holder during repairs to the main holder.

Skipper's Bridge, NY371834, built 1807. A 3-span structure, with 2 large and 1 small segmental arches. The arch rings are of dressed stone and the spandrels rubble. Just to the north are the altered remains of Langholm Distillery, founded 1765.

Townhead Bridge, NY363847, built 1780, widened 1880. A 3-span

30 Horizontal retorts, Langholm Gas Works.

bridge, with flat segmental arches. Footpaths with lattice-girder parapets were added in 1880. Nearby is the single-storey and basement Townhead tollhouse, with projecting castellated central bay.

Foundry and smithy, NY366844, late 19th century. The foundry is a 2-bay, single-storey rubble block, formerly a brewery, with a home-made cupola. The smithy is a single-storey rubble building with a corrugated-iron extension at right angles. It contains 2 hearths with a very complete set of tools. There is also a 3-storey, 5-bay rubble store.

Suspension bridge, NY362845, mid 19th century, engineers E. HERNULEWICZ & CO, London. A wooden span, with light lattice railings, supported by iron-link chains with iron suspenders. The pylons are cast- and wrought-iron on coursed rubble bases.

Tannery, NY360845, 18th century and later. A group of buildings of various dates, including a 2-storey block with louvred ventilators in the upper floor.

Woollen Mill, NY363843, late 19th century. A 1- and 2-storey complex of brick buildings with a circular-section brick chimney, a single-storey engine house and a 3-bay rubble boiler house, with brick arch rings and a cast-iron roof tank.

MORTON

Morton Mill, Carronbridge, NX869976, 1665, 1752, and early 19th century. A large 2-storey and attic rubble mill, with a projecting kiln with a marine-type ventilator. Now a store.

Viaduct, Carronbridge, NS881010, opened 1850 by the Glasgow, Dumfries & Carlisle Railway. A 6-span masonry viaduct, with semicircular arches. Brick parapets have been added.

MOUSWALD

Windmill, Mouswald Grange, NY053734, late 18th century. A large, steeply tapering rubble tower, with a conical slated cap.

PENPONT

Scar Bridge, NX849944, 18th century. A 2-span bridge, with dressed-stone arch ring and rubble spandrels. The arches are segmental and the cutwaters triangular.

Granary, NX847947, possibly a former woollen mill, late 18th to early 19th century. A 3-storey and attic, 5-bay rubble building, now used as a store.

Bridge, Thornhill, NX871954, late 17th or early 18th century. A handsome 2-span bridge, with dressed-stone arch rings and rubble spandrels. The arches are segmental, and the triangular cutwaters are extended up to form pedestrian refuges.

RUTHWELL

Horse-gin house, Summerfield, NY111680, early 19th century. A semicircular rubble building with a slate roof.

SANQUHAR

Eliock Bridge, Mennock, NS804083, early 19th century. A picturesquely situated single-segmental arch, with dressed-stone arch ring and rubble spandrels.

Buccleuch Brickworks, NS781103, 1850s and later. The much reduced remains of an exceedingly interesting complex. The circular kilns with their conical vents are now almost completely demolished, but the large brick moulding and drying shed still survives. The course of the narrow-gauge railway linking the works with the clay-pits can still be traced.

Sanquhar Station, NS781102, built 1850 for the Glasgow, Dumfries & Carlisle Railway. Formerly a 2-platform through station, with the main offices on the down platform in a single-storey rubble building on a U plan, incorporating a dwellinghouse, with an awning between the arms of the U. Six of the original Tudor chimney stacks survive. At the up end is a masonry skew overbridge. The platform edges have now been cut back.

Wanlockhead, NS8713. There are scattered remains of lead mining and smelting round this village. The single-storey houses were mostly built for workers in the lead industry. The most interesting survival is a water-bucket pumping engine at NS873125, of wooden construction, with iron fittings (see frontispiece). This has been taken into Guardianship by the Department of the Environment, and at the time of writing is protected by a wooden cover. At the Bay Mine site (NS868137) there is the stone column for another water engine and the pit of a large waterwheel. Excavations here by Glasgow University Summer Schools in 1972–4 have revealed foundations of engine and boiler houses, including the stone base for an engine built by WILLIAM SYMINGTON (see *Industrial Archaeology*, 1973, **10**, 129).

TORTHORWALD

Horse-gin house, Braehead, Collin, NY033762, early 19th century. A semicircular rubble building, of the typical Galloway windowed type, with a slate roof.

Dunbartonshire

Dunbartonshire falls into two areas: the western division is partly rural, and highland in parts, and includes the major industrial towns of Clydebank and Dumbarton, as well as the textile printing centres of the Vale of Leven. The eastern division has coal and ironstone fields, and its principal town, Kirkintilloch, was a centre of the iron-founding industry. Important rail, road and canal routes pass through the county.

Forth & Clyde Canal, NS785785–650733 and NS513700–449734. The Dunbartonshire section of the canal is divided in 2. The eastern section (built 1768–75, engineer JOHN SMEATON), includes only 1 lock, No 20 at Wyndford (NS776787), which is still intact. There is a fine aqueduct over the Luggie at Kirkintilloch (NS657739), and smaller aqueducts at Castlecary (NS785784), Shirva (NS692754) and Auchendavie (NS674748). Other interesting features are the remains of a canal inn at Auchinstarry (NS720768), the ruin of a standard stable at Shirva (NS691753) (plate 31), and the Hillhead Basin at Kirkintilloch. The western section (built 1787–90, engineer ROBERT WHITWORTH), contains 4 locks, including the 2 sea locks at Bowling (NS449734), 3 bascule bridges, at Bowling (NS451735), Ferrydyke (NS458731) and Dalmuir West (NS478713), and a small 2-span aqueduct over the Duntocher Burn (NS478713). At Bowling there are 2 basins – 1 dating from 1848, the other from the 1880s – a railway swing bridge (1896), a 2-storey custom house, and a basin for sea-going ships.

ARROCHAR

Craig-an-Arden Viaduct, NN322106, opened 1894 by the West Highland Railway. A 7-span masonry viaduct, on a curve, with semicircular arches. The parapets are castellated.

BONHILL

Alexandria Station, NS393799, opened 1850 by the Caledonian & Dumbartonshire Railway. Formerly a 2-platform through station, now cut down to 1. The main offices are on the up platform, in a single-storey, red-and-white-brick building on a rubble base. There is a tall signal-box of similar construction.

Croftingea Printworks, NS394806, founded 1790 by Andrew, John & James Stirling. A group of 2- and 3-storey, red-and-white-brick and sandstone buildings, now mainly a bonded store. The oldest part appears to be a 4-storey, 9-bay rubble block.

Housing, Croftingea, NS393803, late 19th century. Two handsome ranges of workers' housing, associated with Croftingea Printworks. One, 'Foremen's Row' is a 2-storey and attic rubble block, with external open stairs at the rear. The other is a 1-storey and attic group, ashlar-built.

Motor car factory, NS390807, built 1906 by the Argyll Motor Co Ltd (plate 32). A large range of single-storey workshops, with a 2-storey office block. The centre 5 bays of the office project are surmounted by a central clock tower with a dome, flanked by 2 shorter towers. Currently empty, this complex was reckoned one of the largest motor-car factories in Europe when new, but only built cars to 1913.

Balloch Central Station, NS389819, opened 1850 by the Caledonian and Dumbartonshire Railway. A 2-platform through station,

31 Ruins of Forth & Clyde canal stables, Shirva.

32   Argyll motor-car factory, Alexandria.

with the offices on the up platform, in a 2 storey, coursed-rubble block with a single-storey wing. The building has been partly modernized.

Balloch Pier, NS386825, opened in present form 1896 by the Dumbarton & Balloch Joint Line Committee. The steamer pier, a sheet-piled modern structure replaced a timber-piled pier, the shore end of which still exists, supporting a wooden station building, with a bracketted glazed awning.

Road bridge, Balloch, NS391819, late 19th century. A 5-span bridge, with 3 lattice-truss spans and a shorter plate-girder span on each side. The girders are supported on cylindrical masonry piers.

Slipway, Balloch, NS385825, built *c* 1899 by the Dumbarton & Balloch Joint Line Committee. A 2-track 'patent slip', with a wooden cradle with iron outriggers supported on a double central rail, with ratchet in the centre, and single side rails. The rails are all of cast-iron, bolted to longitudinal sleepers, which are in turn held to gauge by widely spaced cross sleepers. At the head of the slip is a single-storey harled winding-engine house, containing a large steam winch.

Bonhill Bridge, NS396798, built 1898, engineers CROUCH & HOGG. A single bowstring girder span, with castellated pylons at both ends.

Dalmonach Print Works, Bonhill, NS395802, founded 1786 and rebuilt 1812–13 by James Black & Co after a fire. A somewhat altered group of 1- and 2-storey sandstone and brick buildings. The oldest part would appear to be beside the river Leven. At the gate is a neat Gothic school, presumably operated in connection with the works.

CARDROSS

Cardross Station, NS344773, opened 1858 by the Glasgow, Dumbarton & Helensburgh Railway. A 2-platform through station, with the main offices on the up platform in a single-storey ashlar building with round-headed windows. The down-platform building is a 1-storey wooden building with an awning, of typical North British Railway pattern.

Dalquhurn Print Works, Renton, NS392776, erected as a bleach-works in 1715 by Andrew Johnstone. A large, much altered group of brick and rubble buildings. The most striking is a 4-storey, 9-bay, red-and-white-brick block at the entrance, while other interesting features include 2 engine houses, 1 with cast-iron roof beams. Now an industrial estate.

Renton Station, NS387783, opened 1850 by the Caledonian & Dumbartonshire Railway. A 2-platform through station, now reduced to a single platform. The main offices are on the up platform, in a 2-storey, red-and-white-brick building, incorporating a dwelling-house. There was a wooden shelter on the down platform, now demolished.

CUMBERNAULD

Lenziemill, NS751719, built *c* 1810. A decaying 2-storey rubble building, with an internal overshot wheel 4ft wide by 12ft 6in diameter (1·2 by 3·8m), with cast-iron rings, hub and axle and wooden spokes and buckets.

DUMBARTON

Dennystown Forge, NS392758, founded 1854. A range of single-storey workshops, clad in corrugated iron and red and white brick, with a 2-storey, 10-bay rubble office block. There is 1 rubble work-shop bay, presumably the original. There is an interesting wooden gate, now disused, with a trussed beam carrying 2 sliding leaves.

Dumbarton (Central) Station, NS397756, opened 1896 by the Dumbarton & Balloch Joint Line Committee. A 4-platform through station on a series of arches. The booking office is at street level, and there are 2 virtually identical platform buildings – red brick with steel-framed glazed awnings. Dumbarton East (NS406751) is similar but has only 1 island platform, and was built by the Lanarkshire and Dumbartonshire Railway.

Dumbarton Bridge, NS393753, built 1765, widened 1884, recon-structed 1934. A 5-span bridge, with dressed-stone arch rings and rubble spandrels and wing walls, extended in concrete. The arches are segmental, increasing in size to the centre, and there are rounded cutwaters extended up to form circular buttresses, now supporting the concrete extensions.

Leven Shipyard, NS402748, founded 1857 by William Denny & Bros. The most interesting survival at this yard is the test tank (1882–3) the first commercial one in the world, which is in a long single-storey brick building, with a stone frontage. Other remains are mainly modern sheds. Nearby are several streets of superior dwellings built by the company from 1882.

Denny Engine Works Offices, NS397757, built 1851 and later. An L-plan block, consisting of an older 2-storey and attic, 2-by-5-bay, pinned-rubble building and more recent 2-storey and attic, 7-bay and 3-storey, 4-by-3-bay range, with an external stairway, part wooden-clad.

Engine of PS 'Leven', NS395753. The single-cylinder, side-lever engine, built by ROBERT NAPIER in 1824, formerly beside Dumbarton Castle, has been moved to the new town centre.

Offices, McMillan's Yard, NS397752, late 19th century. A handsome 2-storey and attic Renaissance building, with the attic recently converted to a third storey. The ground-floor openings are roundheaded, and the doorway is pedimented. Now Electricity Board offices. The shipyard itself, founded 1834, has been obliterated.

Paul's Engine Works, NS392753, built 1847, extended 1866. A 14-bay, single-storey brick building, lit at 2 levels, a tall single-storey, 4-bay erecting shop, and a 10-bay rubble block, also lit at 2 levels. Latterly used as a garage, now empty. On the other side of the street was a 2-storey 9-bay brick office with sandstone dressings (1881).

Workers' housing, Dillichip, NS397790, mid 19th century. A pleasing range of 2-storey, red-sandstone dwellings, with access to the upper floor from stairs at the rear. Almost the last examples of a type once common in the calico-printing villages of the Vale of Leven.

KILMARONOCK

Drymen Bridge, NS474875, erected 1765, widened 1928–9. A 5-span masonry bridge, reconstructed in concrete, but retaining the masonry facing.

Drymen Station, NS478862, opened 1856 by the Forth & Clyde Junction Railway. Formerly a 2-platform through station, with the main building on the down (Stirling) platform. This was a 1- and 2-storey block similar to that at Balfron, but the 1-storey part has been demolished. The corrugated-iron goods shed still stands.

KIRKINTILLOCH

St Flanan's Colliery, NS688749. The extensive ruins of a large late 19th-century colliery, including engine and boiler houses and fan casing, all brick-built.

Lion Foundry, NS655740, founded c 1880 by 3 foremen from the Saracen Foundry, Glasgow. A large group of single-storey brick moulding and fitting shops, with a neat 1-storey and attic, red-and-white-brick office block with cast-iron details. There are 2 solid-bottom cupolas, apparently original.

Old Foundry, NS657737, mid 19th century. An interesting group of 1- and 2-storey rubble and brick buildings. The oldest appear to be 2-storey, 10-bay and 8-bay blocks, with round-headed openings on the ground floor. Now in multiple occupation.

Tollhouse, NS650741, early 19th century. A single-storey, 5-bay, ashlar-fronted rubble cottage, with the central doorway, flanked by toll tables, still partly legible.

LUSS

Arrochar and Tarbet Station, NN312045, opened 1894 by the West Highland Railway. A standard West Highland island-platform station, with brick and wooden 1-storey building, approached by a subway.

Cotton Mill, NS357928, late 18th century. A 3-storey, 5-bay rubble building, on a rectangular plan, with a 1-storey and attic dwelling-house at one end. Now a sawmill.

NEW KILPATRICK

Bearsden Station, NS543717, opened 1863 by the North British Railway. A 2-platform through station, with a 2-storey, 4-bay rubble office and station-house block on the up platform, with a single-storey wing, and a bracketted awning with glazed side screens. The down-platform building is a small brick structure, with the roof overhanging on 3 sides, and glazed side screens.

Tramway substation, Bearsden, NS551715, built 1924. A 1-storey and basement, 3-by-7-bay, red-sandstone rubble building, with turrets on 3 of the 4 corners. Originally housed two 500kw rotary converters to supply the Milngavie tram route, but now gutted and converted to a public hall.

'Gavin's Mill', Milngavie, NS554742, early 19th century. A 2-storey and attic rubble building on a rectangular plan, with a 6-spoke, all-iron overshot wheel, about 3ft wide by 12ft diameter (0·91 by 3·66m). Now a tea room and office.

Milngavie Station, NS556743, opened 1863 by the North British Railway. A 3-platform terminal station, with offices in a single-storey, 7-bay rubble building, extended by a 12-bay, steel-framed glazed awning supported by cast-iron columns. There is a rubble goods shed, and, on the island platform, a small wooden shelter.

OLD KILPATRICK

Bowling Station, NS443737, rebuilt after a fire in 1881. A 2-platform through station, with the main offices on the up platform in a single-storey, wood and brick building with a bracketted glazed awning. The ends of the awning are supported on cast-iron columns which also serve as rain-water pipes. The down-platform building is also wood and brick, with a cantilevered awning. There is a wooden goods shed, now used as a garage.

Littlemill Distillery, Bowling, NS442737, founded *c* 1800, rebuilt 1875 and subsequently. A much altered complex of brick and rubble buildings, mainly 1- and 2-storey, with 2 pyramidal-roofed kilns.

CLYDEBANK

Clydebank Riverside Station, NS499696, opened 1896 by the Lanarkshire & Dumbartonshire Railway. Formerly a 3-platform through station, with the offices on the up platform in a 1-storey brick and sandstone Renaissance building, with a hexagonal tower. This survives, now shorn of awnings.

Clydebank Shipbuilding Yard, NS4969, founded 1870 by J. & G. Thomson (plate 33). The yard in its present form dates largely from *c* 1890–1914, and consisted of 2 sets of berths on either side of a fitting-out basin. Interesting surviving features are the 2 fitting-out cranes, 1 of the 'Scotch derrick' type and the other hammerhead, built 1905 and 1906, the 4-storey brick stores building, and the late 19th-century offices. Now an oil-rig building yard.

33 Fitting-out basin, Clydebank Yard, with 1906 crane and MV *Alisa*, last ship built at the yard.

Rothesay Dock, NS502691, built 1907 by the Clyde Navigation Trust. A large rectangular basin, built in concrete, originally designed for coal shipment and iron-ore importation.

Sewing-machine factory, NS494707, built from 1882 for the Singer Manufacturing Co Ltd. Though much altered in recent years, this very large complex still contains much of interest, including 2 late 19th-century, multi-storey brick blocks, one 4 storey, the other 6 storey, both flat-roofed, and with concrete floors. The original single-storey oil store, with brick chimney-like ventilators also survives. There is some older machinery still in use.

Shipyard, Dalmuir, NS483707, built 1905 by William Beardmore and Co. Some single-storey brick workshops and the fitting-out basin, now used for shipbreaking, are the principal remains of this once great yard.

Faifley Cotton Mill, NS496730, early 19th century. The cut-down remains of an extensive complex, consisting of a 3-storey, 2-by-8-bay block and a single-storey, 12-bay range at right angles, formerly taller. At the rear is the 2-by-2-bay roofless ruin of a large wheel-house. Now converted to a morning-roll bakery.

RHU

Garelochhead Station, NS242910, opened 1894 by the West Highland Railway. A standard West Highland island-platform station, with brick and wooden 1-storey building, approached by a subway.

HELENSBURGH

Helensburgh Pier, NS294822, rebuilt 1861 and 1872. A long straight rubble pier, which was a steamer pier until the opening of Craigendoran in 1883.

Helensburgh (Central) Station, NS298824, opened 1858 by the Glasgow, Dumbarton & Helensburgh Railway, and rebuilt in the late 19th century. A 4-platform terminal station, with glazed steel-framed awnings over the platforms, supported on cast-iron columns and brick side walls. The ends of the platforms and the circulating area are covered by an arched overall roof with an attractive glazed screen. The offices are grouped round this in a 1- and 2-storey, U-plan range, with a 4-bay Renaissance street frontage.

Helensburgh (Upper) Station, NS298833, opened 1894 by the West Highland Railway. A standard West Highland Railway island-platform station, with brick and wooden 1-storey building, unusually approached from a road overbridge.

Granary, NS295823, early 19th century. A somewhat altered 3-storey, 3-bay harled building, now empty.

East Lothian

One of the great farming counties of Scotland, this has significant agricultural-processing industries. The coal industry was early to develop, and it had important salt and lime works. The towns of Haddington and Dunbar, and the smaller communities of Prestonpans and Cockenzie, contain some of the most picturesque industrial monuments in Scotland. The coastal routes between Edinburgh and the south pass through the county.

ABERLADY

Granary, NT465800, late 18th to early 19th century. A 3-storey, 7-bay rubble building with a hoist. Pantiled roof.
Smithy, NY467800. A small single-storey rubble building with a pantiled roof, now disused.

DIRLETON

Smithy, Gullane, NT483827, 18th century. A low single-storey rubble building with a pantiled roof. Now disused.

DUNBAR

Barns Ness Lighthouse, NT723772, established 1901, engineer D. A. STEVENSON. A tall, slightly tapering, circular-section tower, with circular lantern with triangular panes and domed top. The keepers' houses are, as usual, single-storey, flat-roofed structures, harled, with the quoins exposed.
Catcraig Limekilns, NT715772, mid 19th century. A pair of limekilns in a bank, 1 of which is 2-draw, the other 3. Of the 3 arches in the face of the bank, the centre one gives access to draw holes for both kilns. Restored in 1966 by East Lothian County Council.

DUNBAR

Belhaven Brewery, NT665784, rebuilt c 1814 (see plate 3). A most attractive range of 1- and 2-storey rubble buildings, pantile-roofed, except for the 2 pyramidal-roofed malting kilns, which are slated. There is a circular-section brick chimney (1887).

Dunbar Harbour, NT680793 and NT681792. The harbour is in 2 parts. The older section (*c* 1710–30) consists of a basin formed by a curved rubble pier and a shorter straight pier. Some of the masonry is vertically set. A low wharf inside the curved pier was for coal importation (1761). The newer part – the Victoria Harbour (1842) – is formed by a sea wall linking 2 rock outcrops, together with a quay along the shore parallel with the wall. This section has 2 entrances, 1 to the old harbour channel, spanned by a hand-operated, wrought-iron, 2-leaf bascule bridge, and the other, at the north end, is open. There is a 3-storey, 5-bay, harled store (Spott's Granary) on the old short pier.

Barometer, Dunbar Harbour, NT681791, presented 1856 to the fishermen of Dunbar. A handsome masonry pier, with an inscription, a low-relief sculpture of fishermen and a boat, and a wooden barometer case.

Covered boat slip, NT681792, 19th century. A rubble building, with a modern flat roof, covering a building and repairing slip. Situated off the old harbour.

Dunbar Station, NT681784, opened 1846 by the North British Railways. A 2-platform through station with the main offices in a 2-storey 'Tudor' stone building on the up platform. The down-platform building is similar in style, but only 1-storey high.

Grain stores, NT681791, 18th to 19th century. A 3-storey, 8-bay rubble building, with an arched cart entry, and a 3-storey, 7-bay rubble block with 2 hoists, now a joiner's workshop.

Horse-gin houses, NT685784 and NT681786, late 18th to early 19th century. The former is a heptagonal structure, with 3 rubble piers and the barn wall supporting the roof. At the apex of the roof is a weathercock. Preserved. The latter is a hexagonal rubble building. Both have pantiled roofs.

Maltings, NT680792, mid 19th century. A 4-storey rubble block on a U plan, 6-by-9-by-10 bay, harled on the walls facing the harbour. There are 2 kilns with square-section louvred ventilators. Being converted to flats.

Maltings by harbour, NT681791, late 18th century (built as warehouses). A long range of 3- and 4-storey rubble buildings, with 2 pyramidal-roofed kilns. Now disused. Nearby is a detached 3-storey, 10-bay block, with 2 pyramidal-roofed kilns, also disused.

Windmills. There are three windmill stumps in the parish, and a possible fourth. The largest is at West Barns (NT654783), a concave-tapering 2-storey harled structure, now a summer-house, and the smallest the tapering stump of a wind-pump at Dunbarney (NT702763). In Dunbar, at NT670789, is the short stump of a large tower mill, now with a conical roof, and at Meikle Pinkerton (NT703757) is a large-diameter tapering stump, now a dovecote, possibly formerly a windmill. The first 2 are probably late 18th century, and the third possibly 17th century.

Farm chimney, East Barns, NT717762, mid 19th century. A plain circular-section brick chimney, with single-storey rubble engine and boiler houses.

Railway underbridge and culvert, East Barns, NT726754, opened 1846 by the North British Railway. An attractive pair of bridges. The underbridge has a semicircular arch, with dressed-stone arch ring and rubble spandrels and wing walls. The culvert is slightly skewed with a semicircular arch and curved wing walls. The water course has a rubble invert.

Engineering works, West Barns, NT655779, built 1878. A single-storey, red-and-white-brick building on an L plan, the longer wing being 4-by-8-bay. There is a neat square-section, red-and-white-brick chimney.

Maltings, West Barns, NT654781, early 19th century and later. A group of much-altered, rubble-and-brick buildings, with asbestos-clad additions, dominated by a circular-section brick chimney. There is a substantial lade, still flowing, with an aqueduct over a minor road at the rear of the complex. Now gutted and empty.

GARVALD & BARA

Farm chimney, Danskine, NT569673, mid 19th century. A circular-section brick chimney, on a square stone base, with a single-storey engine house.

Smithy, NT590708, early 19th century. A single-storey, 2-bay rubble building with a pantiled roof.

GLADSMUIR

Limekilns, Landridge, NT457754, late 18th to early 19th century. Two large kilns; 1 is 4 draw, the other 3 draw, with arched side wings. Both stone-lined. (See Skinner, *Limekilns*, pp. 32, 38.) Disused.

Longniddry Station, NT446763, opened 1846 by the North British Railway. A 3-platform junction station, with the main offices on the north side. These are in a 2-storey rubble building, with overhanging eaves, entered from the platform side at first-floor level. The original building has been extended by a single-storey range. On the island platform is a brick and wood shelter of typical North British Railway design. To the south is a single-storey dwellinghouse on a T plan. An unusual open-truss footbridge, with wooden boarding, connects the platforms.

Railway underbridge, Longniddry, NT442759, opened 1846 by the North British Railway. Of a standard North British Railway design, with arched cast-iron side girders and steel main girders on rubble abutments.

Farm chimneys, Mains, NT483710 and Samuelston, NT486710, mid 19th century. Both brick-built, the former circular, the latter square in cross section.

HADDINGTON

Farm chimney, Barberfield, NT481719, mid 19th century. A circular-section brick chimney, with a small stone engine-and-boiler house.

Abbey Bridge, NT533746, 16th century. A fine 3-span bridge, with pointed arches and triangular cutwaters. The voussoirs are dressed stone and the rest of the masonry is rubble.

Abbey Mill, NT534747, late 18th century. A 2-storey rubble building with attic on an L plan, with a kiln at the end of 1 arm of the L. The building, now gutted and used as a store, is partly roofed with pantiles.

HADDINGTON

Gimmers' Mills, NS518740, founded 1408, taken over 1897 by John Montgomery. A most attractive 4-storey and attic, 7-bay rubble building, with a pyramidal-roofed kiln, both pantiled, with a modern extension. Associated with the mills is an early 20th-century, 5-storey, 4-by-10-bay coursed rubble block of maltings with a pyramidal-roofed kiln. Produces malt flour for baking.

Nungate Bridge, NT519738, 16th century. A 3-span bridge, with roughly segmental arches and triangular cutwaters. The arch rings and lower courses of the spandrels are of dressed stone.

Poldrate Mill, NS518734, early 19th century. The main mill is a 3-storey, 2-by-2-bay rubble block, with kiln and steam-engine house at the rear. Across a road is a massive 4-storey and attic, 2-by-5-bay granary block, linked to the mill by gangways at 2 levels. The all-iron, 6-spoke, low-breast wheel has now been exposed, and the mill block has been converted to a community centre.

Rosehall Foundry, NS509737, early to mid 19th century. A block of single-storey rubble buildings with pantiled roof. Part in use as a garage.

Simpson's Maltings, Distillery Park, NT514733, mid to late 19th century. A large group of maltings, the main range being a 4-storey and attic, 3-by-12-bay block, with 2 kilns.

Skinnery, NT519739, 19th century and later. A somewhat altered group of 1-, 2- and 4-storey buildings including a 4-storey rubble grain mill converted to a drying shed.

Victoria Bridge, NT518739, built 1900, engineers BELFRACE & CARFRAE. A 2-span bridge, with each span consisting of 8 segmental-arched, cast-iron ribs, supported on rusticated stone abutments and central pier. There is a cast-iron balustrade, and the spandrels of the outer ribs have low-relief serpentine decoration.

Waterloo Bridge, NT518733, built 1817. A graceful single segmental arch, with dressed-stone arch ring and coursed-rubble spandrels and wing walls.

West Mills (flour), NS513734, built 1842–3, converted to tweed manufacture in 1885. The former flour-mill range is a 4-storey, 5-bay, coursed-rubble building, with, at the rear, single-storey weaving sheds and a 2-storey and attic block.

Grain stores, 18th century and later. There are several grain stores in the town. One, at NT513739, has a 1-storey, 3-bay Renaissance office with 3-storey stores at the rear. Another, at NT515738, is more typical: 3-storeys and attic, 9-bay rubble, with a central hoist. The oldest is certainly the superb 3-storey and attic, 3-by-4-bay rubble building with end hoist, at NT520738. There is also a 3-storey, 5-bay rubble block at NT515739.

INNERWICK

Innerwick Station, NT741744, opened 1846 by the North British Railway. Formerly a 2-platform through station, the only surviving structure is a 2-storey, rubble building on an L plan, situated on the down platform. This has the projecting eaves characteristic of early North British Railway buildings. At the south end of the station is a skew overbridge similar to that at Bilsdean (*qv*).

Farm chimney, NT719739, mid 19th century. A circular-section brick chimney with a pantile-roofed engine house.

Railway bridge, NT744741, opened 1846 by the North British Railway. A single-span underbridge, with cast-iron side girders, of slightly bellied form, and steel main girders, supported on rubble abutments with wing walls. Unusual type for North British Railway.

Thornton Mill, Innerwick, NT742741, late 18th to early 19th century. A neat 1-storey and attic rubble building, with a projecting kiln with a circular ventilator. Now converted to a knitwear factory, though the 6-spoke wood and iron overshot wheel, about 2ft wide by 16ft diameter (0·61 by 4·88m), survives.

NORTH BERWICK

Balgone Barns Windmill, NT553828, late 17th century. A classic vaulted-tower windmill stump, standing about 2 storeys high. Of rubble construction.

North Berwick Harbour, NT553856, mainly 19th century. A rectangular basin, formed by an east pier and an 18th-century west breakwater, with quays on the landward side. There are a pair of 18th-century, 3-storey warehouses, now converted to other uses.

North Berwick Station, NT547852, opened 1850 by the North British Railway and subsequently rebuilt. Formerly a 2-platform terminal station, now reduced to 1. The main offices form an L round the buffer stops, and there are substantial wooden awnings, on cast-iron columns, over the curved platforms and round the outside of the office block.

OLDHAMSTOCKS

Bridge, Bilsdean, NT763725, 18th century. Has 2 spans, with segmental arches. The voussoirs are rusticated, and the parapet is castellated. The spandrels and wing walls are of coursed rubble.

Farm chimney, Lawfield, NT752730, mid 19th century. A square-section brick chimney on a square rubble base.

Farm chimney, Oldhamstocks Mains, NT743718, mid 19th century. A circular-section brick chimney on a square stone base. The adjoining engine house is now an implement shed.

Horse-gin house, Nether Monynut Farm, NT728645. A heptagonal rubble building with a slated roof.

PENCAITLAND

Bridge, Begbie, NT491710, late 18th century. A single-segmental arch, with dressed-stone arch ring and rubble spandrels.

Glenkinchie Distillery, NT443668, founded *c* 1840. A group of red-brick buildings, including 3-storey and attic bonded stores. There are several blocks of red-and-white-brick cottages associated with the distillery. The present complex dates from after 1890, when the Glenkinchie Distillery Co was formed.

Bridge, Wester Pencaitland, NT442690, built 1510. A 3-span bridge with pointed arches. The voussoirs are of dressed stone, the outer ones being moulded, while the rest of the masonry is rubble.

PRESTONKIRK

Preston Mill, NT595779, 17th century. A 1-storey and attic rubble range, with a circular kiln. There is a detached single-storey office and granary block. All the buildings have pantiled roofs. There is a 6-spoke, wood and iron low-breast wheel driving 2 pairs of stones. Restored and opened to the public under the auspices of the National Trust for Scotland.

East Linton Station, NT591771, opened 1846 by the North British Railway. Formerly a 2-platform through station, with the main offices on the down platform in a 2-storey building, on a T plan, with a castellated central feature, linked to a 1-storey wood and stone platform building. The main building, which contains a dwelling-house, predates the railway, at least in part.

Bridge, East Linton, NT593771, 16th century. A 2-span rubble bridge, with segmental arches and triangular cutwaters.

Mill, NT593772, 18th century. The much-altered remains of a 2-storey rubble building with a square pyramidal-roofed kiln. Now used by a wall-covering firm.

PRESTONPANS

Prestongrange Pumping Engine, NT373737 (plate 34). The sole surviving beam pumping engine in Scotland. A 70in (1·77m) Cornish engine built by HARVEY of Hayle, for the Summerlee Iron Co in 1874. It was enlarged in 1895, when the cast-iron beam was strengthened. The engine is being restored as the centrepiece of a museum of mining. The former power station of the colliery, a single-storey brick building with round-headed windows, has been reroofed, and is at present being used to house dismantled machinery, pending display. Nearby are the remains of a stoneware pipe works.

Brewery, NT387746, founded 1720. An interesting group of buildings on a rectangular plan, with a 3-storey, 6-bay range of maltings, with pyramidal-roofed kiln, and a 3-storey brewhouse with a roof-ridge ventilator. Now a workshop and store. At NT387745 is a 4-storey, 9-bay, red-brick malting range with a large rectangular kiln, now disused.

Saltworks, NT385746, late 18th to early 19th century. A roughly rectangular group of 1- and 2-storey rubble buildings, part pantile,

34   Prestongrange Pumping Engine.

part asbestos-roofed, with a small circular-section brick chimney. The last salt pan in Scotland operated here until 1959.

SALTOUN

Limekilns, Middlemains, NT473692, rebuilt 1817–20. A block of two 4-draw kilns, rubble-built, with semicircular draw arches. Disused.

Limeworks, East Saltoun, NT484681, opened 1943 by the Scottish Co-operative Wholesale Society. The processing building here is a single-storey brick and corrugated-iron range, with a central silo block. Disused in April 1974. There is a large quarry to the south.

Bridge, West Saltoun, NT458669, 18th century. A single-segmental arch, with dressed-stone arch ring and rubble spandrels and wing walls, the latter with oculi.

STENTON

Horse-gin house, NT621742, late 18th to early 19th century. A hexagonal rubble structure with pantiled roof.

TRANENT

Cockenzie Harbour, NT398757, rebuilt in its present form 1835, engineers ROBERT STEVENSON & SONS. Formed by an L-plan east pier and a west breakwater, both rubble-built, the latter patched in several places.

Cockenzie Waggon-way, NT398757–NT403734, opened 1722 by the York Buildings Co. The track of the first railway in Scotland, part beside the B6371 and part a footpath between hedges.

Port Seton Harbour, NT404759, built 1879–80. Formed by 2 piers with angled heads and a central pier, giving 2 basins.

WHITEKIRK & TYNINGHAME

Sawmill, Tyninghame, NT611790, 19th century (plate 35). An attractive single-storey, 5-bay rubble building, with crow-stepped gables and diamond-paned windows. Machinery driven by a 6-spoke, low-breast wood and iron paddle wheel about 4ft wide by 14ft diameter (1·22 by 4·27m).

Smithy, Tyninghame, NT609791, late 18th to early 19th century. A single-storey, 5-bay rubble building, with pantiled roof. Nearby is a restored village water pump.

Teind Barn, Whitekirk, NT596817, 16th century. A large 3-storey, 4-bay rubble building, with outside stone stairway to the first floor.

WHITTINGHAME

Farm chimney, Overfield, NT597722, mid 19th century. A circular-section brick chimney on a square stone base, with a pantile-roofed, single-storey engine and boiler house.

YESTER

Farm chimney, Duncanlaw, NT541682, mid 19th century. A circular-section brick chimney with a single-storey, pantile-roofed engine house.

35   Tyninghame Sawmill.

Fife

Fife is self-contained to an unusual extent, situated as it is between the firths of Forth and Tay. In the west, it has extensive mineral fields, exploited since medieval times, and in the east it is predominantly agricultural. The great industrial towns of Dunfermline and Kirkcaldy dominate the west as far as manufacturing is concerned. In the east, the towns are smaller, and function more as agricultural markets and fishing communities, though there are pockets of industry, as in Newburgh (floorcloth) and Leslie (paper). Though communications were until comparatively recently mainly of local significance, main road and rail links now traverse the county. There are several important harbours.

ABDIE

New Mill, Parkhill Farm, Newburgh, NO246182, 19th century. A handsome, 3-storey, 3-bay building, with prominent quoins. An overshot wheel with iron rings and axle and wooden buckets and spokes drives 2 pairs of stones. Well kept by the owner, who runs the wheel occasionally.

ABERDOUR

Aberdour Harbour, NT194851, early 18th century and later. A natural harbour protected by an irregular pier built of coursed and uncoursed rubble.

Aberdour Station, NT192853, opened 1890 by the North British Railway. A 2-platform through station, with the main offices in a 1-storey and attic, snecked-rubble building on the up side, with an awning supported on cast-iron columns. The down-platform building is a small rubble structure.

ANSTRUTHER

Cellardyke Harbour, NO577038, built 16th–18th century, improved 19th century, notably in 1829. A roughly rectangular basin, formed by a straight pier, an L-plan pier, and a quay on the landward side, all masonry. The end of the basin is natural beach, presumably for stilling waves entering the harbour.

Anstruther Easter Harbour, NO568034, rebuilt 1866–77 and subsequently partly rebuilt, notably in 1937. A single large basin, formed by a curved breakwater and an L-plan pier, divided into 2 by 2 short straight piers. Much of the works are in reinforced concrete, but there is some rubble masonry. At the seaward end of the breakwater is a neat octagonal concrete light-tower, and on the L-plan pier is a tapering cast-iron light-tower.

Dreel Burn Mill, NO563035, 18th to 19th century. A 4-storey, 3-bay rubble main block, with crow-stepped gables. There is a pantile-roofed, 2-storey kiln and the ruins of two 2 storey and 1 single-storey rubble structures. Each was a lean-to. The axle only of a large overshot wheel survives. Becoming ruinous.

Pittenweem Harbour, NO550023, late 19th century. Two piers with angled heads, forming 2 basins with the shore. An outer pier, acting as a breakwater, lies parallel to the eastern pier.

AUCHTERDERRAN

Engine houses, Lochgelly, NT187946, built c 1850 for the Lochgelly Coal and Iron Co. An interesting pair of ruins. The more complete apparently housed a rotative beam engine. It is now roofless. Of the other, only the west end remains, with a semicircular projection supporting a cast-iron water tank. Inside this 'apse' is a spiral staircase leading to a basement, the newel of the staircase being extended upward in the form of a column to provide additional support for the tank. The masonry work is very fine.

Viaduct, Cardenden, NT219951, opened 1849. A 4-span masonry viaduct, patched in brick, with segmental arches.

AUCHTERMUCHTY

Distillery, NO236120, founded 1829. A large block of 2- and 3-storey rubble buildings, extended in corrugated, asbestos-clad steel, and used as a grain store. The most recognizable part is a 3-storey, 9-bay bonded store.

Foundry and engineering works, NO241116, founded in the 18th century by John White and Son. The oldest building in the present complex is the 2-storey, 2-by-9-bay, stone-fronted brick engineering shop, which had the upper floor added in 1897. The single-storey brick foundry, now asbestos-roofed, dates from 1921. Machinery is modern.

Grain mill, NO239117, late 18th to early 19th century. A much altered 3-storey rubble building, now with an asbestos roof.

Grain store, NO238118, late 18th to early 19th century. A pleasant 3-storey, 2-by-5-bay rubble block with a pantiled roof. At the rear is a single-storey extension, and to 1 side a 2-storey pantile-roofed building.

Linen mill, NO237120, early to mid 19th century. A long rubble range, the older part of which appears to be a 2-storey and attic, 9-bay block, now asbestos roofed. The other part is a 2-storey, 14-bay building, with a projecting porch at first-floor level and a single-storey lean-to extension. Now occupied by a joiner and cabinetmaker.

AUCHTERTOOL

Auchtertool Distillery, NT217907, founded as a brewery in 1650 and converted to a distillery 1845. A group of brick and rubble buildings, dominated by a 4-storey range of maltings with twin kilns. A 2-storey pantiled rubble block at right angles to the maltings is probably part of the brewery. Now used as a bonded store.

BURNTISLAND

Binnend Oil Works, NT241873, founded 1878 by the Binnend Oil Co Ltd. Once a large shale-oil works, ruined workers' cottages are the most substantial remains.

Burntisland Harbour, NY2385, built 1876–1902 for coal exporting. A large harbour, consisting of 2 wet docks and a tidal basin, into which the Burntisland shipyard launches. Interesting features include a wooden-jib post crane and the former waiting room for the ferry from Granton.

Burntisland Station, NT233857, opened 1847 by the Edinburgh & Northern Railway, architect probably DAVID BELL. A 2-platform through station on a curve, with single-storey buildings with awnings on both platforms. On the south side is the magnificent classical 2-storey, 8-bay-front block of the former terminus, with a nonastyle portico and end-pedimented pavilions. Nearby is a fine 5-by-8-bay rubble goods shed, with roof-ridge ventilator and ball finials on the gables. The through platforms were added in 1890 by the North British Railway.

Carron Harbour, NT217858, c 1808. A rubble pier on an L plan with a slipway. Now used for boat-repairing. Originally built to ship lime from Newbigging Limestone Mine (NT210863).

CERES

Bishop Brig, NO400114, 17th century. A single segmental arch, with dressed-stone arch ring, and rubble spandrels and wing walls. The roadway is very narrow, and the bridge is now used as a footbridge.

Fife Folk Museum, NO400114. Two 18th-century weavers' cottages, one with the double window, and the 17th-century weigh house, converted to a museum. The buildings are rubble-built, and the cottages have pantiled roofs. The weigh-house has a low-relief sculpture of a pair of scales above the door.

Meal mill, NO400114, 18th century. A 2-storey rubble building, with a pantiled roof. A beer store since the 19th century.

COLLESSIE

LADYBANK

Bonthrone Maltings, NO307097, late 19th century. An attractive range of malting floors, kilns and offices, with the ruins of another block of floors at the rear. There are 2 pyramidal-roofed kilns.

Ladybank Station, NO307097, opened 1847 by the Edinburgh & Northern Railway, architect probably DAVID BELL (see plate 13). A 2-platform through station, with the main offices on the down platform. These are in a 2- and 3-storey, coursed-rubble building, incorporating a dwellinghouse, and with an unglazed platform awning supported on cast-iron columns. The platform is at first-floor level. The up-platform building is a wood and brick structure, of typical North British Railway design, with a bracketted awning. The platforms are linked by an underground passage.

Pumping Station, Ladybank Waterworks, NO304103, built 1908. An ornate tall single-storey, 3-by-4-bay, red-brick pump house, with stone and coloured brick decoration. The building is lit at 2 levels, and there is a concealed water tank in the roof. An example of a type rare in Scotland.

Railway workshops, NO307101, built c 1848 for the Edinburgh & Northern Railway. A 4-road, 2-by-8-bay, single-storey rubble building with arched doorways and diamond-paned windows. There is a single-storey, 7-bay office block in similar style.

CRAIL

Crail Harbour, NO612073, built 16th–19th centuries. A basin formed by 2 rubble piers. The main (east) pier dates from the 16th–18th centuries, the west pier from 1825–8, engineers ROBERT STEVENSON AND SONS. The enclosed shore was quayed in the 1830s.

CULROSS

Blairhall Colliery, NT004885, sunk 1911. A classic early 20th-century coal mine, with steel-framed buildings with brick infilling, and 2 lattice-girder head-frames. Now out of use, except for the washery.

Comrie Colliery, NT006910, sunk 1936–40 by the Fife Coal Co. A model colliery of its time, with well-designed brick and concrete buildings and 2 headframes of conventional type.

Valleyfield Colliery, NT010683, sunk 1908. A 2-shaft colliery, with brick surface buildings and 'traditional' headgear.

Ice house, NS983859, early 19th century. A large vaulted chamber with a semicircular arch at the seaward end and a rectangular doorway at the opposite end. The earth cover has been eroded. Nearby are the remains of a rubble pier.

Mine shafts, NS980861 and 980856, sunk *c* 1575 and *c* 1590 by Sir George Bruce. The much reduced remains of the celebrated Castlehill and Moat pits (see *Industrial Archaeology*, 1970, 7, 353). The Moat Pit was an early and successful attempt at undersea coal mining.

Ruins, Preston Island, NT007852, built early 19th century by Sir Robert Preston of Valleyfield. A most interesting group of ruined engine houses and other buildings associated with coal-mine and salt-pan complex.

CULTS

Bonthrone Maltings, Pitlessie, NO337096, late 19th century. A 3-storey, 2-by-11-bay rubble range of malting floors, with 3 pyramidal-roofed kilns, and a 3-bay range of malt stores. Now disused.

Cults Limeworks, NO343086 and 352089, 19th century and later. At the former location are a large kiln range, rubble-built, but refronted in concrete in 1936, and a single-storey rubble lime store, now roofed with corrugated iron. There is a similar, but smaller range at the latter location, where there are also twin steel-clad kilns and a modern crushing plant. The kilns are disused.

CUPAR

CUPAR

Cupar Mills, NO371139, early to mid 19th century. A large complex with two 4-storey and attic, 4-bay granaries and a 3-storey, 2-by-4-bay mill block with 2 pyramidal-roofed kilns. Now modernized, with silos for bulk storage of grain.

Cupar Station, NO377143, opened 1847 by the Edinburgh & Northern Railway, architect probably DAVID BELL. A very fine example of a large, early railway station. A 2-platform through station, with the main offices on the down platform. These are in an ashlar block, with a central 2-storey building with an oriel window at first-floor level above a pair of elliptical arches; single-storey wings link this with 2-storey end pavilions. On the platform side is a wooden awning supported on cast-iron columns with lotus capitals. At the south end of the station is a road and foot bridge, with 2 semi-circular arches and a central elliptical span. In the goods yard are a 4-storey, 2-by-5-bay granary, with cart entries on the ground floor, and a range of 5 coal staithes.

East Toll, NO378147, early 19th century. A handsome single-storey building with a semi-octagonal bay projecting from 1 end, with prominent eaves. There is a pedimented Doric porch. Now asbestos-roofed.

Newmill, NO400150, 1780 and later. A 2-storey and attic, 10-bay, rubble building, with a corrugated-iron roof, formerly a flax mill, and a 3-storey, 4-bay building with a pantiled roof and a projecting asbestos-roofed kiln. The 6-spoke, low-breast, wood and iron paddle-wheel for the corn mill survives.

Grain mill, NO372148, early 19th century. A 3-storey, 5-bay rubble building, now occupied by a firm of joiners.

Linen-weaving factory, NO376144, early to mid 19th century. A 6-bay range of single-storey weaving sheds, with associated 2-storey buildings, all rubble-built.

South Toll, NO376138, built 1842. A single-storey rubble building, with a semi-octagonal bay projecting from one end.

Mills, NO374146, 19th century. A 3- and 4-storey, 3-by-9-bay rubble building, with a twin-vented kiln at one end, and a single-vented, pyramidal-roofed kiln at one side.

Horse-gin house, Pittencrieff, NO373159, early 19th century. A circular rubble building with a slated roof.

Russell Mill (flax spinning), Springfield, NO353119, mid 19th century. A range of 4 bays of single-storey, north-light sheds, with a 2-storey rubble office block, a tall single-storey engine house with a pyramidal roof and round-headed windows, and an octagonal red-and-white-brick chimney on a square stone base. Now a concrete-block factory.

Springfield Station, NO349119, opened 1847 by the Edinburgh & Northern Railway, architect probably DAVID BELL. A 2-platform through station, with the main offices on the up platform, in a 2-storey building on an L plan, with a single-storey wing. There is an awning on the platform side, supported on cast-iron columns. The down-platform building is a small wooden shelter, and the platforms are linked by a lattice-girder footbridge. In the goods yard, on the up side, are the bricked up arches of 6 bays of staithes.

DAIRSIE

Dairsie Village, NO415175, 18th to 19th century. Most of the houses in the village, single storey with slate or pantiled roofs, were linen weavers' cottages, and many have the characteristic double window.

DALGETY

St David's Harbour, NT187825, rebuilt 1836. An irregularly shaped basin formed by 2 piers and quays. Was the terminus of Fordell Railway. Now used for shipbreaking.

DUNFERMLINE

Pier, Bruce Haven, NT079830, probably 18th century. An L-plan coursed-rubble pier, forming a basin with a natural reef and a short stretch of artificial breakwater. Now ruinous.

CHARLESTOWN

Broomhall Granary, NT067838, built 1792. A 3-storey, 3-by-5-bay rubble building, with central gable and hoist door. Now houses and shop. To the north is another store block.

Charlestown Harbour, NT064833, 18th century and later. The inner basin was formed by the 5th Earl of Elgin *c* 1770, and the outer basin added later, the north-west pier dating from *c* 1840 and the south-east pier from the late 19th century. Built for coal and lime-stone shipment.

Mid Mill, NT064848, built as a thread mill 1815, converted to a corn mill 1870. A 3-storey rubble building, now modernized internally, with a disused 6-spoke, wood and iron, high-breast or pitch-back wheel, with 3 rings.

Laundry, NT066838, late 19th century. A group of single-storey rubble buildings, with pantiled roofs. Now disused.

Limekilns, NT065835, built from *c* 1761. A long range of 14 kilns, of some complexity, all built of dressed stone. Served by Charlestown Harbour and the Elgin Railway (a horse-tramway) and later by a North British Railway branch, now lifted. The largest group of kilns in Scotland.

DUNFERMLINE

Baldridge Factory (linen), NT083880, built c 1845. A large group of 3- and 4-storey rubble buildings, now disused.

Dunfermline (Lower) Station, NT097871, opened 1877 by the North British Railway and rebuilt in 1890. Formerly a 3-platform through station, now cut back to 2. The main offices are on the down platform in a single-storey stone building with awnings on both rail and road sides.

Dunfermline (Upper) Station, NT094877, opened 1849 by the Stirling & Dunfermline Railway. A 2-platform through station, with the main offices on the down side, in a 2-storey rubble building, incorporating a dwellinghouse. Both platforms have steel-framed awnings, and are linked by a lattice-girder footbridge.

St Leonard's Works (linen), NT097867, built 1851. A magnificent 3-storey, 5-by-17-bay Italian Renaissance building. The other buildings on the site have been demolished.

St Margaret's Works (linen), NT090878, 1870 and later. A large complex, with a 4-storey, 6-by-22-bay front block, extended by a 3-storey, 6-bay building, and a 2-storey, 18-bay range, all in Renaissance style. At the rear are 1- and 2-storey workshops part dated 1893, and across a street (spanned by a covered bridge at first-floor level) is a 16-bay Renaissance range with a balustraded corner tower, built 1900. Behind this is a 2-storey, 23-bay block, dated 1870, and a single-storey, 19-bay block of weaving sheds. Probably the oldest part of the complex is a 3-storey and attic, 5-bay rubble building.

Victoria Works, NT092879, built 1876. A large block of single-storey workshops, with a handsome 2-storey Italianate office block.

Viaducts, NT089878 and 095869, opened 1849 by the Stirling & Dunfermline Railway. Two masonry viaducts, the former with 6 main segmental spans and 2 approach spans, 1 of plate-girder construction. The other, taller, viaduct has 13 spans.

Windmill, Hill House, NT091859, 17th century. The circular rubble stump of a vaulted-tower windmill.

Pier, Limekilns, NT074833, 18th century. A straight coursed-rubble pier, with a central wall, now ruinous.

Roscobie Limekilns, NT093927, late 18th or early 19th century. A striking curved range of 4 2-draw ashlar-built kilns, extended in concrete.

DUNINO

Stravithie Mill, NO536113, built 1856. A 3-storey, 3-bay rubble building, with a projecting kiln with a circular vent. There are 2 pairs of stones, driven by an internal wood-and-iron overshot wheel, about 14ft (4·27m) diameter.

ELIE

Elie Harbour, NT493997, rebuilt *c* 1855. Formed by an island linked to the shore by a causeway, and extended by a pier. There is a 4-storey granary on the pier, probably 18th century.

FALKLAND

Pleasance Linen Works, NO257072, mid to late 19th century. A 2-storey, 8-bay-front block, with 13 bays of contemporary rubble weaving sheds, together with modern brick extensions. There is a circular-section brick chimney.

Freuchie Mill, NO290066, built 1840. A handsome 4-storey, 3-bay rubble building, with a 5-storey, pyramidal-roofed kiln and 1- and 2-storey outbuildings. Now a garage and store.

Jute Mill, Freuchie, NO284070, mid to late 19th century. A 2-storey, 2-by-16-bay rubble front block, with 2 arched cart entries (now blocked up). At the rear are single-storey weaving sheds with sheet-iron ventilators, and a single-storey engine- and boiler-house range with an octagonal brick chimney. Now a warehouse.

Bonthrone Maltings, Newton of Falkland, NO268071, mid to late 19th century (plate 36). An interesting group of buildings, with 2 main 3-storey ranges of malting floors forming an L. The older is 7 bays long with a pantiled roof, rubble-built, and the other 8 bays, with a brick wall. Each range has its own pyramidal-roofed kiln, and there is a circular-section brick chimney. Now disused.

Brewery, Newton of Falkland, NO267070, late 18th century. A 2-storey and attic rubble block with pantiled roof, with a pyramidal-roofed kiln, now blanked off. Used as a garage and store.

FERRYPORT-ON-CRAIG

TAYPORT

Tayport Harbour, NO459291, rebuilt 1847 by the Edinburgh & Northern Railway. A basin formed by a pier and two quays, built as terminus of the ferry to Broughty Ferry (*qv*). Superseded by the Tay Bridge in 1878.

West Lighthouse, NO447293, built 1823 and later. A tall circular tower.

Jute spinning mill, NO465277, mid 19th century. A group of rubble buildings, mostly 1 storey, with a neat engine house and an octagonal brick chimney.

Sawmill, NO461277, 19th century and later. An irregular group of brick buildings, roofed with corrugated iron, asbestos, pantiles and slates, and some slat-sided drying sheds. There is a circular-section brick chimney. The mill is powered by a marine-type steam engine.

FORGAN

Ferry terminal, Newport, NO418277, built *c* 1822. An unusual structure, with 2 semicircular canopies, 1 on each side of a single-storey, 4-bay office. Now used by the University of Dundee, as is the ramped ferry pier, designed by THOMAS TELFORD.

INVERKEITHING

INVERKEITHING

Inverkeithing Harbour, NT132826, 18th century and later. Rubble

36 Bonthrone Maltings, Newtown of Falkland.

quay walls on both sides of a small stream, with sluices for clearing silt. Now much decayed. Was the terminus of the Halbeath Railway, an early 19th-century wagonway.

Inverkeithing Paper Mill, NT130825, built 1914 by Caldwell & Co. A complex of red-brick, 1- and 2-storey buildings, with a 2-storey, 19-bay office block. There are 2 circular-section brick chimneys.

Inverkeithing Station, NT132833, rebuilt 1890 by the North British Railway. A 2-platform through station, with brick and wood offices on both platforms. The main offices are on the down side.

Warehouse, NT132831, mid to late 19th century. A 3-storey, 22-bay harled building, with round-headed windows in the top floor. Now disused.

Halbeath Railway Bridge, NT132832, probably early 19th century (plate 37). A semicircular arch in a bridge crossing the Forth Bridge approach railway, a stream, and the track of the Halbeath Railway, a mineral tramway.

North Queensferry Station, NT132808, opened 1890 by the Forth

37 Halbeath Railway Bridge, Inverkeithing.

Bridge Railway. A 2-platform through station, with wooden buildings on both platforms, with awnings, and a wooden footbridge.

Ferry piers, North Queensferry, NT131802, and 128802, 19th century. Two ramped ferry piers and a wood-piled pier. The eastern ferry pier has a neat hexagonal light tower at its shore end, *c* 1810.

KEMBACK

Blebo Mills, NO415144, *c* 1830. The only surviving part of this flax-spinning complex is a single-storey rubble block on an L plan, now used as a garage.

Yoolfield Crescent, NO415148, *c* 1839. A curved range of 10 single-storey weavers' cottages, all but one with the characteristic double window.

Yoolfield Mill, NO415148, built 1839. The cut-down remains of a small rectangular rubble building, with an intact 1-room office and a square-section stone chimney.

KENNOWAY

Mill, NO351026, early to mid 19th century. A 3-storey, 5-bay rubble block, with pantiled roof. At 1 end is the ruin of a large kiln. Now a launderette.

KETTLE

Balbirnie Estate Sawmill, NO333050, mid 19th century. A 2-storey rubble building, with dressed-stone quoins. There is a detached square-section brick chimney. In the yard is a wooden derrick crane.

Falkland Road Station, NO228058, opened 1847 by the Edinburgh & Northern Railway, architect probably DAVID BELL. Formerly a 2-platform through station. The down-platform building survives, a 1-storey, 11-bay ashlar structure.

Linen weaving mill, Kingskettle, NO333048, mid 19th century. A 9-by-11-bay range of 1-storey weaving sheds, with a circular-section brick chimney, and the ruins of a boiler house. Now empty and decaying.

KILMANY

Horse-gin house, Wester Kinnear, NO400227, early 19th century. A hexagonal rubble building, with a pantiled roof.

KINGHORN

Kinghorn Harbour, NT273869, probably 18th century. The 'kirk' harbour, consisting of the rubble-quayed sides of a small bay.

Kinghorn Station, NT270868, opened 1847 by the Edinburgh & Northern Railway, architect probably DAVID BELL. A 2-platform through station, with the main offices on the down platform in a neat 2-storey, 4-bay rubble building. Some of the lamp-posts are still inscribed 'Edin & North Rail'.

Flax-spinning mill, NT270872, mid 19th century. A 2-storey, 9-bay rubble building.

Pettycur Harbour, NT265861, rebuilt 1792. A rubble pier with a curved end, protecting a natural inlet. Now badly silted. There is a cast-iron capstan on the pier-head with inscription 'Anderson, Leith Walk Foundry, 1813'.

KIRKCALDY

Frances Colliery, Dysart, NT310939, sunk c 1850 (plate 38). The oldest colliery still operating in Scotland. The present steel-framed

38   Frances Colliery, Dysart.

headframe and coal-preparation plant are relatively recent.

Harbour, Dysart, NT302928, 17th century and later. An interesting harbour, built for coal shipment, with 2 rubble piers forming an outer basin, and an inner, gated basin formed in 1831. Now used by pleasure craft, with a 2-storey and basement warehouse converted to a yacht clubhouse. The slipway was used as a shipbuilding yard in the mid 19th century.

Windmill, Dysart, NT299934, late 17th to early 18th century. A short rubble tower about 25ft (7·6m) high, with a subterranean vault.

KIRKCALDY

Abden Works, NT278902, founded 1864 as a linen-weaving factory. A group of 2- and 3-storey harled buildings, with a large circular-section brick chimney, dated 1866. There is an unusual circular brick water-tower.

Bennochy Works (linen), NT273913, built 1865. A handsome 3-storey and attic 3-by-13-bay, coursed-rubble building, with a mansard roof. The 3 western bays have round-headed windows. At the rear are a fine octagonal brick chimney, and 2- and 3-storey stores. The entrance gate has a lamp supported by wrought-iron brackets, and rubbing posts in the form of cannon.

East Bridge Flour Mills, NT285923, early 19th century and later. A complex of buildings of various dates, mostly harled. The oldest part is a 2-storey and attic block, with a converted circular horse-gin house adjoining, linked to a 2-storey and attic, 3-bay, Palladian office block.

Forth and Clyde Roperie, NT278900, early 19th century on. A long stone and brick single-storey building, with roof part pantiled, part corrugated-iron clad. There are some single-storey ancillary buildings.

Kirkcaldy Harbour, NT285920, improved 1843 and 1909. Consists of an inner and an outer basin, the former gated, with two piers. There is a swing bridge over the entrance to the inner basin. The works are executed partly in rubble and partly in concrete and built 1909. Associated with the harbour are 1-, 2-, 3- and 4-storey warehouses of various dates.

St Mary's Canvas Works, NT285921, built 1869, rebuilt 1914. A large complex, with street frontage on an S curve. The main blocks are 3 storey by 19 bay and 1 storey by 15 bay. The 1-storey building has pairs of pilasters separating the bays, round-headed openings, and rusticated quoins.

West Bridge Mills (flax), NT276902, founded 1806. A fine 3-storey and attic, 4-by-17-bay rubble building with mansard roof, built 1856. There are ball finials on the S gable, and 2 quatrefoil windows at attic level. There is a single-storey brick boiler house, with a square-section chimney, and 2- and 3-storey rubble offices and stores. Now disused.

Electricity generating station, NT282924, opened 1903 by Kirkcaldy Corporation Tramways. A tall single-storey ashlar building, with a 2-storey office. Now a store.

Flint mills, NT265902. Of these two mills, Balwearie (c 1840) is on the west, a pantile-roofed rubble building with a high-breast wheel with wood spokes and iron rings, axle and buckets 24ft (7·32m) diameter. Nearby is a vertical stone flint-calcining kiln. Hole Mill (c 1860) is a more complex structure, with some machinery surviving, including a high-breast wheel, 24ft (7·32m) diameter, driving 2 grinders. There are ruins of a calcining kiln and drying floors. Hole Mill is of rubble construction, with a corrugated-iron roof and brick extensions. See *Industrial Archaeology*, 1966, *3*, 170–6, 195. Both mills were converted from 18th-century corn mills, and are becoming ruinous.

Tiel Works, NT278902, built c 1870 by George Brown, engineer. A 2-storey, 11-bay, harled rubble building, now used as bus workshops.

Linoleum works, NT287927, founded 1847 by Michael Nairn for floorcloth manufacture; started making linoleum 1877. A large complex of stone and brick buildings, some with the characteristic tall ground floor of the classic linoleum works. The majority appear to date from the late 19th or early 20th century.

Maltings, NT287923, mid to late 19th century and later. A large group of rubble buildings, mainly 3 and 4 storey, with 3 pyramidal-roofed kilns and 2 most unusual conical-roofed kilns. There are also modern grain silos.

Maltings, NT279922, late 19th century. A range of 4-storey brick malting floors, with 2 pyramidal-roofed kilns. Now disused.

LARGO

Largo Pier, NO417025, 19th century. An irregular rubble pier protecting the mouth of a small stream.

LEUCHARS

Horse-gin house, Clayton, NO430183, early 19th century. A heptagonal structure, with slate roof supported on ashlar piers. Now a store.

Guard Bridge, NO452188, built 1450. A 6-span rubble bridge, with 5 large segmental arches and 1 small. There are triangular cutwaters, carried up to form refuges. Bypassed by a 3-span, segmental-arched concrete bridge.

Inner Bridge, Guard Bridge, NO450198, probably 18th century. A 3-span, coursed-rubble bridge, with 2 wide segmental arches and 1 small. There are massive triangular cutwaters. Now bypassed and used as a footbridge.

Paper mills, Guard Bridge, NO451195, founded 1872 by the Guard Bridge White Pine Co Ltd. A large group of buildings of various dates, mainly brick-built, with 3 tall circular-section brick chimneys.

Leuchars Junction Station, NO449207, built *c* 1900 by the North British Railway. Formerly a 4-platform through and terminal station, having an island platform with a bay at each end. The station building is of brick and wood, with a massive awning, supported on cast-iron columns all round it. The platform is linked with a minor road by an unusual single-track, lattice-girder bridge.

MARKINCH

Cameron Bridge Distillery, NO346002, founded 1824 by John Haig. A large complex of buildings of various dates, with a 4-storey and 2 attic block of malting floors with a pyramidal-roofed kiln.

MARKINCH

Balbirnie Woollen Mills, NO288012, founded 1835 by 'Mr Drysdale'. A 2-storey and attic, 2-by-8-bay rubble building, now asbestos-roofed, with a lower 2-storey addition. There is a square-section brick chimney. Now used as a paper store.

Markinch Station, NO299014, opened 1847 by the Edinburgh & Northern Railway, architect DAVID BELL. A 2-platform through station, with the main offices on the down side, in a 1- and 2-storey building above and behind the platform. There is a wooden shelter on the platform. The up-platform shelter is also wooden. The platforms are linked by a footbridge which is incorporated in a road overbridge.

Markinch Viaduct, NO298010, opened 1847 by the Edinburgh & Northern Railway. A handsome 10-span viaduct, with small single arches at each end and 8 main arches, all semicircular. The arch rings are of dressed stone, rustic ashlar, and the spandrels of coursed rubble. Iron tie-rods have been inserted in the spandrels.

Middle Mill, NO294010, early 19th century. A 3-storey, 5-bay rubble building, now gutted and used as a barn.

Beam-engine house, Thornton, NT292973, late 18th or early 19th century (plate 39). A unique example of the buildings of an 'engine pit' of the period, disused by 1854. These consist of a 3-storey ashlar engine house, with 1- and 2-storey rubble buildings, including a dwellinghouse. Now a farmstead.

NEWBURGH

Newburgh Harbour, NO235187, 19th century. Three masonry piers projecting from a quay wall on the shore line.

Floorcloth factory, NO234185, founded 1891 by the Tayside Floor-cloth Co. A large complex of red-and-white-brick and rubble buildings. Prominent features are 2 towers, 1 a 7-storey, 2-by-2-bay water tower, the other a 5-storey and attic, 3-bay linoleum drying tower. The office is a 1-storey and attic, 3-by-13-bay block, with Renaissance details (1906).

Malt barn, 114 High Street, NO236184, late 18th or early 19th

39 Beam-engine house, Thornton.

century. A much-altered 2-storey, 1-by-2-bay rubble building, forming an L with a 2-storey dwellinghouse.

ST ANDREWS

Boarhills Viaduct, NO567133, opened 1881 by the North British Railway. A 5-span viaduct on a curve, with blue-brick arch rings and coursed-rubble spandrels and piers. There are refuges corbelled out above each pier.

Park Mill, Boarhills, NO566132. The main mill (1804) is a 3-storey and attic rubble building, now gutted and used as a hen house, but formerly containing 3 pairs of stores, driven by a 20ft (6·10m) diameter overshot waterwheel, now also removed. The detached 2-storey, pantile-roofed granary and kiln date from 1819.

Horse-gin house, Bonnytown, NO545127, early 19th century. A circular structure, with slated roof. The roof was carried on rubble piers alternating with cast-iron columns, the spaces between now being filled with old oil drums set in cement.

ST ANDREWS

Argyle Brewery, NO504166, mid 19th century. An attractive group of 2- and 3-storey rubble buildings grouped around a courtyard. There is a 3-storey brewhouse, with an octagonal-section, red-and-white brick chimney built on to it, and a 2-storey range with louvred upper floor behind the main complex. All the buildings have pantiled roofs.

St Andrews Harbour, NO517166, 18th century and earlier, improved *c* 1900. This is formed by 2 straight piers, 1 of roughly squared drystone rubble (*c* 1700) and a stretch of quay wall. An inner harbour has been formed by quaying a stretch of river bank, and is approached through a gated opening, spanned by a rolling suspension footbridge (early 20th century).

Brewery, NO507165, 19th century or possibly earlier. A small group of 1- and 2-storey brick and rubble buildings, round a cobbled courtyard. The brewhouse, a 2-storey structure, had a louvred upper floor. Now a garage and store.

Denbrae Mill, Strathkinness, NO478158, early 19th century. A 3-storey, 4-bay mill block, incorporating a kiln, with a 2-storey extension. There are 3 pairs of stones, but the wheel and drive have been removed. The miller's house incorporates a grain store at first-floor level, and has crow-stepped gables. All these buildings have pantiled roofs.

ST MONANS

St Monans Harbour, NO526015, rebuilt 1865 and *c* 1883. Two basins formed by 3 L-plan piers, part concrete, part masonry of various dates.

Boat-building yard, NO525105, late 19th century. A large weatherboard shed, with lean-to additions, housing building berth and machinery. The boats are lifted into the harbour by a derrick crane.

Windmill tower, NO534019, 18th century. The slightly tapered circular-section rubble tower of a windmill, originally used to pump sea water to salt pans.

SCOONIE

Durie Foundry, Leven, NO377007, founded by Henry Balfour in 1810. The foundry is a tall single-storey building, with brick walls. and steel frame. There is a wooden foundry crane, now electrified. The cupola by Thwaites (1914 pattern) has a receiver.

TULLIALLAN

Kincardine Bridge, NS921869–NS928873, opened 1936. A steel-girder bridge, 2,696ft (822m) long with a central 364ft (111m) swing span, in the form of a steel truss with central bowed portion.

Kincardine Pier, NS928872, completed 1811–13. A rectangular coursed-rubble pier, originally much longer, cut back as a result of land reclamation in 1829. The old sea wall can still be seen.

Ferry pier, Kincardine, NS927873, built 1826–7. A coursed-rubble ramped ferry pier.

WEMYSS

Michael Colliery, East Wemyss, NT332967, sunk 1895 and resunk 1926. The surface buildings and headgear survive here, though the colliery was closed by a fire in 1967. There are 2 steel-girder headframes. Nearby are single-storey harled cottages with pantiled roofs, typical of the model miners' housing provided by the Wemyss estate.

Methil Harbour, NT995375. In its present form dates from 1887 when a small wet dock was built for R. Erskine Wemyss. It was extended between 1895 and 1913 by the North British Railway. It has 2 decayed piers at the north-east end to increase the number of berths available. There are 3 coal hoists still in position, with associated elevated railway lines. The earlier docks are built of stone, the latter of concrete. Both were designed for coal shipment, which finally ceased in 1970.

Miners' Rows, Methil, NT365989, late 19th to early 20th century. A range of relatively modern 2-storey harled cottages, with pantiled roofs. Access to the upper houses by an outside stair.

Harbour, West Wemyss, NT324946, 19th century. Now largely filled in, though the main pier and the entrance to the gated basin are still intact.

Kinross-shire

Kinross-shire is Scotland's second smallest county. It is almost totally rural, with one town, Kinross, which supports a small textile industry.

CLEISH

Cleish Mill, NT103978, probably early 19th century. A rectangular 2-storey rubble building with a kiln at 1 end. The kiln has a pantiled roof and a square louvred ventilator. Now gutted and used as a barn.

FOSSOWAY

Horse-gin houses, Coldrain (NO083003) and Wood of Coldrain (NO084009), late 18th to early 19th century. Both circular rubble buildings with slated roofs. The latter is unusually small.
Bridge, Crook of Devon, NO033003, 18th century. A small hump-backed bridge, with a segmental arch.
Mill, Crook of Devon, NO038003, early 19th century. A 2-storey, rubble building on a rectangular plan, with a projecting kiln. One angle between the kiln and the main block has been filled by a brick extension. Now gutted and used as a cowhouse.

KINROSS

Lochleven Mills, NO119015, built from 1846 as wool-spinning mills. The oldest part appears to be a 2-storey, 4-by-15-bay rubble building, and there is a similar, parallel range. Recently modernized without substantial alteration.
Horse-gin houses, Middle Balado, NO093026 (plate 40) and Tillyochie, NO073029, late 18th to early 19th century. The former is a circular rubble structure with a slated roof; the latter is a hexagonal building with a pantiled roof.

ORWELL

Horse-gin house, Dalqueich, NO081045, early 19th century. An octagonal rubble building with a pantiled roof.
Grain mill, Milnathort, NO119047, mid 19th century. A 4-storey, 9-bay rubble building with a most unusual ribbed concrete roof.

Woollen mill, Milnathort, NO119047, built *c* 1867. The main block has been demolished, but some single-storey sheds and a striking large engine house survive.

Walk Mill, NO099051, 18th century. The shell only of a 2-storey rubble building, with single-storey wings, now used as a store. The long lade can still be traced; it also supplied a waterwheel-driven pump for domestic water supply. The 6-spoke, all-iron overshot wheel still exists, 1ft 7in wide by 5ft diameter (0·48 by 1·52m).

PORTMOAK

Powmill, NO158041, mid 19th century. A 1-storey and attic rubble building, with a pantiled roof, and the skeleton only of an 8-spoke, wood and iron suspended wheel with external rim drive. Disused.

40   Horse-gin house, Middle Balado.

Kirkcudbrightshire

Kirkcudbrightshire is almost entirely rural, the only industrial centres, Gatehouse-of-Fleet and Dalbeattie, now being decayed. Despite its indented coastline there is only one harbour of significance – at Kirkcudbright.

ANWOTH

Bridge, Skyreburn, NX573546, 19th century. A single flat segmental rubble arch, now bypassed.

BORGUE

Brighouse Bay Pier, NX637453, late 18th century. A short rubble pier, with a rounded end, forming an L with a stretch of quayed shore. At the shore end is a former fish house.
Smithy, NX630483, early 19th century. A 1-storey, 3-bay rubble building, with a small roof ventilator, Now disused.
Knockmulloch Smithy, NX622485, early 19th century. A single-storey rubble building with a roof ventilator. Still in use.

BUITTLE

Horse-gin house, West Logan, NX807634, early to mid 19th century. A small circular rubble building, slate-roofed.
Smithy, Little Knox, NX804602, early 19th century and later. A single-storey, 3-bay rubble building, with a later 1-storey range at the rear. Still in use.
Palnackie Harbour, NX822569, 19th century. A small rectangular basin off the river Urr, with wood-piled quays, now badly silted. Nearby is a 2-storey rubble warehouse.

COLVEND

Pier and quarry, Kippford, NX841553, late 19th century. A whinstone quarry, linked with a rubble pier on the river Urr by an inclined railway, the roadbed of which can still be traced.

Barnhourie Mill, Sandyhills, NX889553, late 18th to early 19th century. A small 2-storey, rubble building, on an L plan, now gutted and used as a garage. The 15ft diameter (4·57m), wood and iron, high-breast wheel survives.

Southwick Mill, NX927579, late 18th to early 19th century. An attractive, 2-storey rubble building on an L plan, with single-storey wings. Now part used as a barn, it part houses a turbo-generator with a concrete flume, used to provide electricity for Southwick House.

Horse-gin house, Castle Farm, NX917589, early to mid 19th century. A circular rubble building with a slate roof, of the unusual Galloway pattern, with windows instead of full-height openings.

Bridge, Caulkerbush, NX928572, late 18th to early 19th century. An attractive small single rubble segmental arch with circular cast-iron tieplates.

Farm Mill, Southwick Home Farm, NX937568, 19th century. A 2-storey, rubble threshing barn with a 10-spoke wood and iron suspended wheel, about 4ft 6in wide by 15ft diameter (1·37 by 4·57m), with rim drive. Interior gutted and used as a store.

41 Carding mill, Old Bridge of Urr.

CROSSMICHAEL

Carding mill, Old Bridge of Urr, NX775677, probably late 18th century (plate 41). A neat rectangular 2-storey, rubble building, set into the river bank.

Old Bridge of Urr, NX776677, late 18th century. A 2-span rubble bridge, with semicircular arches and triangular cutwaters.

DALRY

Grennan Mill, NX643803, founded 1506, rebuilt in the late 18th century and again in 1834. A small 2-storey rubble building, with 3 pairs of stones, driven by a 10-spoke, all-iron, high-breast wheel, 3ft 4½in wide by 14ft diameter (1·02 by 4·27m). There are drives from the main vertical shaft to a sack hoist and to a pulley, probably for an oat bruiser. Preserved by owner.

GIRTHON

GATEHOUSE-OF-FLEET

Brewery, NX599563, late 18th or early 19th century. A large 3-storey

42   Thomas Scott & Co's cotton mill, Gatehouse-of-Fleet.

brick and rubble building on an L plan, with a 2-storey dwellinghouse at one end. The brewery part is now a store.

Tannery, NX599562, probably 18th century. A 2-storey, rubble building, with a single-storey dwellinghouse at one end. Now converted to garages.

Barlay Mill, NX602573, 18th century. A 1-storey and attic rubble range, now converted to a garage, with the polygonal wooden axle of a breast waterwheel. Machinery gutted.

Cotton mills, NX599564, built *c* 1785 by Birtwhistle & Sons. The roofless ivy-covered remains of a 3-storey mill and foundation remains of 2 other mills, with lade and wheelpit. The axle hole for the wheel of the former is clearly visible. In Birtwhistle Street (NX601566) is a row of cottages of typically English design built for workers in the mills.

Cotton mill, NX603564, built *c* 1790 by Thomas Scott & Co (plate 42). A 3-storey, 6-bay rubble building, the best preserved cotton mill in Galloway, now a sawmill.

Tollhouse, NX602566, probably *c* 1790 (plate 43). A very handsome

43 Tollhouse, Gatehouse-of-Fleet.

single-storey building on an L plan, with semicircular ends to the wings. (See *Industrial Archaeology*, 1966, *3*, 127.)

KELLS

Ken Bridge, New Galloway, NX640783, built 1821–2, JOHN RENNIE, engineer. A beautiful 5-span masonry bridge, 340ft (103·6m) long, with segmental arches increasing in size to the centre. The cutwaters are rounded.

Suspension bridge, Kendoon, NX603876, built *c* 1934. A footbridge with wooden deck supported from wire-rope main cables. The pylons are of braced-steel-girder construction.

Glenlochar Bridge, NX733645, early 19th century. A 6-span rubble bridge, with segmental arches. There are circular flood-relief holes through the spandrels.

KELTON

Old Bridge of Dee, NX734599, early 18th century. A 4-span rubble bridge, with semicircular arches and triangular cutwaters.

Threave Bridge, NX737604, built *c* 1825. A fine 3-span masonry bridge, with segmental arches and rounded cutwaters. The masonry is rusticated. Replaced Old Bridge of Dee.

Kelton Mill, Rhonehouse, NX746603, early 19th century. A 2- and 3-storey rubble building on an L plan. Now houses a grain dryer.

Tollhouse, NX750612, probably early 19th century. An attractive and unusual single-storey rubble building, 1-by-3-bay, with Gothic windows. There is a modern extension at the rear.

Gelston Mill, NX873589, probably late 18th century. A 2-storey and attic rubble building, with lean-to extensions, now gutted and disused.

KIRKBEAN

Southerness Lighthouse, NX977543, built 1749. A particularly fine 18th-century lighthouse, with a square rubble tower rounded on 3 corners at the top to support a corbelled iron-railed walkway and part-circular, slate-roofed lantern with small panes. Disused since 1867; now preserved.

KIRKCUDBRIGHT

Tongland Bridge, NX692533, built 1804–8, engineer THOMAS TELFORD. An interesting structure, with a segmental arch of 112ft (34·1m) span, flanked on either side by a semicircular 'cutwater', carried up to form a pedestrian refuge, and by three 6ft (1·83m) span pointed flood-relief arches. The parapet is corbelled out, and is castellated, and the voussoirs of the main span are rusticated.

KIRKCUDBRIGHT

Kirkcudbright Old Mill, NX688515, late 18th to early 19th century. A 2-storey and attic, rubble building on an L plan, with a circular-section kiln vent. Now gutted and converted to a studio pottery.

Bridge, NX684513, built 1924. A 5-span, reinforced concrete, bowed-truss bridge of unusual design.

Kirkcudbright Harbour, NX684512, quay built 1910, engineers J. & H. V. EAGLESHAM, Ayr. A well-built, granite-fronted quay, with a small slipway at one end. Nearby are 1- and 2-storey rubble warehouses, that at NX683512 being particularly fine.

Kirkcudbright Station, NX686512, built 1864 for the Kirkcudbrightshire Railway. All that is left of this single-platform terminal station is the main building, a 2-storey, 5-bay rubble building, in Elizabethan style, very similar to the first Ayr station (*qv*) now a coffee shop.

Windmill, Cannee, NX687501, probably 18th century. A 3-storey circular rubble building with 4 string courses, reputedly a wind-powered cider press or mill. Now a dairy.

KIRKMABRECK

Big Water of Fleet Viaduct, NX559644, opened 1861 by the Portpatrick Railway. A 20-span masonry viaduct with segmental arches. The piers have been strengthened in brick and the spandrels are braced with old rails. Now disused.

Kirkdale Sawmill, NX517533, mid to late 19th century. A single-storey rubble building, with a wooden addition. The sawbench has been removed, but the 8-spoke, all-iron overshot wheel, 3ft 9½in wide by 13ft diameter (1·15 by 3·96m) has been repaired and is to be used to drive the sawbench when replaced. Drive is from a gear ring.

KIRKPATRICK DURHAM

Mill, Old Bridge of Urr, NX777677, late 18th to early 19th century. An irregular 2-storey rubble complex on an L plan, sharing a wheel with a rectangular sawmill. The kiln and granary are on the other side of the access road. The wheel is high breast, with cast-iron axle and rings and wooden spokes and buckets, 3ft 8in wide by 16ft diameter (1·11 by 4·88m). Largely gutted.

MINNIGAFF

Smithy, Palnure, NX452633, early 19th century. A single-storey, 2-bay rubble building, with door at the rear.

Suspension Bridge, Minnigaff, NX411665, built 1911, D. H. & F. REID, Victoria Bridge Works, Ayr, engineers. A light lattice-girder span supported from wire-rope cables by iron-rod suspenders. The pylons are also of lattice construction. Similar to the bridges being erected by James Abernethy and Co of Aberdeen at the same period.

Cumloden Waulk Mill, NX414670, founded c 1800. A 3-storey and attic, 4-bay rubble building with a single-storey lean-to, formerly the dyehouse. How a dwellinghouse.

Minnigaff Mill, NX411660, built 1823. A handsome, 4-storey, 4-bay rubble building, with a 2-storey, 2-bay wing. Now gutted and used in part by a local joiner.

NEW ABBEY

Sawmill, Drumburn, NX979621, probably early 19th century. A single-storey and basement rubble building, with wooden extensions. There is an 8-spoke overshot wheel 4ft 1in wide by 14ft diameter (1·25 by 4·27m), with iron rings, axle and buckets, wooden sole and spokes, driving a circular saw. Still in use.

Sawmill, NX960663, converted from woollen mill c 1900. A much-altered complex, with a 2-storey rubble core. There is a disused 8-spoke, wood and iron pitchback wheel 5ft 1in wide by 17ft diameter (1·55 by 5·18m) with gear-ring drive. Nearby is a 3-bay, single-storey rubble block with the site of a waterwheel in series with the main wheel, which may have been a waulk mill.

Monksmill, NX962663, probably late 18th century. A picturesque 2-storey and attic rubble building with kiln and house adjoining. An 8-spoke, pitch-back wheel with wooden axle, buckets and spokes and iron rings and hubs, 5ft wide by 14ft 6in diameter (1·52 by 4·42m), drove 3 pairs of stones (dated 1851). The kiln has a circular vent with a fish wind-vane. Being restored in 1974. (See *Industrial Archaeology*, 1971, *8*, 307.)

TWYNHOLM

Kempleton Mill, NX683552, built 1785. A 2- and 3-storey rubble building with an internal low-breast, wood and iron wheel 3ft 4in wide by 12ft diameter(1·01 by 3·66m) driving 3 pairs of stones.

URR

Newbank Woollen Mill, Springholm, NX805694, built c 1804. An interesting 2-storey rubble building on an L plan, with single-storey outhouses. Now gutted and used as a henhouse and workshop.

Mount Pleasant Paper Mill, Dalbeattie, NX835614, built *c* 1790 by Alexander Wilson. A roofless, 2-storey rubble building, with 1 end still used as a dwellinghouse. Nearby is a 2-storey store and at the rear is a detached square-section brick chimney.

High Pirn Mill, Dalbeattie, NX835614, probably mid 19th century. A substantial 2-storey and attic, snecked rubble building, now partly ruined and used as a bus garage.

Mills, Dalbeattie, NX829604. A large complex of provender mills, mainly modern, but incorporating a 3-storey, rubble block, probably mid 19th century.

Barrbridge Mill, NX839613, built 1837. A handsome, 3-storey, 8-bay rubble range, with extensions. There is a modernized detached kiln with a marine-type ventilator.

Maidenholm Forge, NX841613, built *c* 1835 by John Elliot to make agricultural and other machinery. Two single-storey rubble buildings, with an 8-spoke, wood and iron, high-breast wheel, 5ft 10in wide by 16ft diameter (1·77 by 4·88m) by J. B. A. MCKINNEL of Dumfries. The lade also fed a turbo-generator installed in 1916 by the Dalbeattie Electric Light Co, the concrete flume for which still exists. Now disused.

Lanarkshire

Lanarkshire is Scotland's greatest industrial county. Most of the country's heavy industry is concentrated within its boundaries, or a short distance outside them. Glasgow is the commercial capital of Scotland, and was for long one of the most important manufacturing centres in the world; the Clyde Valley houses almost the whole of the Scottish steel industry. These facts tend to obscure the fact that the county is largely rural, containing extensive tracts of upland agricultural land. Because of its central importance, its communications are of national significance, and Glasgow is still one of the country's main ports.

Forth & Clyde Canal, NS650735 to NS594709, opened 1775, engineer JOHN SMEATON. The short section of the canal in Lanarkshire has, as its main features of interest, a block of stables at NS635731, and some canal cottages at Cadder, NS617722. The original bridges have been replaced by swing, bascule and fixed bridges, from the 1920s. The stable block is the best preserved example of a standard Forth & Clyde type, but is decaying (see also p. 107).

AVONDALE

Craig Bridge, NS713432, 18th century. A 2-span rubble bridge, with segmental arches and triangular cutwaters. Now bypassed and used by pedestrians only.

Powerloom factory (woollen), Craig Bridge, NS713433, probably early 19th century. A small 3- and 2-storey building with semi-circulat stair tower at the rear. The 3-storey part (2-storey at road frontage) was the mill and the 2-storey part a dwellinghouse (c 1850). A lade runs underneath the 3-storey block.

Craig Mill, NS714433, early 19th century. A 2-storey, 3-bay building with a low-breast wheel in a projecting gabled wheelhouse. Machinery gutted.

Limekilns, Drumclog, NS615393, late 18th to early 19th century. A bank of 5 segmental-arched, rubble-built, single-draw kilns, much decayed.

STRATHAVEN

Kilwuddie Weaving Factory, NS703447, founded *c* 1860 as a silk mill. A block of north-light rubble weaving sheds, with the ruins of a 3-storey block. Equipment included belt-driven Anderston Foundry looms. Now closed.

Town Mill, NS705445, built 1831, extended 1877, and remodelled in 1935. The main building is 3 storeys high, by 3 bays, with a kiln, and adjacent is a 4-storey brick granary with massive buttresses. Now empty and decaying.

Engineering works, NS443700, mid 19th century. A 2-storey, 4-bay, ashlar-fronted brick block, with a single-storey brick wing. Now disused.

Hosiery factory, NS702444, founded 1887 by W. Elder & W. Watson. Two 2-storey blocks, one 5 bay, the other 3, and a 2-storey and attic, 3-by-3-bay building, with 6 bays of single-storey sheds at the rear. Equipment includes an 1895 Cornish boiler, a long-disused, single-cylinder horizontal steam engine, a milling machine by JAMES MELROSE & SONS, Hawick and a hydro-extractor by JAMES RITCHIE, Glasgow. There is a square-section brick chimney.

Silk factory, NS701443, built in 1880s by Messrs Frew. A 4-by-8-bay block of red-and-white-brick, north-light weaving sheds, with a 3-storey, 5-bay office and preparation block. Now partly used as a store.

BIGGAR

Biggar Mill, NT039381, late 18th century. A 2-storey rubble building on an L plan, set into a hillside, with access to the granary at first-floor level. The wheel has been removed.

Cadger's Bridge, NT040377, reputed to be of 13th-century origin. A small segmental arch bridge, of light construction, with iron railings, now used for foot traffic only.

Edmonston Mill, NT073416, built 1800. Though roofless, this 3-storey rubble building is notable for its round-headed first- and circular second-floor windows.

Wolfclyde Bridge, NT019362, probably early 19th century. A most unusual bridge, with 2 wide segmental arches and no fewer than 6 smaller flood arches, in groups of 4 and 2. The original rubble and ashlar bridge has been widened in concrete.

Gas works, NT040378, mid to late 19th century. A group of single-storey rubble buildings, with 2 small holders. The smaller holder has 3 guides, the larger 5. The retort house has a Belfast roof. To be preserved as an example of a small horizontal-retort works.

BLANTYRE

Blantyre Mills, NS695585, founded 1785 by Henry Monteith, Bogle & Co. All that remains of the large mill complex here is the curved weir and the lade, together with the end 2 bays of the 3-storey and attic counting-house block. There are 2 ranges of housing, one 2 storey, the other 3, forming a memorial to David Livingstone, the African explorer and missionary. Among the exhibits in the memorial are an excellent model of the mills and a section of a fairly early self-acting mule.

BOTHWELL

Bothwell Bridge, NS711578, a 17th-century bridge, widened and improved in 1826 and 1871. A 4-span masonry bridge, with segmental ribbed arches, and triangular cutwaters. On both sides, iron footpaths with cast-iron parapets have been cantilevered out.

Uddingston Station, NS694609, built 1853–4 by the Caledonian Railway. A 2-platform through station, with the main offices on the down platform in a 2-storey ashlar building with a single-storey wing. There is a small wooden shelter on the up platform.

Viaduct, over Clyde, Uddingston, NS688608, opened 1848 by the Caledonian Railway. A 3-span, cast-iron arch bridge, with 4 ribs per arch, tied by wrought-iron bracing. The arches are supported on masonry piers. Now used as a footbridge. Its steel-truss replacement, also supported on masonry piers, is immediately downstream.

CADDER

Cardowan Colliery, NS665683, sunk *c* 1924. A 3-shaft pit, with the 2 older shafts upcast. These have steam winding engines built by MURRAY & PATERSON, Coatbridge, in 1924, both with piston valves operated by Stephenson valve gear. The western engine is fitted with tailrods. The engines are supplied with steam by 6 Lancashire boilers.

CAMBUSNETHAN

Clydesdale Distillery, Wishaw, NS789552, founded 1825 by Lord Belhaven. A large group of 1- and 2-storey rubble buildings, now all used as bonded stores.

Clydesdale Factory, Wishaw, NS790551, late 19th century. A 4-storey, 9-bay, red-and-white-brick building, with a 3-storey, 8-bay lodging house adjoining. Still a clothing factory.

Goods shed, Wishaw, NS790551, late 19th century. A large rubble building, with full-length awning on the road side, and 3 roof-ridge ventilators. There is a small single-storey office block at the north end.

CARLUKE

Carluke Station, NS840501, rebuilt by the Caledonian Railway *c* 1900. A 2-platform through station, with the main offices on the up platform, in a 1-storey building on an L plan, brick and harl, with wooden insertions in the gables. There is a neat projecting awning, with glazed side screens and an ornamental vallance. The lavatories have prominent roof ventilators.

High Mill, NS849508, built 1797. A tapering 3-storey rubble tower of circular cross section, with a later 2-storey ashlar addition, a brick square-section chimney and outbuildings at the rear. There is the condenser of a steam engine, made by EASTON & ANDERSON, of London, and most of a Tangye gas engine. The interior of the tower is not readily accessible, but is believed to contain some of the mill-work, and is thus the most complete Scottish windmill.

Tileworks, Law, NS832523, late 19th century. A large disused works, with 4 rectangular kilns, of 3 different types, and a circular kiln. There are louvred single-storey drying sheds of brick and wood construction, and a curious moulding shop made of hollow tiles with cement cladding. The works made flower pots as well as the more usual field drains.

CARMICHAEL

Carmichael Mill, NS922416, late 18th century. A large 3-storey rubble mill, with a 2-storey kiln with a square-section vent. A 3-storey, 2-by-3-bay, corrugated-iron-clad store has been added. Behind the mill is the skeleton of a wood and iron, low-breast wheel which drove a threshing mill.

Prett's Mill, NS902402, 19th century. A 2-storey rubble block, forming an L with a kiln and dwellinghouse range. There are 3 pairs of stones, situated on a half-floor, and belt driven by 2 turbines (installed 1914). There are also a roller mill by RICHMOND & CHANDLER, Manchester, and an Albion Patent Grinding Mill by HARRISON, MCGREGOR & CO LTD, Leigh, Lancs. Disused, but intact.

CARNWATH

Carnwath Mill, NS998453, probably late 18th century. A 2-storey, 3-bay, rubble mill building, with a gabled wheelhouse. At right angles to the mill is a 2-storey granary and kiln block. The 6-spoke, low-breast, paddle wood and iron wheel, 3ft 6in by 12ft diameter (1·06 by 3·66m) is unusual in having a circular wooden axle.

Cleugh Mill, NS953534, late 18th or early 19th century. A 2-storey rubble building on an L plan, with a wheelhouse forming a T. The kiln is at the end of the main range. The 8-spoke, pitch-back wheel, with iron rings and axle and wooden arms and buckets, 4ft 5in wide by 15ft 6in diameter (1·34 by 4·72m), drove 2 pairs of stones. Intact, but in poor structural condition. One lintel dated 1722 is probably an insertion.

Viaduct, Spittal, NS992449, opened 1867 by the Caledonian Railway. A three-span rubble viaduct, with segmental arches. Now disused.

Tarbrax Village, NT026552, built 1904 for the Tarbrax Oil Co. A group of rows of single-storey shaleworkers' cottages. The shale bing, all that is left of the oil works here, is being removed for hard-core.

Wilsontown Ironworks, NS951549, built 1781. The much ruined remains of this ironworks were demolished in June 1974. They consisted of the front walls of 2 engine houses, a limekiln, the ruins of a large square blast furnace, a 3-arched wagonway bridge, and a section of culvert over the Mouse Water.

CARSTAIRS

Carstairs Station, NS953454, rebuilt 1913–14 by the Caledonian Railway. An island-platform through station, with single-storey offices with round-headed openings, and extensive steel-framed glazed awnings supported on cast-iron columns.

COVINGTON

Thankerton Bridge, NS978384, built 1778. An impressive 2-span structure, with segmental arches of unequal and unusually large size. The arch rings are of dressed stone, with rubble spandrels. The cutwaters are triangular.

CRAWFORD

Leadhills, NS8815, active 17th century to early 20th century. A lead-mining village, with the small rubble cottages of the lead miners. Interesting features are the warning bell (NS885148) and the Miners' Library. Round the village are complex remains of lead mining, though virtually no complete structures survive.

Viaduct, Leadhills, NS901158, opened 1901 by the Leadhills & Wanlockhead Light Railway. An 8-span viaduct on a curve, with reinforced-concrete arch rings and brick piers and spandrels.

CULTER

Coulter Mill, NT024338, early 19th century. A large 4-storey, 3-bay

rubble building, now gutted and used as a garage and store.
Bridge, NT024339, built 1831. An attractively situated single-segmental-arched bridge, with dressed-stone voussoirs and rubble spandrels. Unusually, iron railings are fitted.

DALSERF

Avon Sanitary Engineering Works, Birkenshaw, NS769493, founded 1895 by Jackson, Elphick & Co. A complex of single-storey, steel-framed buildings. Had in 1968 a disused solid-bottom cupola and a demounted Tropenas converter.
Caledonian Brickworks, Birkenshaw, NS770491. A late 19th-century brickworks, with a 16-chamber kiln, making composition bricks.
Garrion Bridge, NS793510, built 1817. A 3-span rubble structure with segmental arches and rounded cutwaters extended up to form semicircular pedestrian refuges. At the south end is a plaque.
Larkhall Silk Factory, Larkhall, NS766511, founded 1879 by James McAuley & Co. The present building dates from 1898, and is a block of single-storey, red-and-white-brick weaving sheds.
Avonbank Bleach Works, Millheugh, NS725508, founded as a print works c 1796, converted to a bleachworks c 1836. The main block is a 3-storey, 4-by-10-bay building, and there is a superb 2-storey, 9-bay beetling mill dating from 1839, with the original beetling stocks. A single-storey beetling shed was added in 1898.
Broomhill Viaduct, Millheugh, NS754503, built 1904 by ARROL BROS for the Caledonian Railway. A 6-span, steel-truss bridge 530ft (381m) long and 170ft (51·8m) high, with masonry piers.

DALZIEL

Lanarkshire Steel Works, Flemington, NS767564, founded 1899 by the Lanarkshire Steel Co Ltd. The 2-storey and attic, 4-by-19-bay, snecked-rubble office block is dated 1899 and it is probable that the steel-framed, open-hearth melting shop is also original, as is some of the equipment.
Motherwell Mill, NS756580, dated 1785, but rebuilt in mid to late 19th century. A 2-storey and attic rubble mill block, with a lower asbestos-roofed kiln. There is an internal iron high-breast wheel about 20ft diameter (6·10m), fed from a pond with an arched dam, driving 3 pairs of stones through bevel gearing, with a power take-off for driving ancillary machinery. At right angles to the mill block is a 1-storey and attic, harled office and granary building. Disused but intact.

DOUGLAS

Folkerton Mill, NS856359, early 19th century (see plate 2). A 2-storey mill on a T plan, set into a hillside, with access to the granary at first-floor level. An 8-spoke, all-iron, overshot wheel, about 3ft wide by 14ft diameter (0·91 by 4·27m), drove 2 pairs of stones, which are situated on a half floor below the first floor. Not in use, but in very fair condition.

EAST KILBRIDE

Busby Station, NS582563, opened 1866 by the Busby Railway. A 2-platform through station. The down-platform building is a single-storey rubble structure on a T plan, with a bracketted awning. The platforms are linked by a lattice-girder footbridge. There is a handsome rubble goods shed with round-headed openings.

Printworks, Busby, NS578562, mid 19th century. Once a very large complex, there are fragmentary remains of several buildings and a few intact, of which the largest is a 3-storey and attic, 6-bay, red-brick building with a single-storey wing.

Millhouse Mill, NS602507, early 19th century. A 3-storey rubble building on an L plan, with a wood and iron overshot wheel about 14ft (4·27m) diameter and the remains of a turbine. Disused but relatively intact. Upstream is a narrow single-span bridge, reputed to have been a pack bridge.

Limekilns, Thorntonhall, 18th century and later. An interesting group, including double kilns at NS591549 and 592552, and a single kiln at NS585547.

Dripps Mill, Waterfoot, NS569552, dated 1761, but since rebuilt several times. A 2-storey and attic rubble range, on an irregular plan, with 2 internal overshot wheels, one by A. & W. SMITH, Glasgow, driving a feed mixer, and the other driving a single pair of stones and a girdle (heated pan) for roasting peas before grinding to pease meal. The only water mill making pease meal in Scotland.

GLASGOW

Forth & Clyde Canal, NS594709–NS513700 (main line) and NS572690–NS593667 (Glasgow branch). The main line from the east to NS572690, Stockingfield Junction, opened in 1775, engineer JOHN SMEATON, and was extended to Hamiltonhill Basin (NS586672) in 1777. A further extension to Port Dundas (NS593667) was opened in 1790 at the same time as the westerly extension of the main line to Bowling, engineer ROBERT WHITWORTH. Notable surviving features include Kelvin Aqueduct, NS562679, a 4-arch structure (1787–90), and smaller aqueducts at NS578689 (1775), NS587671 and NS572690 (1790), NS587671, NS575680 and NS567688 (1879–81). Original bascule bridges survive at a few sites, such as NS586672. There are interesting flights of locks at Maryhill, NS563690, 5 with basins and dry dock, and at Knightswood, NS534705, 3 locks. The canal office at NS588666 (1812) is particularly attractive, with its pediment and Doric porch.

Albert Bridge, NS584644, built 1870–1, engineers BELL & MILLER. A 3-span arch bridge, with 6 wrought-iron and 2 cast-iron ribs per span. The spandrels and cast-iron parapets have gothic tracery and are decorated with coats of arms.

Anderston Brass Foundry, 32 Elliot Street, NS575655, built 1870–1, for Steven & Struthers. A handsome block with single-storey moulding shop and 3-storey office. There is a fine arched doorway with a semicircular glazed fanlight. Now a chemical works.

Anderston Grain Mill, 27 Washington Street, NS582652, built pre-1845 as a cotton store. A 4-storey sandstone rubble building, 6-by-4-bay, extended in brick by a further storey. To the south is a striking 5-storey, 6-by-3-bay, red-and-white-brick grain store (1845). Now a rice mill.

Bishop Mills, 206 Old Dumbarton Road, NS562662, rebuilt *c* 1853 for William Wilson. A 4-storey, 2-by-10-bay rubble building with carved wheatsheaves on the gables. There is a brick wheelhouse on the south end. Disused.

Botanic Gardens Garage, 16–18 Vinicombe Street, NS568673, built 1911 for A. K. Kennedy, architect D. V. WYLLIE. The finest early garage in Glasgow, with a 2-storey, 5-bay, green-and-white-tiled frontage and unusual steel roof trusses.

Broomward Cotton Work, 19–21 Kerr Street, NS606642, built *c* 1815 for James Dunlop & Sons, cotton spinners. The remains of a 5-storey, 31-bay, red-brick building, cut down to 2 and 3 storeys. Internally, wooden floors are supported on slender cast-iron columns. At the rear are weaving sheds, and to the north a 3-storey and attic, 4-by-15-bay weaving factory (*c* 1867). DAVID ELDER, the famous marine engineer, designed the millwork for the 1815 mill.

Burnside Works, 109–15 Brook Street, NS610642, founded *c* 1871 by Walker, Birrell and Co, power-loom cloth manufacturers. The main 4-storey, 17-bay block and the weaving sheds to the north date from 1885. The sheds are good examples of a once-common type.

Caledonian Ironworks, 64 Strathclyde Street, NS614629, built

1889 for Penman & Co, boilermakers. The main block is a tall single-storey, cast-iron-framed engineering bay, with side aisles, reputedly built as the engineering hall at the Glasgow Exhibition of 1888. It has a typical red-and-white-brick frontage with a large arched doorway.

Cathcart Mill, Snuffmill Road, NS585601, built in the 18th century as a meal mill and rebuilt as a cardboard and snuff mill, 1812–14. A block of low single-storey buildings, to be restored by the city parks department.

Central Station, Union, Gordon and Hope Streets, NS587652, built 1879–1905 for the Caledonian Railway. The roof is of the ridge type, carried on flat trusses (1879 part) and on elliptically arched trusses (1899–1905 part). The 5- and 6-storey station hotel was designed by ROWAND ANDERSON, an Edinburgh architect, and the stonework of the extension was by JAMES MILLER. The destination indicator is arguably the finest in Britain. The station is supported on an undercroft which houses parcels and mail offices, shops and stores. There is a low-level station (1896) closed in 1964.

City of Glasgow Grain Mills, 204–44 North Spiers Wharf, NS588667, built c 1851–70 for John Currie & Co and others. An impressive range of 5- and 6-storey sandstone buildings.

College Passenger Station, High Street, NS598651, opened 1871 by the North British Railway. A classic train shed of the mid 19th century with wrought-iron roof trusses supported on the south side by a brick wall, and on the north by a row of 10 heavy cast-iron columns, linked laterally by flat-arched, cast-iron girders. Closed 1886 and now disused.

Cranstonhill Foundry (iron), 58 Elliot Street, NS574655, built c 1854 for James Aitken & Co, engineers, millwrights and founders. An interesting tall single-storey building with 4 narrow round-headed windows on each side of a large arched central doorway with glazed fanlight. No longer a foundry. One of the oldest purpose-built foundry buildings in Scotland.

Crookston Station, Crookston Road, NS520634, built c 1885 by the Glasgow & South Western Railway. The up-platform building is particularly attractive, a 1-storey, snecked-rubble building with a glazed screen protecting the entrance to the offices.

Custom House, 198 Clyde Street, NS589649, built 1840, architect G. L. TAYLOR. An attractive 2-storey and attic classical building, with a sculpture of the royal arms at roof level.

Daily Record Printing Works, St Vincent Lane, NS588654, built

1900, architect CHARLES RENNIE MACKINTOSH. A notable 'modern movement' building consisting of linked 6-storey and basement, 4-bay and 3-storey and basement, 4-bay glazed-brick blocks.

Dalmarnock Gas Works, 122 Old Dalmarnock Road, NS612632, founded 1843 by the City & Suburban Gas Co. Much reduced remains include a large gas-holder with cast-iron guides built in 1872.

Dalmarnock Ironworks, 85 Dunn Street, NS613636, founded c 1868 by William Arrol. This large complex was built, in the main, between 1889 and 1911, and from it came some very large structural iron and steel work including the Central Station Bridge and parts of the second Tay Bridge.

Eagle Pottery, 60 Boden Street, NS614638, built from 1869 for Frederick Grosvenor. The most complete of the Glasgow pottery buildings, a 3-storey, 3-by-23-bay, red-and-white-brick block, now in multiple occupation.

Eglinton Engine Works, 120 Tradeston Street, NS583642, built from 1855 for A. & W. Smith & Co, engineers. The oldest part is a 3-storey, 4-by-17-bay sandstone building (1855) now offices, and there are 3 wide bays of red-brick workshops, dating from the early 1870s. Now the only sugar-machinery works in Glasgow.

Fairfield Shipbuilding Yard & Engine Works, 1048 Govan Road, NS548660, founded 1863 by Randolph & Elder (see plate 7). The most interesting parts of this large complex are the particularly fine engine works (c 1874) with braced cast-iron columns supporting wooden roof trusses, and the French Renaissance office block, with ornamented main-office entrance, designed by J. KEPPIE, 1889.

Glasgow Bridge, NS587647, built 1898–9, engineers BLYTH & WESTLAND. This 7-arch masonry bridge has a granite facing, part of which came from an earlier bridge on the same site by Thomas Telford.

Glasgow Railway Engineering Works, 87 Helen Street, NS553653, built c 1891 for D. Drummond & Sons, railway engineerings. Famous for its foundation by the great Dugald Drummond, locomotive engineer, this block of single-storey buildings has a 1- and 2-storey brick frontage.

Glasgow Saw and File Works, 24 Elliot Street and **Glasgow Turning Works,** 22 Elliot Street, NS575655, built 1870 and 1872. A striking pair of red-and-white-brick, 2-storey and attic buildings, 7-by-12 and 12-by-4 bay respectively with round-headed openings. The former is still in the hands of its original owners.

Govan Graving Docks, Stag Street, NS561654, built 1869–98 for the Clyde Navigation Trust. Three large graving docks, each of which could, when built, take the largest ships afloat.

Greenhead Brewery, 31 Blackfaulds Place, NS604640, founded c 1800 by Robert Struthers, and reconstructed 1887–1914. A group of 2-storey, red-and-white-brick buildings round a courtyard with malting kilns adjacent to the south. The most complete pre-1914 brewery in the city, this is now a bottling plant.

Greenhead Works, 45 Greenhead Street, NS604640, founded on this site in 1859 by R. & J. Dick, gutta-percha manufacturers. This large complex, now in multiple occupation, includes an 1840 cotton mill, and 2 blocks facing Glasgow Green which were built to resemble residential tenements (1872–3, 1886). The Dick Brothers became well-known philanthropists.

Harbour Tunnel, Tunnel Street to Plantation Place, NS571650, built 1890–6. Three parallel tunnels, 2 of which were used for vehicular traffic. At each end is a circular brick terminal, with a domed roof, which housed hydraulic lifts. The pedestrian tunnel is still open.

King George V Bridge, NS586648, built 1924–8, engineers T. M. SOMERS and CONSIDERE CONSTRUCTIONS LTD. A 3-span, reinforced-concrete, continuous-beam bridge, faced with Dalbeattie granite.

Kingston Engine Works, 71 Milnpark Street, NS572645, founded c 1866 by Smith Bros, engineers and ironfounders. A 3-storey, 4-by-19, red-and-white-brick building (c 1873) with rounded-headed windows. A classic example of an engine works of the period.

Kingston Grain Mills, 21–3 West Street, NS584648, built 1875–6 for Stevenson & Coats. A striking 4-storey and basement, 9-bay polychrome-brick range in Italian Renaissance style. Now a store.

Kinning Park Sewage Pumping Works, 100 Seaward Street, NS575645, built 1909–10 for Glasgow Corporation, engineers D. & A. HOME MORTON. A tall 1-storey, 1-by-5, terra-cotta-brick building originally housing steam pumping engines.

Lancefield Cotton Work, 87 Lancefield Street, NS576652, built c 1826 for the Lancefield Spinning Co. A 5-storey attic and basement, 5-by-23-bay rubble building now used as a store. The last cotton mill in the area.

Linthouse Shipbuilding Yard, Holmfauld Road, NS540660, founded 1869 by Alexander Stephen & Sons. The most interesting part of this large complex is the original cast-iron-framed engine works of 1872.

Meadowside Granary, Castlebank Street, NS545664, built from

1911 for the Clyde Navigation Trust. The first part was completed in 1913, and is 13 storeys high, 6 by 13 bays. Part was designed for bulk storage in silos, the rest for storage of bagged grain.

Milton Colour Works, 58–70 Dobbies Loan, NS595660, built 1873 for James Steel Jun & Co, oil and colour merchants. A 2-storey, 9-bay, red-and-white-brick building with central entrance and tower. An attractive example of a small factory of the period, now a joinery.

Museum of Transport, Albert Drive, NS581633, built 1894–1912 for Glasgow Corporation Tramways Department as tram depot and workshops. A large triangular block of brick and sandstone buildings, part used as a very fine transport museum.

Netherlee Road Bridge, NS585602, built in the 18th century. A 2-span rubble bridge, with the road on an incline. The southern arch is narrow and semicircular, the northern wide and segmental.

North British Diesel Engine Works, 739 South Street, NS533668, built 1913–14 for Barclay, Curle & Co. The main shop is a steel-framed brick building, with a 'flattened mansard' roof having a strong resemblance to Peter Behrens's celebrated AEG factory.

North Woodside Flint Mill, 125 Garriochmill Road, NS573673, built 1846 for Kidston, Cochran & Co. The mill was demolished *c* 1964 but the ruins have been excavated and consolidated by the Corporation Parks Department. There is a pyramidal kiln.

Parkhead Forge, Old Shettleston Road, Duke Street and Earl Wellington Street, NS624644, founded *c* 1837 by Reoch Bros & Co. Most of the present large complex of steel-framed buildings dates from 1884–1914. Machinery includes a late 19th-century cogging mill driven by a 2-cylinder horizontal steam engine (1942).

Partick Bridge, NS565664, built 1877–8 for the Glasgow & Yoker Turnpike Trust to carry a horse-tram line, engineers BELL & MILLER. A cast-iron, skew-arched bridge with 9 ribs. Its predecessor, built 1800, is immediately to the north, a masonry structure with 3 river arches and 1 over Bunhouse mill lade.

Partick Sewage Pumping Station, 35 Dumbarton Road, NS564664, built 1904 for Glasgow Corporation in connection with Dalmuir Sewage Works. An ornate red-sandstone building which housed, until *c* 1960, 3 sets of triple-expansion pumping engines. At the rear is a fine octagonal brick chimney stalk.

Pinkston Power Station, North Canal Bank Street, NS597667, built 1900–1 for Corporation Tramways Department, engineer HARRY B. MEASURES. A large red-brick building, with 3 main bays, dominated by a pair of large chimneys, which had ornamental caps until recently.

Pollok House Bridge, NS549617, built *c* 1750, architect probably JOHN ADAM. An elegant single-segmental arch with well-proportioned balustrades.

Pollokshaws Viaduct, NS560613, built *c* 1847 for the Glasgow, Barrhead & Neilston Direct Railway, engineer NEIL ROBSON. A 5-span masonry viaduct, with segmental arches. There are 2 wide river spans and 3 land spans, 1 over a minor road. The nearby Pollokshaws West Station, with a 2-storey brick and sandstone building, on the up platform, is now the oldest in the city.

Pollokshields West Station, Terregles Avenue and Fotheringay Road, NS575628, built *c* 1894 for the Cathcart District Railway. The wooden station building here is unusual, with a booking hall at street level approached by footbridges, and the other offices below, at platform level. Maxwell Park Station, to the west, is almost identical.

Port Dundas Distillery, 76–80 North Canal Bank Street, NS593668, founded *c* 1870 by J. Gourlay & Co. A large complex of 2 to 7 storey buildings, mostly dating from before 1914.

Port Dundas Electricity Generating Station, Edington Street, NS587667, built 1898 for the Corporation Electricity Department, architect ANDREW MYLES. A large range of red-brick buildings with a central French Renaissance tower. The finest of the early Corporation power stations.

Port Dundas Sugar Refinery, 256 North Spiers Wharf, NS588668, built 1865–6 for Murdoch & Dodrell. A 7-storey, 16-bay, ashlar-fronted building. The only surviving Glasgow refinery building.

Portland Street Suspension Bridge, NS589647, built 1851 and 1871, stonework by A. KIRKLAND, architect, metalwork by GEORGE MARTIN. Classical masonry pylons support flat-link chains with a light lattice-girder deck. Clear span is 414ft (126m).

Prince's Dock, NS565650, built 1893–7 for the Clyde Navigation Trust. A large tidal dock, with 3 basins, lined with 2-storey transit sheds. At the east end is the former hydraulic power station, with a Gothic accumulator tower and the stump of an octagonal chimney with a sculptured frieze.

Queen Street Station, North Queen Street, NS592655, opened 1842 by the Edinburgh & Glasgow Railway. The fine wrought-iron arched roof, carried on cast-iron Corinthian columns, was built 1878–80, engineer JAMES CARSEWELL. The rest of the station has recently been rebuilt. The 2 bridges spanning the cutting beyond the station are worth noting, as is the tunnel (1842) leading to Cowlairs. Underneath the main-line station is the much-modernized, low-level station (1886).

Queen's Dock, NS570653, built 1872–80 for the Clyde Navigation Trust. The oldest surviving Glasgow dock, with 2 tidal basins lined with single-storey transit sheds. At the west end is the now empty hydraulic power station, with its prominent Italianate accumulator tower. Closed 1969.

Queen's Tea Store, 23 York Street, NS586650, built 1843 for William Connal, architect J. STEPHEN. A 4-storey, attic and basement, 17-bay block with 'fireproof' interior. The front elevation is heavily ornamented.

St Andrew's Suspension Bridge, NS600640, built 1853–5, engineer NEIL ROBSON. Cast-iron classical pylons support flat-link chains from which are suspended a light truss deck.

St Enoch Underground Station, St Enoch Square, NS599650, built 1895 for the Glasgow District Subway Co. A 2-storey, 3-by-3-bay, red-sandstone building in Jacobean style, designed by JAMES MILLER as the headquarters of the company.

Scotia Leather Works, 108 Boden Street, NS614636, founded 1873 by Hamilton Caldwell. The surviving 4- and 5-storey buildings date from 1873–1906, and indicate the large scale of leatherworking in Glasgow.

Sentinel Works, Jessie Street, NS597625, built 1903–14 for Alley & McLellan, engineers. The original home of the Sentinel steam lorry. The most interesting part is the 4-storey, 3-by-12-bay, rein-forced-concrete block, architect ARCHIBALD LEITCH, designed as pattern shop and offices in 1903, and the first reinforced-concrete building of any size in the city.

Shieldhall Factory, Renfrew Road, NS532660, built from 1887 for the Scottish Co-operative Wholesale Society. A large complex of mainly red-brick buildings, which housed a remarkable assortment of manufactories, many of which have now closed. The most impressive part faces Renfrew Road, a 6-storey, 6-by-12-bay, sandstone-fronted range in French Renaissance style.

Springburn Tram Depot, 81–3 Keppochhill Road, NS603674, built 1893–4 for the Corporation Tramways Department, engineer WILLIAM CLARK. A 5-bay, single-storey, sandstone-fronted brick block of car sheds, with, at the rear, the building of the experimental power station for Glasgow's first electric tram route (1898).

Sun Foundry, 280 Kennedy Street, NS597661, built 1870–1 for

George Smith & Co, artistic ironfounders. A rectangular block of 1- and 2-storey buildings, now in multiple occupation, but in its time the largest architectural iron foundry in Glasgow and probably in Scotland.

Victoria Bread & Biscuit Works, 30 Wesleyan Street, NS609645, built from 1880 for John McFarlane & Sons. The oldest of the large machine-bread-making bakeries surviving in Glasgow. The earliest extant part is a 4-storey and attic, 8-bay block with arched doorways (1886) and the main block, 5 storey and attic, 4-by-5-bay, dates from 1895.

Victoria Bridge, built 1851–4, NS592645, engineer JAMES WALKER. A 5-arched sandstone bridge, encased in granite, with a balustraded parapet. Reckoned the finest of the Clyde bridges in Glasgow.

Washington Grain Mills, 90 Washington Street, NS577651, founded c 1849 by J. & R. Snodgrass. The oldest part, at the rear, is a 4-storey, 4-bay rubble block, while the front buildings include a 5-storey, 4-bay block built as a warehouse (1865) and a 6-storey, 7-bay Italian Renaissance block (1874).

Bakery, McNeil, Adelphi, Moffat and Ballater Streets, NS599639, built 1886–1916 for the United Co-operative Baking Society. A large and elaborate block of red-and-white-brick buildings, part Flemish, part French Renaissance and part Glasgow Factory in style. Designed by BRUCE & HAY.

Body-building works, 44 Kilbirnie Street, NS582639, built 1913 for William Park, body-builder, architect R. HENDERSON. An interesting 3-storey, 6-by-9-bay, reinforced-concrete building with a central well.

Cabinet works, 53 Kent Road, NS578657, built 1879 for Wylie & Lochhead, architect J. SELLARS. A 4-storey, attic and basement, 3-by-10-bay French Renaissance building with 'fireproof' interior. There are later additions to the rear.

Carpet factory, 62 Templeton Street, NS603641, founded on this site 1857 by James Templeton & Son. The most spectacular part of this large complex is WILLIAM LEIPER'S 4-storey and attic, 4-by-11-bay, Venetian Gothic, polychrome-brick block (1888–92) built for weaving spool Axminster carpets, but other buildings are also of interest, including a cut-down cotton mill of c 1823.

Contractors' depot, 38 West Street, NS583647, built 1895 for Wordie & Co, haulage contractors, architect W. TENNANT. A classic example of a large contractors' stable, 3-storeys, 12-by-15-bay, of red brick, with a central courtyard and horse ramps to the upper floors. As built had 151 stalls. Now a store.

Cotton mill, 100 Duke Street, NS603651, built 1849 for R. F. & J. Alexander, thread manufacturers, architect CHARLES WILSON. A 6-storey, 22-bay sandstone building in Italian Renaissance style. The central entrance was added in 1909 when the building was converted to a workingmen's hotel. The interior is fireproof, of jack-arch construction.

Cotton spinning mills, Carstairs Street and Swanston Street, NS611628, built 1884–9 for the Glasgow Cotton Spinners Co, Ltd, architect JOSEPH STOTT, Oldham. Two massive red-brick mills, one 5-storey, 11-by-28-bay, and the other 4-storey, 10-by-31-bay, with a tall circular section. The largest yarn mills in Glasgow in their day, now a carton factory.

Engineering works, 47 Broad Street, NS610642, built from 1896–7 for Mavor & Coulson Ltd. This firm were pioneer electrical engineers, and the original single-storey works, with side aisles and galleries (1896–7, architect A. MYLES) still stands. At the rear is part of Mile End Thread Works (1854 and 1878, built for John Clark Jun & Co).

Horse-tram depot, 105–15 Admiral Street, NS574645, built c 1893 for Glasgow Corporation Tramways Department, engineer W. CLARK. Typical of the new depots built by the Corporation at the time, this is a 2-storey, 6-bay building, originally with stables on the first floor and cars on the ground floor. Now a store.

Paint warehouses, 106 Tradeston Street, NS583645, built for Blacklock, McArthur & Co. A 4-storey, 9-bay, sandstone block dates from 1886, architects H. & D. BARCLAY, while the more distinctive 4-storey, 4-by-8-bay, Venetian Gothic corner block was added in 1900, architect W. J. MCGIBBON.

Printing works, 50 Darnley Street, NS580634, built 1901 for Miller & Lang, art publishers, architects GORDON & DOBSON. An extraordinary 3-storey, 5-bay, *art nouveau* building.

Railway bridges, Dalmarnock, NS613625. The older of the 2 bridges, built c 1858, engineer GEORGE GRAHAM, has 3 wrought-iron arched girders on sandstone piers. The more recent one (1893–7) has 3 bowed lattice-girder spans on triple cast-iron piers. Both have short approach spans.

Sawmill and power station, Pollok House, NS540616, probably built c 1880–1900 on an older water-power site. The mill is a 1-storey brick building, with machinery driven by an 1888 Holyoake (Francis) water turbine. The adjacent electric power station, now disused and partly gutted, still contains a Waverley turbine by CARRICK & RITCHIE of Edinburgh. The complex is to become a museum.

Sewing machine factory, 116 James Street, NS606638, built 1871–2 for the Singer Sewing Machine Co. A 4-storey, 6-by-22-bay, stone-fronted building, which housed Singers until their move to Kilbowie in 1882.

Stables, 21–25 Carlton Court, NS587646, built c 1895 for the Clyde Shipping Co Ltd. A fine example of a city-centre stable, 3-storey and attic, 9-bay with wooden horse ramps in a central well. Now a store.

Stables and workshops, Berkeley, Elderslie Streets and Kent Road, NS575658, built 1870–3 for John Wylie, architect J. SELLARS. A rectangular block of 2-storey and basement buildings, 19-by-20-by-17 bay, with 3-storey corner pavilions. The roof trusses are wrought-iron, of unusual design. Now a garage.

Subway power station, 175 Scotland Street, NS578641, built c 1895 for the Glasgow District Subway Co, architect JOHN GORDON. The original cable-winding engines were housed here. Three bays of single-storey brick buildings with a 1-storey office block. Now part of James Howden & Co's engineering works.

Tollhouse, 1 Cross Street, NS557610, built c 1800. A perfectly circular building, with a conical roof and central chimney stack. Now preserved as a monument, in the centre of a roundabout.

Tollhouse, Dalmarnock Road, NS614631, built c 1820. A small single-storey and basement building with a central semi-octagonal projecting bay.

Tramway stables, 58–72 Tobago Street, NS604643, built c 1877–83 for the Glasgow Tramway & Omnibus Co. The main block of stables and grain stores, with car shed beneath, was built in 1883, and is 4-storey, 5-by-12-bay. At the rear are older buildings.

Warehouse, 105–69 Bell Street, NS598650, built 1882–3 for the Glasgow & South Western Railway. A massive 6-storey, 4-by-31-bay block, with rusticated ground floor. The interior has cast-iron columns supporting cast-iron beams with mass-concrete arches. Part still used as a bonded warehouse, with hydraulic hoists operated from a small pumping station to the east, with an Italianate accumulator tower.

Warehouses, James Watt Street, NS585650. A group of 4 fine classical warehouses built as grain and general stores. Nos 68–72 built 1847–8 for William Connal & Co and 65–73 built c 1848 for Harvie & McGavin are externally alike, with centre pilastered porticos, though the former has a 'fireproof' interior while the latter has conventional wood and cast-iron. Nos 41–45 was built 1854 for A. Harvie and enlarged in 1910–11, when the interior was reconstructed in reinforced concrete. The finest of the group is 44–54, built 1861 for Thomas Mann, a 4-storey, 13-bay block with end pilastered porticos.

Weaving factory, 11 Graham Square, NS607647, built *c* 1825 for G. Grant Jun. An early power-loom weaving factory, 6-storey and attic, 3-by-9-bay, with wooden floors supported by slender cast-iron columns.

Workshop, 35 Carrick Street, NS583650, probably built *c* 1840 for Tod & MacGregor as a marine-engine works. A 1- and 2-storey, 3-bay, sandstone-fronted building, with 3 gables. There are arched recesses to receive the door leaves when open and circular windows between the doors. Now disused.

GLASSFORD

Limekiln, Cot Castle, NS734457, early 19th century. A neat semicircular draw arch, with superstructure removed.

HAMILTON

Avon Bridge and tollhouse, NS735547, built 1820, engineer THOMAS TELFORD. A single segmental arch of dressed-stone construction. The tollhouse is a pleasing 1-storey and basement ashlar structure, with a bow front and diamond-paned windows, recently tile-roofed.

Avon Bridge (old), NS733547, 17th century. A handsome 3-span bridge, of dressed-stone construction, with 3-rib segmental arches and triangular cutwaters. Now carries a private road.

Avon Mill, NS734547, early 19th century. The ruins of a 3-storey and attic rubble building on an L plan, with the skeleton and some paddles of a 6-spoke, low-breast paddle wheel, about 3ft wide by 16ft diameter (0·91 by 4·88m), with wood spokes and paddles, and iron rings and axle. There is also a turbine, now inaccessible.

Avon Viaduct, NS731546, opened 1860 by the Caledonian Railway. A 4-span viaduct, with segmental arches of dressed-stone construction.

Hamilton Cloth Factory, Peacock Cross, NS711559, founded 1855 by Mitchell Bros. A group of single-storey, red-and-white-brick buildings with stone dressings. Some of the windows are round-headed, the rest have segmental-arched heads. Now in multiple occupation.

LANARK

Bonnington Power Station, NS883417, built 1927 by the Clyde Valley Electrical Power Co Ltd. A tall single-storey, 3-by-7-bay, reinforced-concrete building with round-headed windows, and ancillary 3- and 2-storey blocks in similar style. Stonebyres (NS850442) is very similar.

Clydesholm Bridge, Kirkfieldbank, NS869439, built 1694–9. A very attractive 3-span rubble bridge, with semicircular arches, and triangular cutwaters extended up to form pedestrian refuges. Now bypassed and used as a footbridge.

Hyndford Bridge and tollhouse, NS914414, built 1773, engineer ALEXANDER STEVENS. A 4-span bridge, with segmental arches of unequal size. The arch rings are of dressed stone, with rubble spandrels and parapets. There are rounded cutwaters extended upwards to form refuges. Below the parapet is a dentilated cornice. The tollhouse is at the south end of the bridge, and is a plain 1-storey cottage with a modern wooden porch.

LANARK

Lanark Station, NS886437, built 1867 by the Caledonian Railway. A 2-platform terminus, with a 1-storey and attic, coursed-rubble building on the down platform, with a bracketted awning, and a 1-storey wooden building on the up platform with a bracketted glazed awning round 3 sides.

Box works, NS886437, mid 19th century. An attractive 2-storey and attic, 3-by-9-by-9-bay, red-and-white-brick building on an L plan, with a square-section brick chimney. Now an agricultural-engineering works.

Cartland Bridge, NS869444, built 1822, engineer THOMAS TELFORD. A beautiful 3-span, dressed-stone, bridge, with semicircular arches on slender piers. The sockets for the centring can be seen near the tops of the piers. Concrete footpaths have been cantilevered out. Can only be properly viewed in winter, owing to the tall trees in the valley.

Tollhouse, Braxfield Road, NS884432, late 18th century. Tollhouse for the New Lanark turnpike, a 1-storey harled building, with a projecting semihexagonal bay.

Tollhouse, Lanark Racecourse, NS902426, built c 1820, architect THOMAS TELFORD. A typical Telford tollhouse, a single-storey stone building, with a central bowed bay with a door flanked by 2 windows. There is another example at NS805596.

Mousemill Bridges, NS869443, possibly 17th century, and probably early 19th century. Two small segmental-arched bridges, with dressed-stone arch rings. The older has been reduced to little more than the ring.

New Lanark, NS880426, founded 1784 by David Dale and Richard Arkwright (plate 44). Important group of houses, mills and community buildings. No 1 mill (1787) cut down to 3 storeys from 5 is rubble-built, with a projecting staircase block with paired Palladian windows. No 2 is 5 storeys high, extended in brick *c* 1905, and No 3 is 5 storeys high, externally as built *c* 1826. The houses are mainly 3 and 4 storey, all with a 'sunk floor' owing to the steeply sloping site. There are 2 community buildings: the Institute for the Formation of Character (1816) and the School (1817), both 2 storey and basement, and both with central pediments. Other buildings of interest are the 3-storey store, the 4-storey Nursery Buildings, and the 3-storey mechanics shop. Perhaps the most striking is, however, the 4-storey New Buildings (*c* 1799) with its bellcote. Some of the housing, Nursery Buildings, and the store have been renovated, and plans are in hand for more renovation [see J. Butt (ed), *Robert Owen :*

44   Caithness Row (left), Nursery Buildings (centre) and the Store, New Lanark.

Prince of Cotton Spinners, David & Charles, Newton Abbot, 1971.]
New Lanark Gatehouses, NS884428, probably *c* 1810. Two 2-storey, 3-bay buildings, with pedimented, slightly projecting central bays, facing each other. Stylistically they appear to date from Robert Owen's tenure of the mills, and may have been a traffic control introduced by him. Modernized internally, and windows altered slightly.

LESMAHAGOW

Auchenheath Brick and Tile Works, NS815437, late 19th century. A single-storey range of drying sheds, on a U plan with louvred sides, roofed with asbestos and pantiles, with 2 kilns, each with 24 brick vents. Disused.
Crossford Bridge and toll, NS827465, built 1793. A 3-span bridge, of dressed-stone construction, with the voussoirs and piers rusticated. The arches are segmental, and the cutwaters rounded. The tollhouse is a neat 1-storey building, with a semi-octagonal bay and a projecting double window at one end.
Mill, NS815407, late 18th to early 19th century. A 2 storey and attic rubble building, with later extensions. There is an internal wheel, still in use.
Viaduct, NS813404, opened 1883 by the Muirkirk & Lesmahagow Junction Railway. An 8-span viaduct, with segmental arches. The arch rings are of blue brick, with masonry spandrels. At the north end was a plate-girder approach span, now removed.

NEW MONKLAND

Gartlea Foundry, Airdrie, NS763652, late 19th century. A long rectangular single-storey moulding shop, partly brick, lit at 2 levels, with a solid-bottom cupola. There is also an old machine shop. Was part of Gibb & Hogg's engineering works.
Martyn's Foundry, Chapel Street, Airdrie, NS761659, late 19th century. A rectangular red-and-white-brick moulding shop, lit at 2 levels, with a single-storey pattern and sand store and a square-section brick chimney. There is a hand-charged cupola, probably early 20th century. In the yard are 2 derrick cranes, 1 by BUTTERS BROS, Glasgow, 1917.
Caldercruix Paper Mill, NS817676, founded 1848 by T. R. & G. Craig. A group of red-and-white-brick buildings, mainly 1 and 2 storey, with a tall circular-section building. At the rear is a reinforced-concrete block of early 20th-century construction. Now disused.

OLD MONKLAND

Brickworks, Bargeddie, NS704643, late 19th century. A most interesting group of buildings with a number of rectangular Hoffman kilns and a circular pipe kiln, now partly disused. There are 4 large brick chimneys.

Bleachworks, Carmyle, NS652616, early 19th century. A group of 1- and 2-storey, red-brick buildings, now used for storage.

Clyde Iron Works, NS638622, founded 1786. The present plant dates basically from the late 1930s, No 1 furnace being completed in 1939 and No 2 in 1940. The first battery of coke ovens was finished in 1939. No 3 furnace followed in 1948 and the second battery of coke ovens was added in 1952.

Viaduct, Clyde Ironworks, NS637618, opened 1865 by the Caledonian Railway. A 5-span viaduct, with dressed-stone arch rings and coursed-rubble spandrels and piers. The arches are segmental and the cutwaters rounded.

Clydebridge Steel Works, NS631618, founded 1887, by the Clydebridge Steel Company. The present melting shop, with a mixer furnace and 6 open-hearth furnaces, dates from 1916, when it was installed by Colvilles. The furnaces have since been updated. Most of the rest of the plant is modern.

Coatbridge (Sunnyside) Station, NS732656, built 1888 for the North British Railway. A 2-platform through station on a curve, with the booking office in a wooden building on an overbridge. There is a single-storey brick building on the up platform, dated 1888, with a glazed awning supported on cast-iron columns.

Coatbridge (Central) Station, NS729652, rebuilt *c* 1900 by the Caledonian Railway. A 3-platform through and terminal station, with the main office in a 2-storey, Renaissance stone and brick building with the platform at first-floor level. There is an awning over the entrance and a substantial awning over the platform.

Sheepford Boiler Works, NS747647, founded *c* 1876 by Thomas Hudson. A large single-storey, corrugated-iron-clad steel workshop, with lower buildings. Interesting features are a gantry for suspending boiler shells over a rivetting machine, and a large hydraulic accumulator. The small brick office block has *art nouveau* features.

Engineering works, Coatbridge, NS732657, late 19th century. A tall single-storey, 6-by-18-bay, red-brick building, with a steel and corrugated-iron extension and a smaller single-storey foundry block (now adapted to other use) with a prominent roof-ridge ventilator. The 2-storey office block has recently been obscured by an addition.

45   Steam hammer, Fleming's Forge, Rutherglen.

Engineering works, Coatbridge, NS734643, founded 1900 by Murray & Paterson. Three bays of single-storey engineering shops, the centre bay built 1900, with cast-iron columns, and the 2 side bays added *c* 1910, with steel frames. There is a small brick single-storey brass foundry, and a 2-storey, 3-by-4-bay office block.

RUTHERGLEN

Brattice Cloth Factory, Farmeloan Road, NS623617, mid 19th century and later. The main block here is a 3-storey rubble building, much altered, which housed the weaving section. The proofing section is housed in a group of red-brick, single-storey buildings, with a 3-storey wood and brick drying tower.

Eastfield Ropery, NS623618, mid 19th century. A long single-storey brick rope walk, with a 2-storey, 4-bay office block and 1- and 2-storey ancillary buildings.

Fleming's Forge, Main Street, NS612617, early 19th century and later (plate 45). A disused single-storey rubble shoeing forge, with partially collapsed roof, and a 1-storey, 8-bay, red-and-white-brick steam forge, with a 1910 steam hammer by R. G. ROSS & SON, Glasgow, at the rear. The half door and shuttered windows of the shoeing forge still face the main street. The steam forge has a prominent full-length louvred roof ventilator.

Richmond Park Laundry, NS625615, early 20th century. A 10-bay block of red-brick, single-storey workshops and garages, with a 3-storey office block. Was one of the largest laundries in Scotland, but now occupies only a part of the complex.

Joinery works, NS613618, late 19th century. A 2-storey, 7-bay, red-and-white-brick building with an external wooden stair at the rear. In the upstairs workshop is a hand-operated Mathieson mortising machine.

SHOTTS

Shotts Iron Works, NS879598, founded 1802 (see plate 6). An interesting group of structures, dominated by a long L-plan rubble furnace bank, with a partly buried ironstone calcining kiln and a tall brick water-tower used to provide cooling water for the furnace. There are the remains of an engine house, probably of the 1830s or 1840s, and behind that the remains of an earlier engine house, with a D-shaped, wrought-iron roof tank. The principal surviving building is a tall single-storey, corrugated-iron-clad steel foundry, dated from *c* 1900, but retaining the cupola arches from an earlier building

(1828). Behind this are single-storey pattern stores and a brass foundry, probably mid 19th century in origin. One of the 2 small curved gatehouses also survives. Now the most important monument of the Scottish coke-smelting iron industry.

Shotts Station, NS873598, opened 1869 by the Caledonian Railway. A 2-platform through station, with the main offices on the down platform, in a 1-storey ashlar building on a T plan incorporating a dwellinghouse. A dormered attic has been added. The up platform building is a single-storey rubble building. The platforms are linked by a lattice-girder footbridge.

Paper Mill, Caldercruix, NS817675, founded 1848 by Thomas, Robert & George Craig, greatly extended *c* 1890. A large group of 1-, 2- and 3-storey buildings, now used in part as a bonded warehouse. The older buildings are of red-and-white-brick, with round-headed openings. There is a tall brick chimney. The reinforced concrete blocks, of pre-1914 construction, are of interest.

Tollhouse, Auchinlee, NS805596, *c* 1820. A typical Telford tollhouse with central bowed bay, flanked by single windows.

STONEHOUSE

Limekilns, Cot Castle, NS737455, early 19th century. A pair of single-draw limekilns set into a bank, with elliptically arched draw holes and projecting buttresses.

Cander Mill, NS766470, early 19th century. A 2-storey rubble building on an L plan, with a square kiln-vent. Electrified.

Bridge, Linthaugh, NS751473, late 18th century. A 2-arch bridge, with dressed-stone arch rings and rubble spandrels. The arches are segmental and the cutwaters triangular.

Stonehouse Viaduct, NS757476, built 1904, by ARROL BROS for the Caledonian Railway. A steel-truss bridge with 8 spans on a curve.

Weavers' cottages, NS758468, late 18th to early 19th century. Two long rows of single-storey cottages, many with the characteristic double window.

SYMINGTON

Woodemailing Mill, NT003357, early 19th century. A rubble building on an L plan. The wheel and machinery have been removed, but the bottom stones remain on the hurst, which is supported on cast-iron columns.

WANDEL & LAMINGTON

Bridge, Lamington, NS971303, built 1836. A handsome 2-span bridge, with segmental arches, dressed-stone voussoirs and rubble spandrels.

WISTON & ROBERTON

Mill, Wiston, NS957316, early 19th century. A large 2-storey rubble building, on an L plan. Now gutted and used as a store.

Midlothian

Midlothian contains the capital of Scotland, and has long had a reputation for coal mining, brewing and paper making. There has also been an important lime industry. The main routes between Edinburgh, the rest of Scotland and England all pass through the county, and its major port, Leith, is one of the largest in the country.

Edinburgh & Glasgow Union Canal, NT246728–206702 and 196701–105706, built 1818–22, engineer HUGH BAIRD. The stretch of the Union Canal in Midlothian is split by infilling at Wester Hailes. Included are: one major aqueduct, at Slateford (NT220727) and half another, at NT105706, a selection of standard bridges, and an unusual vertical lift bridge at Gilmore Park (*qv*), NT244727. Both large aqueducts have cast-iron troughs, that at Slateford having 8 arches and the other having 5 arches. With a height of 86ft (26·2m) the latter is the tallest aqueduct in Scotland (see plate 11).

COCKPEN
Carpet factory, Bonnyrigg, NT307655, late 19th century. The street frontage consists of a 2-storey, 9-bay building and a 2-storey, 13-bay block, both with Renaissance features. At the rear are single-storey brick sheds, and a circular-section brick chimney.

CRANSTON
Cousland Lime Works, NT376689, operated from 16th century. A large quarry, with a modern crushing plant. The sign at the works entrance consists of 3 quarry tubs, mounted on a raised piece of track and painted with the name of the firm. Nearby are ruins of a bank of 3 limekilns (NT375686).

Lothian Bridge, NT391646, built 1827–31, engineer THOMAS TELFORD. A 5-span bridge with segmental arches, built of dressed stone. The design is similar to that of Dean Bridge, Edinburgh, with flat-segmental arches carrying the footpaths and smaller-radius arches supporting the carriageway.

Limekiln, Magazine, NT410628, early 19th century. A single 3-draw rubble kiln in good condition, disused.

CRICHTON

Limekilns, NT392616, probably early 19th century. Two very substantial 3-draw kilns, at right angles to each other, with a range of single-storey offices/houses nearby. Now used as a store.

Smithy, NT385620, early 19th century. A single-storey, 3-bay rubble building, now disused.

CURRIE

Balerno Paper Mills, Balerno, NT164663, founded 1810. A large group of steel-framed brick buildings, with a circular-section brick chimney. The 2-storey and basement, snecked-rubble, baronial office block is dated 1916.

Malleny Mills (flax spinning), Balerno, NT171657, early 19th century. A 2-storey and attic, 3-by-5-bay rubble building, now converted to a dwellinghouse. Nearby, at NT169657, is a fine square-section ashlar chimney, with some fragmentary remains of walls, part of another flaxmill.

Paper mill, NT188680, founded 18th century. A large complex of buildings of various dates, mostly modern, with a very tall red-brick, circular-section chimney.

Smithy, Long Hermiston, NT179703, early 19th century. A single-storey, 4-bay rubble building, now used as a store.

DALKEITH

Dalkeith Mills, NT331676, mid 19th century. The main mill range here has been completely rebuilt, except for the pyramidal-roofed rubble kiln, with its square louvred vent. Other buildings on the site are 2-storey and attic, 4-bay, 1-storey and attic, 3-bay, and a 2-storey block on an L plan. The 2 latter have crow-stepped gables.

Newmills Bridge, NT329676, built 1756, widened in 1814, and improved in 1839, engineer JAMES JARDINE. A 3-span rubble bridge, with segmental arches.

Iron mill (flour), NT326671. A 3-storey and attic rubble building on an L plan, with Gothic windows. Now gutted and disused. The water supply came from a substantial masonry weir a short distance upstream.

Railway bridge, NT324672, opened 1849 by the Edinburgh & Hawick Railway. A large single semicircular masonry arch, with substantial steel reinforcement.

Railway overbridge, NT327670, mid 19th century. An unusual bridge, with a slightly curved, slender riveted wrought-iron plate girder and massive cast-iron parapets.

Water-tower, NT327671, built 1879. An octagonal brick tower, with a louvred wooden top.

EDINBURGH

Bell's Mills, Belford Road, NT238737, late 18th century. The 3- and 4-storey main ranges here were demolished in 1971 after an explosion, but the former granary, a 3-storey attic and basement, 3-by-7-bay rubble block (1807), survives as an automobile paint shop. This building has a central pediment with a sculptured wheatsheaf in the tympanum.

Bernards Maltings, Salamander and Seafield Road, NT283760, mid to late 19th century. Two ranges of maltings, the older 4 storey and 2 attic, 3-by-13-bay, with 2 pyramidal-roofed kilns and a 6-bay silo block, and the other, of snecked rubble, 5 storey, 6-by-20-bay.

Bonnington Mills, Newhaven Road, NT263761, 18th and 19th centuries. An interesting pair of rubble buildings, consisting of a 3-storey, 2-by-5-bay granary, with a pantiled roof, and a 4-storey, 6-bay mill, with a Belfast roof, linked to the granary by 2 gangways. The internal structure of the mill is most unusual, with cast-iron columns and beams supporting wrought-iron joists and iron-plate floors. There is a bevel-gear drive to 3 pairs of stones, installed by ALEX MATHER, Fountainbridge, from a low-breast paddle-wheel, 6ft wide by 11ft diameter (1·83 by 3·35m), in a brick wheelhouse. Now disused.

Bonnington Tannery, Newhaven Road, NT264760, late 19th century. An extensive complex, the oldest part of which is probably a 3-storey, 14-bay, snecked-rubble block, dated 1879, with drying sheds at the rear. The other important buildings are 4-storey, 6-bay, and 4-storey, 4-bay structures, both rubble-fronted, with a red-and-white-brick water-tower. There are other, smaller buildings at the rear. Now disused.

Burdiehouse Limekilns, NT277673, probably early 19th century (see plate 9). A range of 3 coursed-rubble kilns, 1 semi-hexagonal, 3 draw, 1 circular, single draw, and 1 rectangular, 2 draw.

Caledonian Brewery, Slateford Road, NT231720, late 19th to early 20th century. A complex of red-and-white-brick buildings on a triangular site, dominated by a circular-section brick chimney. The main block of maltings, 4 storeys and attic by 8 bay, with twin pyramidal-roofed kilns, is now converted to other uses. The brewhouse is 4 storeys high.

Caledonian Distillery, Dalry Road, NT239731, built 1855 by Menzies and Company, and subsequently extended. A very large distillery complex, with a 5-storey, 8-by-13-bay range of malting floors and a double kiln. There is a tall circular-section brick chimney.

Craigmillar Maltings, Peffer Place, NT290720, late 19th century. A 4-storey and attic, 3-by-9-bay, red-and-white-brick block of maltings with a single large pyramidal-roofed kiln, a flat-roofed 5-storey block, with a smaller kiln, and two 3-storey ancillary ranges. Formerly a much larger complex. There is a tall circular-section brick chimney.

Cramond Harbour, NT188770, built 18th century. The quayed mouth of the river Almond, with rubble quay walls extending some distance up the river. At Cockle Mill (NT188766) is a small dock.

Cramond Old Bridge, NT179754. A 3-span medieval masonry bridge, with segmental arches and triangular cutwaters. The west-most arch is ribbed. Rebuilt and repaired on several occasions in the 18th and 19th centuries.

Croft-an-Righ Brewery, Croft-an-Righ, NT270741, mid to late 19th century. Now reduced remains of a large brewery complex. A 5-storey, 4-by-9-bay rubble block of maltings survives, as do two pyramidal-roofed kilns, but the classic brewhouse has disappeared.

Leith Custom House, Commercial Street, NT271766, built 1811, architect ROBERT REID. An elegant, 2-storey classical building, with a pedimented portico, and single-storey end pavilions.

Dean Bridge, Queensferry Road, NT243740, built 1829–31, engineer THOMAS TELFORD. A magnificent 4-span, dressed-stone bridge, with heavy segmental arches supporting the carriageway and flatter arches supporting the footpaths.

Dean Tannery, Damside, NT240738, late 18th and 19th century. A large complex of buildings of various dates, mostly pantile-roofed, with a 3-storey range of drying sheds, and another 3-storey, 7-bay block, probably the oldest on the site.

Deuchars' Brewery, Duddingston Road West, NT287718, late 19th century. All this once large complex has been demolished, except a 2-storey, 7-bay, red-and-white-brick range.

Dryborough's Brewery, Peffer Bank, NT287717, late 19th century. A large group of buildings, some modern, the most interesting of which is a 4-storey and attic, 11-bay range of red-and-white-brick maltings, with a pyramidal-roofed kiln and a 2-bay silo block. There is a water-tower with an ogee cap and round the top of the maltings a Greek key-pattern string course.

Duddingston Mill, Willowbrae Road, NT293732, early 19th century. A 3-storey block on an L plan, with arched cart entries at ground level, probably a granary, and a much altered 2-storey block, both rubble-built. At the rear of the 2-storey block are the pit and fragmentary remains of a 10-spoke, high-breast bucket wheel, with cast-iron axle and rings, wooden spokes and sole, and sheet-iron buckets, about 3ft 6in wide by 20ft diameter (1·06 by 6·10m).

Edina Works, Edina Place, NT271747, built 1878 for Morrison and Gibb, printers and bookbinders. A 2-storey, 20-bay, flat-roofed brick building, with a cornice, and a 2-storey, 2-by-3-bay office block, with a pediment surmounted by an urn.

Fairafar Mill, Cramond, NT187765. The most complete of the Cramond iron mills, converted from a grain mill to a forge in 1770. The walls stand 1 storey high. There is a substantial weir built by 1839 which supplied water to a 13ft (4m) diameter undershot wheel and 2 smaller wheels. (See Patrick Cadell, *The Iron Mills at Cramond,* Edinburgh, 1973.)

Fountain Brewery, Fountainbridge, NT267738, late 19th century. Despite modernization, the old 3-storey and attic and 2-storey buildings facing the street survive here.

Gorgie Mill, Gorgie Road, NT225721, early 19th century. A 3-storey and attic, 6-bay rubble building, with a 2-storey extension. Now an upholstery workshop.

Granton Harbour, NT2377, built 1835 on, by the Duke of Buccleuch, engineers WALKER AND BURGESS, London. Consists of a wide central pier, completed 1845, protected by east and west (*c* 1863) curved breakwaters. Used by railway ferry steamers to Burntisland from 1848–90.

Haymarket Station, Haymarket Terrace, NT240731, built 1840–2 for the Edinburgh & Glasgow Railway, architect JOHN MILLER. Now a 4-platform through station, in a cutting with the main offices in a 2-storey and basement, 7-bay building at street level. This is the original office block of 1842, with Doric tetrastyle portico. Behind the main offices is the original 9-bay, cast-iron and wood train shed, now used as a car park. The present platforms had extensive wood-framed awnings, now cut back, and, in the case of the island platform, wooden waiting rooms. Under threat of redevelopment.

Heriot Brewery, Roseburn Terrace, NT231731, mid to late 19th century. A complex of buildings of various dates, the oldest of which are the 4-storey, 7-bay brewhouse, with louvred top floor and circular-section brick chimney, and the 2-storey office block with corner tower.

Holyrood Laundry, London Road, NT273743, late 19th century. A 2-storey, 12-bay block and a 3-storey, 3-by-5-bay block, with ancillary buildings, and a graceful circular-section brick chimney with a flared top.

King George IV Bridge, NT257735, built 1829–34, engineer THOMAS HAMILTON. A series of semicircular masonry arches.

Leith (Central) Station, Leith Walk, NT271758, opened 1903 by the North British Railway. A very large building, with 4-bay steel-framed roof and coursed-rubble walls. Now disused.

Leith Co-operative Society Warehouses, Links Place, NT276762, late 19th century. A 4-storey and basement, 6-by-22-bay Renaissance block, with a plainer 6-bay section and a detached 3-storey, 10-bay building at the rear.

Leith Flour Mills, Commercial Street, NT266767, mid 19th century. An interesting classical group on a triangular site. The main blocks are 7 storeys, 10 bays, with an 8th storey added: 6 storeys, 8-by-4 bays; and 6 storeys, 2-by-6 bays. The 7-storey block has pediments over the end pairs of bays. There is a tall circular-section chimney with an octagonal base, rising from a 2-storey boiler house. To the rear of the main complex is a 3 storey, 4-by-8-bay block, cut down from a taller block.

Leith Harbour, NT2777. The original harbour was the quayed mouth of the Water of Leith, protected and extended by piers, and this was first modernized by the construction of the East and West Old Docks (1800–6 and 1810–17, engineer JOHN RENNIE). These have been filled in, but the entrance gates and 2-leaf, cast-iron swing bridge at the entrance to the East Dock (NT270767) survive. The Victoria Dock (NT268768) followed in 1847–51 (engineer J. M. RENDEL). The Prince of Wales Graving Dock (NT272769) was added in 1858, and the Albert Dock was completed in 1869 (NT274768, engineers RENDEL AND ROBERTSON), the first dock in Scotland with hydraulic cranes. The Edinburgh Dock (NT227767) was built for coal shipment in 1877–81, and the final wet dock, the Imperial Dock (NT273772) was completed 1896–8. A second large graving dock, the Alexandra, was added beside the Prince of Wales Dock in 1896, engineer PETER WHYTE. Interesting features include a hydraulic crane (plate 46) on Albert Dock, 2 hydraulic pumping stations, 1 on Edinburgh Dock (1898), the other beside the drydocks, an iron

46   Hydraulic crane, Leith Docks.

bowed-truss swing bridge between the two sides of the harbour, and a mobile hydraulic crane at the west end of Victoria Dock (COWANS SHELDON, 1903). Along the south side of the Old Docks is a long 4-storey rubble range of bonded warehouses, with, at the east end, a 4-storey and attic, 7-by-12-bay office and warehouse block.

London Road Foundry, London Road, NT273744, mid to late 19th century. A large group of moulding and machine shops, with a handsome 1- and 2-storey frontage to London Road, incorporating a now disused round-headed doorway, with glazed fanlight.

Lothian Road Station, Lothian Road, NT247733, built c 1870 by the Caledonian Railway. A large stone-fronted train shed, with a 2-storey office block, latterly part of Lothian Road Goods Depot.

Moray Park Maltings, Marionville Road, NT274745, late 19th century. A 7-storey range of malting floors, with a remarkable castellated frontage, rubble-built.

Newhaven Harbour, NT256771, built 1812 on. A basin enclosed by an L-plan pier (1825) and a curved concrete breakwater (1876–8). There is an octagonal lighthouse on the end of the pier, and on the east side of the pier is an 11-bay, gabled, wooden fish market.

North Bridge, NT259739, built 1896–7, engineers BLYTH AND WESTLAND. A 3-span bridge, with steel segmental arches on masonry piers. The spandrels of the outer ribs are faced with cast-iron panels decorated with swags and arcades.

North British Distillery, Wheatfield Road, NT229724, late 19th century. A large group of mainly rubble buildings, including a 5-storey, 4-by-23-bay block of bonded stores.

North Leith Station, Commercial Street, NT267766, opened 1846 by the Edinburgh, Leith & Granton Railway. Formerly a terminal station, with a cast- and wrought-iron overall roof, now cut back to 1 bay and bricked in. The surviving block is in the classical manner, 1 storey high, with 2 porticos. Now used as a public house and a brass and copper works. Adjacent to the passenger station is a rubble goods shed, now used as a warehouse.

Quayside Mills, Quayside Street, NT268765, 18th century and later. An interesting group of brick and rubble buildings, the oldest of which are 4-storey and attic rubble blocks, 1 with a tower having a wooden top of a traditional Scottish design. The brick buildings consist of a 3-storey and attic, 6-bay mill block and a 5-storey and attic, 6-bay store. The circular-section brick chimney is now demolished.

Raeburn Brewery, Niddrie Mains Road, NT291717, late 19th century. A very pleasing group of rubble buildings, with a single malt kiln and a circular-section brick chimney.

Regent Bridge, Waterloo Place, NT260741, built 1816–17, architect ARCHIBALD ELLIOT, and engineer ROBERT STEVENSON. A tall single semicircular arch of dressed stone. Surmounting the parapet on each side is a triumphal arch flanked by pairs of columns. Designed as a memorial for the dead of the Napoleonic Wars.

St Ann's Brewery, Abbeyhill, NT269741, early 19th century on. An extensive and irregular complex of buildings, mostly rubble, the oldest of which is probably a 3-storey, 6-bay block at the entrance. Behind are ranges of malting floors, kilns and brewhouse. Now used as a store.

St Leonard's Brewery, St Leonard's Street, NT264730, main part built 1889–90, architect P. L. HENDERSON. A most unusual group of 3-storey and 4-storey and attic rubble buildings. The main block is 4 storey and attic, 2-by-7 bay, in Scots baronial style, with, at the rear, 3 pyramidal-roofed kilns. Now disused.

St Leonard's Station, St Leonard's Street, NT266728, opened 1831 by the Edinburgh & Dalkeith Railway. A 3-storey, 2-by-17-bay rubble warehouse, with elliptical-arched cart and railway entrances and 4 hoists. Traces of tracks and a loading bay can be discerned. Now disused.

St Leonard's Warehouse, Holyrood Park Road, NT268727, late 19th century. A 4-storey, 18-bay rubble range, part harled, with corner turrets, and a row of 2-storey stores, the longest 16 bays long.

Scotland Street Tunnel, Canonmills, NT254748–257740, opened 1847 by the Edinburgh, Leith & Granton Railway, engineers GRAINGER AND MILLER. Constructed on a gradient of 1 in 27 and worked by cable haulage. Closed since 1868, but still intact. The southern entrance is now obscured, but the monumental northern portal is still visible.

Shrubhill Tramway Workshops and Power Station, Dryden Street, NT263752, power station opened 1898. A tall 8-bay, 1-storey and basement ashlar block, 3 wide single-storey bays, and a single-storey, 4-bay rubble block with round-headed windows and 8 circular windows. All these have roof-ridge ventilators. The complex is dominated by an octagonal brick chimney, with decorated top section on a square masonry base. The power station housed the haulage engines for cable-tramway operation.

Slateford Laundry, Slateford Road, NT713226, built c 1894 by the Caledonian Railway. A 6-bay, single-storey range, with a 9-bay frontage to Slateford Road. There is a neat circular-section chimney with a flared top.

Slateford Maltings, Slateford Road, NT228716, late 19th to early 20th century. Two 6-storey and attic, 6-by-10-bay, red-brick blocks, with low-relief arch mouldings. At the rear, each block has its own kilns, and there is a modern range of concrete silos to the west.

Slateford Viaduct, Inglis Green Road, NT220707, opened 1848 by the Caledonian Railway. A 14-span viaduct, with segmental arches. The rock-faced masonry has been patched with brick.

South Bridge, NT260736, built 1786–8, engineer ALEXANDER LAING. A 19-span viaduct, partly concealed by buildings, carrying an elevated street over the valley to the south of the old city of Edinburgh.

Swanfield Roller Flour Mills, Bonnington Road, NT266761, mid to late 19th century. A large complex of 1-, 2-, 3- and 4-storey rubble and brick buildings, with a range of reinforced-concrete grain silos. Now in multiple occupation.

Trinity Station, York Road, NT249768, opened 1846 by the Edinburgh, Leith & Granton Railway. Formerly a 2-platform through station, with the main offices on the up platform, in a 1-storey and basement ashlar block on a U plan, with an awning in the gap. Now a dwellinghouse.

The Vaults, Giles Street and Henderson Street, NT268763, built 1682, vault perhaps 1785. A 4-storey and attic, 9-bay rubble building. The fourth storey was added in 1785.

Waverley Station, Waverley Bridge, NT258738, rebuilt by the North British Railway, 1892–1902, engineers BLYTH AND WESTLAND. A 19-platform through and terminal station. The main part consists of a large island platform, with bays at both ends, and there is a subsidiary island for suburban trains, outside the main station wall. The roof of the main station is overall, of the ridge type, and there is a 2-storey office block with a large booking hall in the centre of the island.

West Mill, Dean Path, NT238737, built 1805–6. A handsome 5-storey, attic and basement, 3-by-7-bay rubble building, with 2 wheel arches in the basement, and a 3-storey, 3-by-6-bay granary adjoining at the rear. Now converted to flats.

Bonded warehouses, Breadalbane Street, Bonnington Road and Anderson Place, NT264760. A large rectangular group of warehouses, on the site of the old Leith Distillery. The most impressive are two 8-storey, red-brick blocks – one 8-by-8 bay, the other 3-by-12 bay. There are 2 lower ranges, one 5-storey and attic, 5-bay, rubble-fronted brick, the other 4-storey and basement, 5-by-20 bay, all rubble.

Bonded warehouses and blending plant, Great Junction Street, NT268761, mid 19th century. A roughly rectangular group of buildings, the largest of which are a 3 storey, bay block, with low-relief arches in the middle 6 bays; a 5-storey, 3-by-11-bay ashlar building; and a neat 5-storey, 3-bay rubble building, with a central hoist.

Brewery, off Canongate, NT265737, late 18th to early 19th century. A group of 1-, 2- and 3-storey whitewashed rubble buildings, round a courtyard, with a 3-storey office block on an L plan. Approached from Canongate through a segmental-arched cart entry.

Brewery, Holyrood Park Road, NT267726, mid to late 19th century. A large group of rubble buildings altered and added to, with a 5-storey, 19-bay range of maltings, with a single kiln. The east 9 bays of this block have been raised by 2, and in part 3 storeys.

Brewery, Pleasance, NT263734, mid 19th century. A rectangular group of 2- and 3-storey rubble buildings, now a physical education college.

Bridge, Canonmills, NT253751, mid 19th century. A 3-span bridge of dressed stone, with segmental arches.

Bridge, Deanhaugh Street, NT254739, mid 19th century. A single segmental arch, with dressed-stone arch ring and snecked-rubble spandrels. There is a central armorial panel, and the bridge is flanked by pilasters with cruciform imitation arrow slits.

Cable-tram depot, Henderson Row, NT250748, built 1888 for the Edinburgh Northern Tramways Co and extended in 1900. A single-storey ashlar building, with a wide central entrance surmounted by a 1-storey and attic Renaissance office block. Now a police garage.

Canal bridge, Gilmore Park, NT244727, early 20th century. A most unusual bridge over the Union Canal, with riveted steel framework and a short lifting span. The control cabin is situated inside the framework. On the east side is a lattice-girder footbridge for the use of pedestrians when the bridge was lifted.

Chimney, Bonnington, NT262760, late 19th century. An extraordinary circular-section brick chimney with 7 bands of white-brick decoration.

Flour mill, Carpet Lane and Broad Wynd, NT272764, built 1828. A 6-storey and attic rubble building on a Z plan. The middle block is 24-by-9 bay, with low-relief arches running up to fifth-floor level, with brick insertions. The east wing is 4-by-5 bay, with round-headed openings on the ground floor, and the west wing is a 2-bay structure, partly a wing of the main block and partly an extension. Now a seed store.

Footbridge, Bell Place, NT248750, probably mid to late 19th century. An unusual structure, with a curved, riveted-plate span supported on cast-iron columns, with rustic wooden railings.

Granite works, Canonmills, NT254751, mid to late 19th century. A 19-bay, single-storey wooden workshop, incorporating parts of an older block, now harled. There is a lean-to wooden addition. In front is a neat segmental-arched gateway. At the rear are other workshops, and 2 steel derrick cranes.

Maltings, Calton Road, NT265739, mid 19th century. A 3-storey, 8-bay rubble range of malt floors, with a neat pyramidal-roofed kiln. Now a garage.

Maltings, Musselburgh Road, NT328731, late 19th century. A large 4-storey and 2 attic, 2-by-18-bay rubble block of malting floors, with 2 pyramidal-roofed kilns, and some modern concrete silos.

Mills, Canon Street, NT253750, late 18th to early 19th century. Two blocks, 1 with a 4-storey, 2-by-3-bay front building, and a 4-storey, 6-bay harled building at the rear, and the other a 3-storey, 6-bay harled structure. Now converted to other uses.

Power station, McDonald Road, NT261752, built 1898. A tall single-storey, steel-framed yellow brick, 4-by-8-bay range, with a handsome ashlar frontage with a central pediment. Steel 'tusks' have been left for a possible extension. Adjacent to this range is a lower 7-bay brick building with a 2-storey office block in front. There is an octagonal brick chimney with an ornamental top.

Printing works, Tanfield, NT251751, mid 19th century. A single-storey, 11-bay coursed-rubble-front block, with twin gables at each end. At the rear is an apparently older 3-storey, 5-by-9-bay building, with 2 pediments.

Printing works, Warriston Road, NT254754, built 1902 for George Waterston and Sons Ltd. A 3-storey, 4-by-14-bay, Renaissance-front block, with a 2-storey, 18-bay, flat-roofed building.

Stables, Burlington Street, NT265760, built for the Leith Provident Co-operative Society, late 19th to early 20th century. An interesting 3-storey and attic, 2-by-4-bay cart shed and stables block, with outside ramped stair to the first and second floors. There is an attractive ventilator with a cupola.

Tollhouse, Prestonfield Avenue, NT279717, late 18th to early 19th century. A 1-storey rubble building, with a projecting central bay.

Viaduct, Warriston Road, NT253753, built 1841–2, by the Edinburgh, Leith & Granton Railway, engineers GRAINGER AND MILLER. A very handsome 3-span viaduct, of dressed stone, with skew segmental arches and rounded cutwaters. One of the arches is over a minor road, and is shorter in span than the others.

Warehouses, Leith. Leith contains the finest collection of general and bonded warehouses in Scotland, though some of the oldest have been demolished in recent years. The 3 main surviving groups are in the Timber Bush–Tower Street area, in the Constitution Street–Mitchell Street area and in the Water Street–Broad Wynd–Maritime Street area. Individual buildings are too numerous to note in detail, but there are representative buildings from the late 18th century onward, up to 6 storeys high, mainly rubble, later brick-built. Many are now disused. Interesting examples are: 17–19 Timber Bush, a 4-storey and attic, 6-by-5-bay double warehouse, with twin hoists; 50–53 Timber Bush, a pair of 5-storey, 5-bay blocks, with central gabled hoists and opposite the wood and iron skeleton of a typical warehouse; No 9 Bond (NT270766), a 5-storey and attic, 3-by-7-bay, coursed-rubble block, with a central hoist; a group of 3 buildings in Constitution Street (NT271761), one 4 storey, 12-bay, ashlar-fronted, with a central-arched cart entry and a pediment, the middle one 3 storey and basement, 5 bay classical, and a 4-storey and basement, 7-bay, coursed-rubble building; a striking group of 3 warehouses in Wellington Place, forming a U, the older being two 6-storey blocks, one 4-by-7 bay, the other 5 bay, and the newer a 5-storey and attic, 3-by-7-bay, coursed-rubble block with round-headed doorways with ropework decoration; and, in Maritime Street, a 2-storey and attic, 13-bay block in Renaissance style, with 3 oriel windows at first-floor level and rusticated ground floor. These examples are arranged in rough sequence of date, from late 18th to late 19th century.

Windmill tower, Tower Street, NT272767, built 1685–6, architect ROBERT MYLNE. A 5-storey, circular, coursed-rubble structure with corbelled crenellations. A 19th-century, 4-storey and attic tenement has been built on to the north side.

Workers' housing, Elgin Place, etc., NT235731, mid 19th century. Though Haymarket Flour Mills were demolished in 1966–7, the single-storey brick rows of 2-roomed cottages built for workers still survive. There are 4 rows with a total of 50 houses and 1 shop.

Workshops, off Logie Green Road, NT254752, opened *c* 1842 by the Edinburgh, Leith & Granton Railway. A single-storey, 11-bay block, with masonry pillars and brick infilling. Now disused.

KIRKNEWTON

Limekilns, Raw Camps, NT095683, late 18th century. A most interesting group of kilns. The northern block consists of a single-draw kiln and an unusual 4-draw kiln with a semicircular tunnel giving access to the rear draw hole. The southern block, much decayed, has three 4-draw kilns, 1 with curved tunnel. All have segmental draw arches. (See Skinner, *Limekilns*, pp 32, 47, Plate III.)

LASSWADE

Polton Paper Mill, Polton, NT291650, founded 1750 (plate 47). A complex of brick and rubble buildings. The oldest block seems to be a 2-storey, 7-bay rubble building, with small-paned windows, extended by 1 storey in red-and-white brick. Adjacent to this block is a red-and-white brick, 2-storey, 3-by-9-bay building, with round-headed windows.

Springfield Paper Mill, Polton, NT287647, founded 1742. A large complex of buildings of various dates. The oldest part appears to be a 3-storey rubble block with small-paned windows, now used as a

47 Polton Paper Mill.

garage. Other 18th- or 19th-century parts are a long 2-storey rubble block and the 3-storey, 9-bay office building. Now in multiple occupation.

Viaduct, over North Esk, Lasswade, NT296655, opened 1867 by the Esk Valley Railway. A 6-span stone viaduct, with semicircular arches. Disused.

LIVINGSTON

Livingston Mill, NT033668, built *c* 1770. A 2-storey and attic rubble building on an L plan, with a 6-spoke, low-breast paddle wheel, with wooden paddles, rings and spokes and iron axle, 3ft 8in wide by 16ft diameter (1·11 by 4·88m). An internal toothed gear-ring formerly drove a threshing mill. An unusual ancillary feature is a dairy with the remains of an internal overshot wheel, 2ft 3in wide by 7ft 6in diameter (0·69 by 2·28m), which formerly drove a butter churn. Restored and open to the public.

MIDCALDER

Howden Bridge, NT061672, built 1764. A 2-span bridge, with dressed-stone arch rings and rubble spandrels. The southern arch is considerably wider than the other; both are segmental.

Midcalder Station, NT104672, opened 1848 by the Caledonian Railway. A 2-platform through station, with the main offices on the up platform. These are in a 2-storey, coursed-rubble building on an L plan, with a wooden shelter in the angle of the L. The building, with crow-stepped gables and ball finials, incorporates a dwelling-house. There is a wooden shelter on the down platform, and the platforms are linked by a diagonally braced steel footbridge, with wood infilling.

Wallace Mills, NT073679, probably early 19th century. Though largely modern in construction, there is an old 3-storey rubble nucleus.

MUSSELBURGH

Esk Net Mills, NT339723, built from 1867 for W. & S. Stuart (plate 48). This extraordinary complex originally consisted of a 4-storey, 10-by-10-bay spinning and doubling mill, with harled back and sides, and an 8-bay classical facade, with pilasters through the first and second floors supporting statuary at third-floor level, and single-storey doubling and net-making sheds round a rectangular court-yard. The spinning mill has a tall 3-bay engine house, a small brick clock tower with a cast-iron crown, and an ornate cast-iron fire escape.

The single-storey ranges are rubble-built, with round-headed windows, and dentilated cornices. The packing block, opposite the main range, has a fine Greek doorway. Later additions include a small single-storey Greek office building, and the inspection block, with a frontage of massive cast-iron columns supporting arched girders, terminating at the rear in a circular turret with an ogival roof.

Fisherrow Harbour, NT334730, rebuilt 1806 (east pier) and *c* 1850 (west pier). Formed by a straight west pier and an east pier with an angled head.

Musselburgh Station, NT342725, opened 1847 by the North British Railway. Formerly a single-platform terminal station, with a wooden overall roof (now removed) and a 2-storey, 3-by-3-bay ashlar office and dwellinghouse block with single-storey wings. The wooden goods shed also survives, as does the 2-span truss bridge over the river Esk at the entrance to the station.

New Bridge, NT342727, built 1806–7, engineer JOHN RENNIE, widened 1924–5. A 5-span bridge, built of dressed stone, with flat-segmental arches and rounded cutwaters.

48   Esk Net Mills, Musselburgh.

Old Bridge, NT341724, early 16th century. A 3-span rubble bridge, with roughly segmental arches and triangular cutwaters. Now a footbridge.

Bakery, NT341726, late 19th century. A 2-storey, 10-bay, ashlar angled block with a lower 4-storey brick extension.

Brewery, NT346728, late 18th to early 19th century. A small 3-storey rubble building with louvred ventilators in the top floor. The roof is pantiled. Now used as a store.

Tollhouse, NT350730, late 18th to early 19th century. A single-storey rubble cottage, with bowed ends and a central arched entrance, now converted to a window.

NEWBATTLE

Newbattle Mill (paper), Newtongrange, NT326648, founded 1795. A 3-storey, 10-bay main block, with outbuildings.

Dalhousie Viaduct, Newtongrange, NT325650–NT329648, opened 1849 by the Edinburgh & Hawick Railway. A 23-span viaduct, with brick arch rings, and coursed-rubble piers and spandrels. The last arch at the southern end is a skew road arch with a masonry arch ring.

Lady Victoria Colliery, Newtongrange, NT333636, sunk 1890–4 by the Lothian Coal Co Ltd (plate 49). The surface buildings here are extensive and are steel-framed, with brick cladding or infilling. There is a very fine steam winding engine, built by GRANT, RITCHIE & CO LTD, Kilmarnock in 1894, with 3ft 6in by 7ft (1·06 by 2·13m) cylinders and Cornish drop valves. This is supplied with steam by a bank of 7 Lancashire boilers. There is a tall circular-section brick chimney.

Lingerwood Brickworks, NT337637, early 20th century. The overgrown remains of a regenerative kiln, with a tall circular-section brick chimney.

Lingerwood Colliery, NT337635, sunk 1798. This colliery was closed in 1967, but one shaft, 'Dickson's Pit', is retained for access to Lady Victoria Pit. This has an electric winder made by FULLERTON, HODGART & BARCLAY of Paisley. The steam winder formerly used here, a Corliss and drop valve engine, survives in derelict condition, as do most of the surface buildings.

PENICUIK

Penicuik Station, NT238598, opened 1872 by the Penicuik Railway. A single-platform terminal station, with a 1-storey, 13-bay, red-and-white-brick building. Adjacent to this is a medium-sized goods shed of similar construction. Closed.

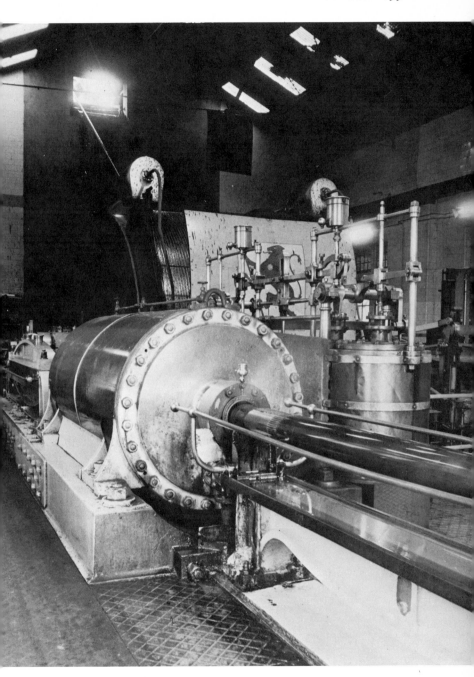

49 Winding engine, Lady Victoria Colliery, Newtongrange.

Valleyfield Paper Mills, NT238598, founded 1708. A large complex of buildings of various dates, with a tall circular-section brick chimney. Closed July 1975.

PORTOBELLO

Portobello Pottery, NT304742, founded *c* 1879. Formerly a complex of 1- and 2-storey brick and rubble buildings, some with pantiled roofs. The buildings have been demolished, leaving the 2 bottle kilns, dated 1906 and 1909, which are to be preserved as free-standing monuments.

RATHO

Ratho Station, NT133722, opened 1842 by the Edinburgh & Glasgow Railway. Formerly a 2-platform through station. The up-platform building, a single-storey structure, on a U plan, still survives.

Peeblesshire

Peeblesshire is almost entirely rural, but the towns of Peebles and Innerleithen are significant outposts of the Border woollen industry.

EDDLESTON

Bridge, Eddleston, NT242721, early 19th century. A single-segmental arch, with dressed-stone arch ring and rubble spandrels.

Eddleston Station, NT241471, opened 1855 by the Peebles Railway. Formerly a 2-platform through station, with the main building on the down platform. This, a wooden single-storey structure, is preserved in a railway enthusiast's garden. The neat 1-storey station house, with its projecting porch, also survives.

Railway bridge, Earlypier, NT244500, opened 1855 by the Peebles Railway. A single, slightly bowed, iron-plate girder span.

INNERLEITHEN

Viaduct, over Tweed, Horsbrugh, NT299391, opened 1864 by the North British Railway. A 5-span viaduct, with slightly bowed plate girders on masonry piers.

Road bridge, over Tweed, Innerleithen, NT333360, mid 19th century. A 4-span bridge, with slightly bowed steel trusses on masonry piers. At the Walkerburn end a small semicircular arch spans a lade.

INNERLEITHEN

Caerlee Mill, NT332370, built c 1788–90 by Alexander Brodie and subsequently extended. The main structure here is a 4-storey, 2-by-16-bay block, with single-storey weaving sheds and ancillary buildings. The first 'modern' woollen mill in the county.

Innerleithen Station, NT332363, opened 1864 by the North British Railway. Formerly a 2-platform through station. The main building is on the down platform – 2 storey, 3 bay with a 1-storey wing, and a projecting platform awning. Now a dwellinghouse.

Rosebank Mill, NT334364, mid 19th century. A complex of buildings, with a 3-storey main block and a very typical 9-bay block of weaving sheds. There is a tall circular-section chimney.

St Ronan's Mill, NT335379, built 1846 by George Roberts & Son, of Selkirk, architects ROBERT HALL & CO, Galashiels (plate 50). The main building is a 3-storey and attic, 2-by-11-bay rubble building, with dressed quoins, with the site of a large waterwheel at the north end. Beyond this is a more recent 2-storey, 2-by-11-bay block. Behind the main block are single-storey engine and boiler houses with a circular-section brick chimney on a stone base. To the south of the main block, and also across the road, are 1-storey stores. Water supply to the wheel, and to a later turbine, was by a high-level lade, which still flows. Now disused. The mill was designed for wool-spinning.

Old Bridge, NT333372, built 1701. A small single-segmental arched rubble bridge with a hump.

Bridge, over Tweed, Walkerburn, NT361368, mid to late 19th century. A 4-span bridge, with bowed steel trusses on masonry piers (except one, which consists of 2 circular riveted steel piers linked by cross bracing).

Ballantyne's Mill, Walkerburn, NT360371, founded 1855. A large

50   St Ronan's Mill, Innerleithen.

complex of buildings, the oldest of which appears to be a 4-storey, 8-bay block with a castellated clock tower. The rest are mainly 2 storeys in height. There is a fine octagonal brick chimney with a flared top. (See *Industrial Archaeology*, 1972, 9, 432.)

KILBUCHO, BROUGHTON & GLENHOLM

Rachan Mill, NT114344, early 19th century and later. A 2-storey rubble building, with a water turbine at the rear fed by a deep wooden flume. The rotor of the turbine is horizontally mounted, with a wrought-iron pulley for belt drive to the mill. Now disused.

KIRKURD

Sawmill, Blyth Bridge, NT131448, early 19th century. A single-storey rubble building, with a wooden extension. The overshot wheel, about 4ft 6in wide by 14ft diameter (1·37 by 4·27m), has been removed.

LINTON

Bakery, West Linton, NT150518, mid to late 19th century. A 2-storey-front building with a one-storey and attic bakehouse at the rear. Now converted to a tea room. The 2 brick 'Scotch ovens' and implements have been retained as 'features'.
Limekiln, Macbiehill, NT184522, probably early 19th century. A large 2-draw kiln on a rectangular plan, with semicircular arched draw holes. Extensive limeworkings in the vicinity.
Weaving Village, Carlops, NT161560, founded 1784 by Robert Brown of Newhall. Two ranges of single-storey harled cottages, one of 4 houses, the other of 6, and a 2-storey block of 4 houses. The Allan Ramsay Hotel, a 2-storey, 8-bay building which may have been a wool store, dates from 1792.

LYNE

Bridge over Lyne, NT202404, probably early 19th century. A 4-span bridge, with 2 main segmental arched spans, and one semi-circular arch on each side. The arch rings of the main spans are of dressed stone, the remainder of the construction is rubble.

MANOR

Kirkton Manor Mill, NT221379, late 18th or early 19th century. A substantial 3-storey rubble building on an L plan, with an additional bay added to 1 arm of the L. There is an all-iron, 6-spoke, high-breast bucket wheel, 4ft wide by 14ft diameter (1·22 by 4·27m), driving 2 pairs of stones.

Kirkton Manor Smithy, NT221379, built *c* 1800 and subsequently extended (plate 51). A picturesque single-storey rubble building, with large square-section chimney stack. Now disused.

NEWLANDS

Blyth Bridge, NT132452, built 1819. A single-segmental arch, with dressed-stone arch ring and rubble spandrels.

Blyth Mill, Blyth Bridge, NT132453, built 1817. A 2-storey rubble building on an L plan, with an 8-spoke, low-breast shrouded paddle-wheel with wooden spokes and paddles and iron axle and rings, 4ft wide by 15ft 6 in diameter (1·22 by 4·72m). The building has been converted to an inn, and the wheel has been retained as a feature.

Romanno Bridge, NT159480, built 1774. A 3-span bridge, with a large segmental arch and 2 much smaller, 1 spanning a lade. The main span has a dressed-stone arch ring and a dentilated string course. The nearby tollhouse is a simple 3-bay building, and dates from *c* 1830.

51 Kirkton Manor Smithy.

Mill, Romanno Bridge, NT161481, probably early 19th century. A 2-storey and attic, 7-bay rubble building, with a 2-storey, 3-bay dwellinghouse attached. Now converted to an annexe to the nearby hotel.

PEEBLES

Farm chimney, Edderston Farm, NT241394, mid 19th century. A circular-section brick chimney on a square stone base, with engine and boiler house attached.

Manor Bridge, NT229394, built 1881–3. A graceful 5-span bridge, with flat segmental arches on slender piers with rounded cutwaters. The arch rings are of dressed stone and the spandrels of snecked rubble.

Manor Water Bridge, NT232394, built 1702 by the Earl of March. A single narrow segmental rubble arch, with a pronounced hump.

Viaduct, Neidpath, NT233402, opened 1864 by the Symington, Biggar & Broughton Railway. A superb 7-span curved skew viaduct in a magnificent setting. The construction is similar to that at Lyne Station (*qv*).

PEEBLES

Ballantyne's Mill, NT250408, mid 19th century. A large group of single-storey weaving sheds. At a lower level is a detached 10-bay block of weaving sheds.

Footbridge, NT252407, mid 19th century. A very light truss bridge, with inverted king-post bracing supported on cast-iron columns.

Suspension footbridge, NT253403, late 19th century. A curved truss span supported by wire-rope cables supported on lattice-girder pylons.

Tweed Bridge, NT251403, late 15th century, widened 1834 and 1900. A 5-span masonry bridge. The original structure has almost semicircular arches – the widened parts have flatter segmental arches. The dolphin lamp standards from the 1900 widening have been retained.

Woollen mill, NT253406. The older part (1883) is a 2-storey block, on an L plan with a 3-storey, 3-by-1-bay terminal. This was extended in 1910 by a 3-storey, 12-bay building with a corner oriel with an ogival cap. Behind these frontages is a single-storey weaving shed.

STOBO

Bridge, over Lyne, Drochhill, NT163429, late 18th or early 19th century. A single-segmental arch, with a much smaller arch over a lade. The arch ring on the larger span is of dressed stone, with rubble spandrels.

Bridge, over Lyne, NT186407, late 18th or early 19th century. A slightly hump-backed bridge with a single rubble segmental arch.

Bridge, Lyne Station, NT209401, late 18th or early 19th century. A 2-span rubble bridge, with segmental arches of unequal size, the smaller being a flood arch.

Viaduct, Lyne Station, NT209400, opened 1864 by the Symington, Biggar & Broughton Railway. A handsome 3-arch masonry skew viaduct, with a plate-girder approach span over a minor road. The arches are elliptical, with slender piers with rounded cutwaters, from which pilasters extend to parapet level. Neat cast-iron railings.

Stobo Station, NT170359, opened 1864 by the Symington, Biggar & Broughton Railway. Formerly a 2-platform through station, with the main building on the down platform. This is a single-storey snecked rubble building, now converted to a dwellinghouse. There is also a substantial rubble goods shed.

Smithy, Stobo, NT170359, early 19th century. A neat 3-bay, single-storey rubble building, with small-paned windows, and, unusually, a small louvred roof ventilator. Now converted to a house.

TRAQUAIR

Railway viaduct, Haughhead, NT341367, opened 1866 by the North British Railway. A 6-span viaduct on a skew, with slightly bowed plate girders on masonry piers.

Scots Mill, NT274393, built 1802. A 2-storey and attic rubble building on an L plan with a large pyramidal-roofed kiln forming 1 arm of the L. Immediately adjacent to the mill is a 2-storey granary of similar construction. The machinery has now been removed. The mill cottage, across the road, is a notable example of the Gothic 'cottage ornée' style of architecture.

Brewhouse, Traquair House, NT331354. Consists of 2 rooms in a service block built *c* 1700, 1 containing boiler, mash tub and 2 cooling trays, and the other with 3 fermenting tuns. Still used occasionally.

Walkerburn Station, NT361368, opened 1866 by the North British Railway. Formerly a 2-platform through station, with the main building on the up platform. This is a single-storey rubble building with a wooden-platform front and cantilevered awning, of typical North British Railway pattern. There is a substantial rubble goods shed, with an awning for road traffic.

Renfrewshire

Renfrewshire in the early nineteenth century was the cotton capital of Scotland, and its major town, Paisley, still has an important thread industry. Its other industrial towns – Greenock, Port Glasgow, Johnstone, Barrhead and the village of Neilston – had varied industries, including textiles, but also engineering, shipbuilding, linen-thread making, and rope-making. Johnstone was the machine-tool manufacturing centre of Scotland, and Port Glasgow houses its most productive shipyards. Communications are of local importance only, though Greenock is a port of national stature.

ABBEY

Glenpatrick Carpet Works, Elderslie, NS445623, built as a paper mill 1815, converted to carpet manufacture *c* 1860. The oldest parts of the complex are a 3-storey, 6-by-9-bay block and a 15-bay block of single-storey weaving sheds.

Cartside Mill, Milliken Park, NS415625, built *c* 1790. One of the finest surviving early Scottish cotton mills, a 6-storey and attic, 20-bay rubble building, with margins. On the south frontage are 2 semi-octagonal bays, and on the north, in the same position, are Palladian windows. Internally, slender cast-iron columns support longitudinal wooden beams, which support cross beams and wooden floors. Now houses paper-coating machines with festoon dryers. There was originally a central waterwheel, later replaced by a turbine, which is now removed. The lade, however, is maintained to provide process water. At the rear is a 2-storey and attic, 27-bay block, and in front a more modern 3-storey, 6-by-14-bay, flat-roofed brick block.

JOHNSTONE

Empress Works, NS432633, built early 19th century as a cotton mill, rebuilt mid 19th century as engineering works. A 2-storey, 3-bay, coursed-rubble office block, a 3-storey and attic, 4-by-10-bay block, now a pattern shop and store, and a block of single-storey engineering shops. The 3-storey and attic block has a wall crane.

Johnstone High Station, NS433629, opened 1840 by the Glasgow,

Paisley, Kilmarnock & Ayr Railway, rebuilt *c* 1890. A 2-platform through station, with the main offices on the up platform in a 1- and 2-storey sandstone range. There was formerly a wooden platform shelter on the down side, and a glazed awning on the up side. These have been removed, as has the glazed cover of the plate-girder footbridge.

Bootlace factory, NS423633, founded mid 19th century by William Paton. The 'Old End', built as Corse, Burns and Co's cotton mill in 1782, is a 6-storey, 9-bay rubble building, the ground-floor windows of which have been enlarged, and similar windows inserted in the gable. At the base of the gable is the circular hole for the waterwheel shaft. From this period, a range of 2-storey stores, with an arched cart entry, also survives. The more modern part is a 5-storey and attic, 6-by-12-bay building, with a water-tower with a balustraded top. There are several smaller outbuildings, and a large circular-section brick chimney. The 'Old End' has wooden cross beams, strengthened by longitudinal sections supported on cast-iron columns. The newer part has cast-iron columns supporting wooden beams and floors.

Cotton mills, late 18th and early 19th century. Johnstone had a large number of cotton mills, mainly spinning. Apart from those noticed separately, the following survive: New Mill (NS430634), 2-storey and attic, 9-bay (stone) and 8-bay (brick) blocks; at NS431633, a 2-storey and attic, 4-by-13-bay, red-and-white-brick block; at NS429634, a 2-storey, 11-bay, red-and-white-brick building; and Laigh Mill (NS428635) a 2-storey and attic, 16-bay structure, now a tyre store.

Engineering works, NS433635, built *c* 1897 by John Lang and Co, machine-tool makers. A range of 11 bays of single-storey brick workshops. A model machine-tool factory of its day.

Foundry, NS430632, founded 1816 by Robert Donald. A group of single-storey moulding shops, incorporating rubble buildings from the early 19th-century and mid to late 19th-century brick buildings.

Linen-thread mill, NS425634, founded 1849 by Finlayson, Bousfield and Co, but incorporating earlier structures. The oldest building in this large complex is a 3-storey and attic, 2-by-23-bay structure, with jack-arch interior. Across the river is a 4-storey, 4-by-22-bay rubble building, with the end 3 bays at each end projecting to the rear. There is a small square tower at one corner, and a tall red-brick engine house with round-headed windows. Behind the old block is a group of red-and-white-brick buildings, with a square tower, and a tall circular-section chimney. The main office range was 2 storeys high, with a central 8-bay block with a cart entry. The complex is now in multiple occupation.

EAGLESHAM

Millhall, NS584512, late 18th century. The cut-down remains of a small cotton mill, now 2 storey and basement, 2 by 5 bay, with a Belfast roof. There is a fine masonry arch dam about 25ft (7·72m) high, with the truncated iron flume for a water turbine emerging from the base.

EASTWOOD

Thornliebank Village, NS547596, founded 1778 by John Crum. Though the great print works here has been demolished, some of the 2-storey rows of houses, with external stairways, built by the Crum family in the mid 19th century, still survive. In Rouken Glen Park, at NS547587, is a tall arch dam impounding water for the works, now a picturesque feature.

GREENOCK

Glebe Sugar Refinery, NS276768, founded on this site in 1831. A 5-storey, red-and-white-brick, flat-roofed building, with a rounded front and round-headed windows. The bays are separated by pilasters. Now a store.

Greenock Central Station, NS283759, built 1889 for the Caledonian Railway. A 4-platform station, with 2 through platforms and a double bay at the east end. The station is on a sloping site. The main offices are on the up platform, in a single-storey building with Gothic features. The main frontage has 5 arched openings, 1 now blocked up. There are substantial glazed awnings over both platforms.

Fort Matilda Station, NS257775, built 1889 for the Caledonian Railway, architect JAMES MILLER. A 2-platform through station, with the main offices on the up platform, in a single-storey brick building with 3 gables to the street, and an integral awning with glazed side-screens.

Shaws Water Mill, Greenock, NS272753, founded 1840 by Fleming, Reid & Co. A large group of red-brick buildings, the oldest being a handsome 6-storey, 22-bay block, built in 1881. The 2-storey gate-house with its clock tower is also pleasing. The mill was sited to derive its power from the Shaws Water Works, and still uses water turbines.

Shaws Water Works, built 1825–7, engineer ROBERT THOM. A remarkable system of open cuts constructed to supply Greenock with water for domestic and industrial use for power. The main line of the cut is from the principal reservoir, Loch Thom (NS2672), to Upper Greenock (NS267748). There the cut splits into two. Other cuts at the west end link Loch Thom with other reservoirs, and streams on the route add to the supply. There are several small rubble accommodation bridges over the cut. No longer used for water supply, but preserved by the Lower Clyde Water Board.

Bonded Warehouse No 15, Kerr Street and Clarence Street, NS277766, late 19th century. A 7-storey, 6-by-11-bay, red-and-white-brick block, with a dentilated cornice.

Custom House, NS283762, built 1818, architect WILLIAM BURN. A 2-storey and attic, 6-by-13-bay building on a U plan. There are pedimented tetrastyle Doric porticoes on the north and east faces, and pilastered corner features.

Drydock, NS288758, built 1810 by Scott and Son. A small masonry dry dock, still in use, now the oldest on the Clyde. The adjoining shipyard has some much-altered 19th-century buildings.

Engine works, NS288756, founded 1845 by John Hastie and Son. The oldest block here is a tall single-storey, cast-iron-framed red-and-white-brick building, 2-by-12-bay block, with round-headed windows and small rectangular windows above.

Joinery works, Dellingburn Street, NS283756, late 19th century, for John Drummond and Sons. A 3-storey, 4-by-7-bay, red-and-white-brick building on an L plan, with Belfast roof and a circular turnpike stair in the angle of the L. There is a square-section brick chimney.

Sugar refineries, NS278753 (Westburn) and NS275763 (Walker's). Westburn refinery was damaged by bombing during the Second World War, and partly rebuilt, but some classic red-brick, 6- and 7-storey blocks remain. Walker's complex includes a very fine red-and-white-brick, 8-storeys, 8-bay block, as well as other smaller buildings of late 19th-century date.

Sugar refinery, Roxburgh Street and Sir Michael Street, NS276763, mid 19th century. A 6-storey and attic, 6-by-6-bay rubble block with a 3-storey and attic store. Now a warehouse.

Tobacco Bond, Hood Street and Clarence Street, NS277766, late 19th century. A 5-storey and attic, 6-by-10-bay, red-and-white-brick building, with 4 arched cart entries, now blocked up, pilasters between the bays, and a dentilated cornice.

Warehouses There are several late 18th to early 19th-century warehouses in the east end of Greenock. Perhaps the best are: at

NS283759, a long 4-storey and attic rubble building, with a 3-bay, gabled street frontage; at NS287757, a 5-storey, 4-bay ashlar block; at NS284759 a 3-storey and attic, 3-by-5-bay rubble structure, now disused; at NS286757, a 3-storey and 2 attic, 6-bay rubble building and a 4-storey and attic, 5-bay block, and at NS283759 (Bogle Street), a 5-storey and attic, 6-bay rubble block.

Warehouse No 4, East India Harbour, NS285759, late 19th century. A large 5-storey and attic, 4-by-11-bay, red-and-white-brick building with segmental-arched windows. The bays are separated by slightly projecting piers.

Victoria Harbour, NS287759, built 1846–50, engineer JOSEPH LOCKE. A rectangular basin formed by a pier shared with the East India Harbour, south and east quays, and two short piers at the seaward side. On the south quay is a single-storey, 3-bay hydraulic pumping station with a 3-storey accumulator tower, now disused, and on the north quay is a 1-by-10-bay transit shed. The works are all ashlar.

Steamboat Quay, NS283763, built 1788, rebuilt and extended 1809–18. A stretch of quay, with a wood-piled frontage, facing the river. At the east end is the 2-storey, 3-by-4-bay waiting- and refreshment-room block (now offices) with 4 oriel windows at first-floor level on the seaward side. On the west side is a 17-by-2-bay, iron-framed wooden transit shed, with an ornamental facade, and a 2-storey and attic, 4-by-4-bay, iron-framed, red-and-white-brick building, with round-headed windows. Dated 1859, this is the earliest dated red-and-white-brick building in Scotland known to the author. Another feature is the cast-iron column supporting a clock and a lantern, made by RANKINE AND BLACKMORE. A westernly extension is known as the West Pier (NS282763), with a similar iron-framed, transit shed, 2-by-20 bay.

East India Harbour, NS285760, built 1805, engineer JOHN RENNIE, A rectangular basin, with a dry dock off the west end. The quay faces are partly masonry, partly wood-piled. On the north quay is a single-storey, iron-framed, wood-clad transit shed. Now used mainly for laying up ships.

James Watt Dock, NS297757, 1879–86, engineer W. R. KINIPPLE. A roughly rectangular gated basin, with a short pier at the east end giving additional berthage. Along the south quay is a fine range of red-and-white-brick warehouses, with two 5 storey and attic, 7-bay blocks, with central hoists, and two 3-storey and attic, one 9 bays, the other 11. The lower buildings have ridged roofs, with circular windows in the attics. Immediately adjacent to the north are the Great Harbour (1880 on) and the Garvel Graving Dock (1871), engineer W. R. KINIPPLE.

HOUSTON

BRIDGE OF WEIR

Bridge of Weir Station, NS391653, opened 1869 by the Greenock & Ayrshire Railway. A 2-platform through station, with the main offices on the up platform in a low single-storey, 10-bay rubble building.

Gryfe Tannery, NS385658, late 19th century. The main block here is a 5-storey, 4-by-9-bay brick structure, and there is a large complex of 1- and 2-storey buildings of various dates. On the site of High Gryfe Cotton Mill (1792).

Leather works, NS389656, late 19th century, for the Bridge of Weir Leather Co. A 3-storey, 4-by-12-bay, brick building, with a similar 5-bay structure at right angles. There is a circular-section brick chimney. In a retaining wall beside the river is the base of Laigh Gryfe cotton mill (1793) with the cast-iron bearing box for a large waterwheel. Upsteam, at NS385657, is a similar, but larger, building on the site of Gryfe Grove and Shanks's Mills.

Viaduct, NS384658, opened 1869 by the Greenock & Ayrshire Railway. A 5-span skew viaduct, with segmental arches. The arch rings are dressed stone, the spandrels coursed rubble. At the south end is an approach span over a minor road.

INCHINNAN

Aircraft factory, NS474684, built 1916 for William Beardmore and Co Ltd. This large complex was converted to a rubber factory in the 1930s, and the airship shed, which housed the famous R34, demolished. The largest surviving structure is a tall 3-bay, steel-framed, brick-clad block.

INVERKIP

Gasworks, Ardgowan, NS218732, mid 19th century. Two single-storey buildings, now derelict. The former retort house has a 3-bay pedimented frontage with a circular ventilator in the tympanum. The stone edge of a circular holder tank can be discerned.

Cloch Lighthouse, NS203758, built 1797 (plate 52). A short circular-section tower, with corbelled walkway and triangular windows. There appear to be two generations of keepers' houses, the older now used as stores, the more recent having crow-stepped gables.

GOUROCK

Gourock Pier and Station, NS243779, opened 1889 by the Caledonian Railway. A long pier, with wood-piled frontage. The station is parallel to the pier, and is typical of Caledonian Railway design of the period, brick and harl, with wood trimming.

Gourock Ropeworks, NS244773, built 1771. A 3-storey and attic, 5-bay block, now much altered, harled, and used as an ex-servicemen's club.

Boat shed, NS242779, early 19th century. A small 1-storey and attic rubble building, probably predating the railway. Now used as a store.

Tollhouse, NS254775, mid 19th century. An attractive 1-storey and attic rubble building with a projecting porch. There are finials on the angles of the porch and at the ends of the front. The attic window in the west gable is Gothic.

Dunrod Farm, NS223732, early 19th century. A 2-storey and attic

52 Cloch Lighthouse, Inverkip.

rubble building, part of the steading, with an 8-spoke, braced, all-iron overshot wheel, about 2ft wide by 10ft diameter (0·61 by 3·05m), disused, but in fair condition. Apparently drove a threshing mill, now removed.

Wemyss Bay Station and Pier, NS193685, rebuilt 1903 by the Caledonian Railway, architect JAMES MILLER, and engineer DONALD MATHIESON. Noted as one of the finest stations of its period. A platform terminus, with glazed awnings over the platform. There is a circular booking office, with steel ribs radiating from it to support a curved glazed roof. The approach from the street is through a single-storey, stone and harl building with a clock tower in similar style. There is a gently sloping ramp to the pier, with glazed sides and roof.

KILBARCHAN

Locher Printworks, Bridge of Weir, NS395646, established 1780–90. An interesting group of 1- and 2-storey buildings, mainly 19th and early 20th century. The oldest appears to be a 2-storey and attic, 8-bay block with a semicircular stair tower projecting from one gable, probably c 1820–30. Now a tannery. Nearby are some old 1-storey and attic cottages.

Handloom weaver's cottage, NS401632, built 1723 for a linen weaver and draper. A 2-storey and attic rubble building, with irregular fenestration, restored by the National Trust for Scotland, and open to the public. There is a handloom, on which demonstrations of weaving are made.

Weaving shop, NS402633, early 19th century. A neat 2-storey, 6-bay rubble building, with a brick chimney stack. An external stone stair gives access to the upper floor. There were several handloom shops of this pattern in Kilbarchan: this is the best preserved.

Linwood Paper Mill, NS444645, early 19th century and later. Embedded in this large complex is a section of the once large Linwood Cotton Mill, a rubble structure with cast-iron window frames.

LOCHWINNOCH

Garthland Bridge, Howwood, NS394607, built 1767. A handsome single-segmental arch, built entirely of dressed stone.

Midtownfield Bleachworks, Howwood, NS407603, founded 1835 by John McNab. A range of 1- and 2-storey brick buildings, with a 2-storey, 21-bay frontage. Now disused.

Mill, Howwood, NS408612, early 19th century. A 2-storey rubble building on an L plan, now converted to a dwellinghouse and office.

Lochside Station, NS360579, opened 1840 by the Glasgow, Paisley, Kilmarnock & Ayr Railway. A 2-platform through station, with the main offices on the up platform, in a single-storey rubble building on a T plan. The platforms are linked by a lattice-girder footbridge. At the up end of the station is an elliptical arched overbridge of standard GPK & A design.

LOCHWINNOCH

Burnfoot Bleachfield, NS348589, late 18th century and later. A complex of 1- and 2-storey rubble and brick buildings, the largest being a 2-storey and attic, 7-bay, red-brick structure and a 3-storey and attic, 3-by-4-bay rubble building. Latterly used as a barrel store, after a period as a silk-printing works.

Calder Cabinet and Chair Works, NS350588, built 1880 for James Hunter and Sons. A 3-storey and attic brick block, on an L plan, with a small square-section brick chimney. Now out of use.

Calderbank Bleachfield, NS350600, early 19th century. A group of 1-, 2- and 3-storey rubble buildings, some ruinous. The largest intact part is a 2-storey, 2-bay and a 2-storey, 3-bay range, now used as a store, and there are the roofless remains of a 2-storey, 5-bay building. In private grounds.

Calderhaugh Mill, NS350588, built 1789. A 4-storey and attic, 11-bay rubble building, cut down from a longer building. At the rear is a 2-storey engine and boiler house, with the stump of a square-section brick chimney. There is also a range of single-storey weaving sheds. Now a silk-weaving factory.

Weir and lade, Calderpark Mill, NS348594, built *c* 1790 by Henston, Burns and Co. The arch dam, 19ft 8in (5·99m) high by 85ft (25·90m) circumference (OSA) is a very early example of the type and is well preserved, as is the now disused lade.

Lochhead Cabinet Works, NS352587, probably 1880s. A group of 2-storey and attic, red-brick buildings, with a small circular-section chimney. Now a cooperage.

Meikle Millbank Mill, NS340574, late 18th to early 19th century. A 2-storey and attic building on a T plan, with the kiln forming the down stroke of the T. There were 2 pairs of stones, driven by an internal 8-spoke overshot wheel, with wooden spokes and buckets, and iron rings and axle, 3ft 6in (1·06m) wide by 19ft (5·79m) diameter. Now much decayed.

Viewfield Cabinet and Chair Works, NS351588, built 1887 for Joseph Johnstone. Two 3-storey and attic, yellow-brick buildings round a courtyard with a 6-storey stair and water-tower. Now a cooperage.

Bridge, NS354584, early 19th century. A handsome 3-span bridge built entirely of dressed stone, with segmental arches and rounded cutwaters. The side arches are smaller than the centre one.

Smithy, NS349587, early to mid 19th century. A 1-storey and attic rubble building, with a single-storey extension. Still in use.

Weavers' cottages, NS349587, late 18th to early 19th century. A range of 1- and 2-storey rubble cottages, several with the characteristic double window.

Dam, Roebank Print Works, NS359553, early 19th century. The remains of a small arched masonry dam, all that survives of this once-extensive site.

MEARNS

Netherplace Bleachworks, NS521557, 18th century. A complex of buildings of various dates, mostly 2 storey. Until 1970, there was an electricity-generating station with 4 high-speed engines, 1 of which is now preserved by Glasgow Museums. Most of the machinery is now modern.

Patterton Station, NS537577, opened 1903 by the Lanarkshire & Ayrshire Railway. A 2-platform through station, with the main offices on the up platform, in a single-storey, brick and wood building with a bracketted awning and glazed side-screens. The down-platform building is similar but smaller.

Pilmuir Mill, NS517544, early 19th century. A rectangular 2-storey and attic rubble building, with a brick lean-to extension, and a brick wheelhouse. The axle only of a large overshot wheel survives. Now derelict.

Lower Mills, Busby, NS578567, founded c 1780. The 4-storey, 19-bay rubble main mill was burned out in 1968, but some of the smaller buildings survive.

NEILSTON

Barrhead Station, NS499593, opened 1847 by the Glasgow, Barrhead & Neilston Direct Railway. A 2-platform through station on an elevated site. The main offices are on the down (now up) side, in a 2-storey, coursed-rubble building, and the up-platform building is similar but smaller. Both buildings have wooden bracketted awnings, at platform level, and have flat gabled roofs with prominent eaves.

Cross Arthurlie Mill, Barrhead, NS498588, built 1790. A 3-storey and attic, 19-bay rubble building with 4 sanitary towers on 1 side and 1 on the other. Internally there are wooden beams and floors supported on cast-iron columns.

West Arthurlie Bleachworks, Barrhead, NS497587, founded 1773. A group of 2- and 3-storey buildings, now harled, the largest being a 3-storey and attic, 4-by-13-bay block. Now a skinnery.

NEILSTON

Broadlie Cotton Mill, NS477577, built 1790. A 3-storey, 2-by-10-bay rubble building, with a circular-stair tower at one end. The top floor was damaged by fire in 1970 and a fourth storey added during reconstruction. The route of the high-level lade which supplied this site can still be traced. Now a leather works.

Crofthead Cotton Mill, NS473574, founded 1792, mid to late 19th century in its present form. A group of multistorey buildings, the largest of which is a 6-storey, 15-by-8-bay, flat-roofed block, with a tall engine house with round-headed windows. There is also a 5-storey, 19-bay range. Now a thread mill.

Gateside Cotton Mill, NS489583, built 1786 (see plate 4). Two 4-storey and attic rubble blocks, one 18-bay, the other 14-bay, with various smaller buildings. Now a waterproofing works.

Housing, NS474569, mid 19th century. A group of single-storey brick rows of 3-roomed cottages, built in connection with Crofthead Cotton Mill.

Skew Bridge, Gateside Mill, NS487582, opened 1847 by the Glasgow Barrhead & Neilston Direct Railway, engineer NEIL ROBSON. A single-segmental span, with dressed-stone arch ring and parapets and rubble spandrels.

PAISLEY

Abbey Bridge, NS485638, built 1878–9. A 2-span, wrought-iron bridge, with cast-iron ornamental facing panels and railings. There are semicircular cutwaters, extended up to support lamp standards.

Abercorn Rope Works, Clark Street, NS463649, founded 1884 by Jas. Picken. A 2-storey, 4-bay ashlar office block, with a single-storey brick ropewalk still in use, and a finishing shed. The machinery in the ropewalk appears to be original.

Anchor Mills, Seedhill, NS490635, founded 1812 by J. and J. Clark. The main 5-storey, red-brick Atlantic and Pacific Mills were demolished in 1972–3. These fine buildings were built in 1872 (spinning) and 1878 (twisting) respectively. A central tower linking the 2 was added in 1886. The main surviving buildings are now the 5-storey, 18-by-16-bay spool shop, and the 6-storey, 8-by-18-bay Mile End block, with its two towers (1899–1900, W. J. MORLEY of Bradford, architect). The 2 enormous chimneys also survive. One of the more interesting smaller buildings is the 3-storey and attic L-plan 8-by-18-bay rubble 'Old Embroidery' block, which was a shawl factory before Anchor Mills were founded.

Blackhall Factory (silk throwing), Blackhall Street, NS489633, founded c 1848 by David Speirs and Co. Two parallel, 4-storey and attic, red-brick buildings, one 4-by-13 bay, the other 3-by-13 bay, with a brick water-tower with a crown.

Blacklandmill Bleachworks, Park Road, NS475620, founded c 1830. A group of mainly 1-storey brick buildings, with a 2-storey, 6-bay block. There is a circular-section brick chimney. Now a whisky-bottling plant.

Caledonia Works, McDowall Street, NS477646, founded 1868 by A. F. Craig. A large complex of red-brick and corrugated-iron-clad steel buildings, incorporating the original works of 1868. The light machine shop and fitting shop are in a 2-storey, 37-bay block, and there is an 11-bay heavy machine shop, lit at 2 levels by round-headed windows. At the other end of this group is the L-plan foundry, part steel-framed, with a 3-storey, 5-bay frontage. At the rear is a large steel-framed fitting shop dating from 1910, built by SIR WILLIAM ARROL & CO. On the other side of the street are the much-altered single-storey boiler shops.

Carlile Quay, New Sneddon Street, NS484647, built 1836–40. A small rubble quay, on an L plan, with the remains of a post crane (1827) and a cobbled cart track. Both the quay and the small basin it forms are badly overgrown. At the south end is a Scherzer rolling-lift footbridge, built 1911 by SIR WILLIAM ARROL & CO. The mechanism was removed c 1942.

Ferguslie Mills, Maxwellton Road, NS467634, founded 1826 by James Coats (plate 53). A very large complex of buildings of various dates. The oldest block is roughly on an E plan, with magnificent 4-storey and attic, 43-by-44-bay frontages. In the centre of each front is a 3-storey engine house, that in the north front being pedimented, formerly with a bellcote. The end bays (5 in 3 cases, 4 in the other) are extended up by another storey. The other 2 wings of the E are formed by a beautiful 2-storey and basement, 3-by-5-bay engine house, and by a 4-storey, 13-bay harled building. The complex was built between 1826 and 1858. Of the other buildings the most im-

53   No 1 engine house, Ferguslie Mills.

pressive are No 1 Spinning Mill (1887), a 5-storey, 14-by-33-bay building in French Renaissance style, designed by WOODHOUSE AND MORLEY of Bradford, and No 8 Mill, a similar, but simpler building, 29 bays long, built 1890. Also of interest are: the west gatehouse, with a large and ornate glazed fanlight and hydraulic gates (1858); a stretch of the Glasgow, Paisley & Ardrossan Canal (the last surviving part), with 2 semicircular-arched overbridges; and the remarkably ornate half-time school (1887), architects WOODHOUSE and MORLEY.

Greenhill Oil Works, Murray Street, NS475647, founded 1880 by Hugh Highgate and Co, oil refiners. Two reinforced-concrete-framed blocks, with curved roofs, one 2-storey, 2-by-6-bay, the other 4-storey, 3-by-6-bay, and 2 older 2 storey and attic, red-brick blocks, also with curved roofs.

Paisley Gas Works, Well Street, NS472643, founded 1827. A complex group of buildings. The most interesting features are a 2-storey, 3-bay building, probably the original manager's house, a 3-storey, 9-bay building, with round-headed windows, and 1 of the gas-holders, which has cast-iron columns.

Paisley Harbour, East Road, NS483653, built 1891. A widened part of th(White Cart Water, with coursed-rubble quay walls on both sides of the river, and brick transit sheds. Now closed and becoming derelict.

Paisley (Canal) Station, Causeyside Street, NS482634, opened 1885 by the Glasgow & South Western Railway. A 2-platform through station in a cutting (on the course of the Glasgow, Paisley & Ardrossan Canal), with offices in a single-storey wooden building, on an overbridge, with an attractive glazed frontage. There is also a substantial 1- and 2-storey block on the up platform, with an awning supported on steel joists.

Paisley (Gilmour Street) Station, NS483642, built c 1840 for the Glasgow & Paisley Joint Railway, and extended in c 1890. A 4-platform through station, raised on masonry arches. The main offices are in the original 2-storey, 10-bay castellated building on the down side. The platforms are covered for most of their length by glazed awnings supported by lattice trusses, of which alternate ones run from wall to wall with a central cast-iron support. The platform buildings are wooden, on sandstone bases.

Royal Starch Works, Falside Road, NS481623, founded 1856 by Brown and Polson, rebuilt early 20th century. Much of this large complex has been demolished, but the red-and-white-brick front blocks remain. These are 3-storey, 13-bay; 4-storey, 4-bay; 3-storey and attic, 10-bay; and 3-storey, 13-bay.

St James Bridge, NS484640, improved 1883. Two segmental arches, built of dressed stone, with semicircular cutwaters extending up to form pedestrian refuges.

St James's Street Dyeworks, St James' Street, NS481643, early 19th century, converted from a mill *c* 1868 by D. and A. Campbell for wool dyeing. A 3-storey and attic, 4-by-6-bay rubble building, with single-storey workshops at the rear. The ground floor of the main building and the workshops have been much modified since 1920 by A. and M. Pottie, motor dealers.

St Mirren Works, McDowall Street, NS478645, built *c* 1860 as a soap works. A 3-storey, 4-bay, coursed-rubble office block, built round a tall circular-section brick chimney, and a range of red-brick buildings: 6 storey, 4-by-5 bay, with a projecting stair and water-tower; 4 storey, 8 bay; 2 storey, 3 bay; and 4 storey, 17 bay. Disused.

Saucel Brewery and Distillery, Saucel Street, NS485636, early 19th century and later. *Brewery.* A 3-storey, 13-bay block, probably originally maltings, with 2 kilns, now with vents removed. Now a bonded store. *Distillery.* A group of rubble and brick buildings, with a 2-storey and attic, 2-bay gabled street frontage.

Saucel Ironworks, Lonend, NS475636, mid 19th century. Two 2-storey, 5-bay front blocks, now harled, and 1 with a cart entry, with single-storey, steel-framed workshops behind and to one side. Across a road is the former stockyard and the area where ships were assembled prior to movement, in whole or in pieces. Closed since 1969.

Saucel Mills, Bladda Lane, NS485637, rebuilt 1868. A 3-storey attic and basement rubble building, with 2 bays, one 5, one 7 bays long, with 2 kilns, and 2- and 3-storey stores, now converted to a hotel and restaurant.

Seedhill Tannery, Seedhill, NS487637, founded 18th century, acquired 1872 by W. J. and W. Lang. Though this complex has been much altered in recent years, the 4-storey, 7-by-5-bay, rubble drying shed still survives.

Soho Engine Works, Murray Street, NS477647, built *c* 1880 for Campbell and Calderwood, engineers. A tall single-storey, red-brick building with gable end to the street, and a roof-ridge ventilator. There are also a 2-storey, 6-bay office block and lower single-storey workshops, 1 with a Belfast roof.

Underwood Mill, Underwood Road, NS478642, founded in the 1780s, and rebuilt in the 1860s as a thread mill. The main building is a 3-storey and attic, 3-by-14-bay structure, with 7- and 8-bay blocks of north-light weaving sheds at the rear. Other 3-storey parts were destroyed by fire in 1971. Now a wool store, after a period as the Arrol-Johnson motor-car factory.

Vulcan Works, Renfrew Road, NS486644, founded 1838 (plate 54). The main workshops consist of 5 single-storey, red-brick bays, with arched doorways, all but one of which are disused. There is a 3-storey office block in similar style, with a doorway surmounted by a bellcote. On the other side of the road are the former foundry buildings, the heavy bays (2) being similar to the main workshop bays, except that one has a roof-ridge louvred ventilator. The light bay, a 3-by-21-bay rubble structure, lit at 2 levels by cast-iron-framed, small-paned windows, and with a full-length roof-ridge ventilator, is probably the finest early foundry building in Scotland. The main workshops contain several interesting heavy machine tools, including a Shanks horizontal and vertical planing machine.

Aqueducts, NS494634, NS495635, built *c* 1810 for the Glasgow, Paisley & Ardrossan Canal, engineer JOHN RENNIE. A single, dressed-

54 Light foundry, Vulcan Works, Paisley.

stone segmental arch, dated 1810, converted to a railway bridge in 1885, and a small segmental arched accommodation bridge, with curved spandrels and wing walls, on an abandoned canal loop.

Brass and copper works, Murray Street, NS478647, built by John Morrison and Sons, c 1880. A single-storey brick coppersmiths' shop, with 2-storey front offices, and a roof-ridge ventilator, and a later cross-bay forming a T. Across a yard is a small rectangular brick brass foundry with an asbestos roof and a square-section brick chimney.

Bridge, Gilmour Street, NS484642, built c 1840 for the Glasgow & Paisley Joint Railway, and widened c 1890. A single segmental arched span, with dressed-stone arch ring. The older part is on the south side.

Carpet factory, Inchinnan Road, NS482651, founded in 1870 by Ronald, Jack and Co Ltd. An unusual 3-storey, 2-by-18-bay, red-and-white-brick building with deeply recessed windows and decorative string courses, dated 1912, and an older 3-storey, 4-by-14-bay, red-and-white-brick block, with north-light ridged roof.

Colinslee Works (clothing), Neilston Road, NS483622, late 19th century, for the Scottish Co-operative Wholesale Society. A tall 3-storey and attic, 8-bay building with a Renaissance frontage. There is a block of single-storey, north-light sheds at the rear, and a lower 3-storey, 6-bay front block.

Coachbuilding works, New Sneddon Street, NS484646, founded 1875 by Lowrie and Clark. Two 2-storey, red-and-white-brick blocks, one 7 bay, the other 5-by-5 bay, with a cement-rendered front. This has a semicircular window at attic level. The offices are in a magnificent 18th-century town house.

Jam factory, Stevenson Street, NS481633, founded 1866, by James Robertson. The front buildings include two 3-storey, red-brick blocks, one 9, one 10 bays long, with panelled fronts, one dated 1914. At the rear are other, plainer, red-brick buildings.

Slater's Workshop, New Sneddon Street, NS484646, c 1870. A curious 1-storey and attic building, extending back to a quay on the White Cart. This old-established concern retains some relics including hand-barrows, slate drills and picks for slate-dressing.

Stables, Henderson Street, NS476642, built 1893 for the Underwood Co-operative Coal Society. A 2-storey, 9-bay, red-and-white-brick building, with round-headed windows on the ground floor. Now a workshop.

Viaduct, Underwood Road, NS478643, opened 1840 for the Glasgow,

Paisley & Greenock Railway. A 3-span viaduct, sharply skewed, with dressed-stone arch rings and coursed-rubble spandrels and wing walls. The central arch is over the carriageway of the road, the smaller side arches span the footpaths. All are segmental.

Warehouses, Forbes Place, NS484638, early mid 19th century. A handsome group of 3-storey ashlar buildings, one 5-bay, others 10-bay (2) 5-by-6 bay, and 8-by-12 bay, L plan. Originally occupied by Paisley shawl merchants.

PORT GLASGOW

Castle Shipyard, NS331743, founded *c* 1870 by Blackwood and Gordon. A most interesting example of a small 19th-century shipbuilding and repairing yard, complete with engine works, relatively little altered. Several 19th-century plateworking and other machine tools are still in use. There are 2 'patent' slips at the east end of the yard, added *c* 1900 and later.

PS 'Comet', Port Glasgow, NS321746 (plate 55). A replica of the *Comet* of 1812, the first successful European steamship, built to the order of Lithgows Ltd, for the 150th anniversary celebrations. Now displayed in a pond.

Glen Shipyard, NS317747, late 19th century. The only significant survival here is a 4-storey, 8-bay ashlar office block with rusticated ground floor. At the rear are 2 semicircular stair bays.

Gourock Ropeworks, NS326745, founded on this site 1797. An interesting group of buildings, dominated by a 7-storey and attic, 8-by-15-bay, red-and-white-brick structure, originally a sugar refinery (1860s). The oldest part is probably the 2-storey ropewalk which is largely 18th century in construction. The 2-storey, 16-bay ashlar office block, with its round-headed windows, is also noteworthy.

Newark Sail Cloth Co, NS314748, early to mid 19th century. The remains of a large complex, consisting of single-storey weaving sheds, with cast-iron columns supporting wooden roofs with wrought-iron tie rods. Now part of the Kingston Shipbuilding Yard.

Port Glasgow Harbour, NS322748, 19th century. All that is left of this once important harbour is a stretch of quay on an L plan, with a tapered cast-iron light tower. A short distance off-shore is a reef with a small circular light-tower.

Port Glasgow Substation, NS310749, *c* 1900. A brick building, with 2 wide bays, each with 3 round-headed openings in the gable. There are roof-ridge ventilators.

55   Replica of PS *Comet*, Port Glasgow.

Engine works, Kingston Yard, NS308750, late 19th century. A 2- and 3-storey, 3-bay brick block, now altered by the driving of a road through the centre bay, and the bricking up of most of the windows.
Railway bridges, NS318745, and 316746, opened 1840 by the Glasgow, Paisley & Greenock Railway. Two 3-span rubble bridges, each with an elliptical road arch flanked by semicircular arches for footpaths. The western bridge has the footpath arches blocked up.

RENFREW

Inchinnan bridges, NS492679, built 1812, engineer ROBERTSON BUCHANAN. Two bridges, similar in style, spanning the Black Cart water and the old course of the White Cart water. Both are ashlar-built, with elliptical arches and pointed cutwaters supporting pairs of Doric pilasters and architraves, which in turn support pedestrian refuges. There are round-headed, flood-relief holes between the pilasters. Both have 3 spans, with the central span larger than the others.
Bascule bridge, Inchinnan, NS493678, built 1924. A Scherzer rolling-lift bridge over the Cart Navigation, of steel-girder construction.

RENFREW

Clyde Navigation Trust Depot, NS511681, early 19th century and later. A 6-bay range of single-storey workshops, with 2 transverse bays, and a slipway for repairing dredgers and other maintenance craft. The east side of a creek known as the 'Pudzeoch' is quayed, and used for laying up vessels.
Renfrew (Fulbar Street) Station, NS497670, opened 1836 by the Paisley and Renfrew Railway. Formerly a 2-platform through station, with the main offices on the up platform, in a single-storey ashlar building on an L plan, now a dwellinghouse. The platforms are linked by a lattice-girder footbridge.
Engine of PS 'Clyde', NS554659. Two-cylinder, simple disconnecting side-lever engines from PS *Clyde*, a Clyde Navigation Trust tug/tender, built by A. & J. Inglis in 1851, preserved on a pedestral in memory of their designer, at one time Provost of Renfrew. Believed to be the first disconnecting paddle engines made.
Shipyards, NS505685, founded 1857 by James Henderson and Son and 1860 by William Simons and Co. These twin shipyards have been closed since 1963, but some of the 1- and 2-storey buildings survive, as does the late 19th-century set of shearlegs, the last surviving in the west of Scotland.

Roxburghshire

Roxburghshire is largely rural, but contains two manufacturing towns, Hawick and Jedburgh. Hawick is the centre of hosiery manufacture in Scotland, but Jedburgh is now much reduced in importance. The third town, Kelso, is principally a market for the surrounding agricultural community. The county is notable for its fine bridges.

ANCRUM

New Bridge, Bridge End, NT639238, early 20th century. A 3-span concrete bridge, with a masonry facing.

Old Bridge, Bridge End, NT639238, 18th century. A 3-span, segmental-arched bridge, of dressed-stone construction, with rusticated voussoirs and a dentilated string course. The triangular cutwaters are extended up to form pedestrian refuges. Now bypassed and closed to all traffic.

BOWDEN

Joinery, Bowden, NT353304, early 19th century. A single-storey, 4-bay rubble building with a brick gable wall.

Smithy, Bowden, NT353306, early 19th century. A neat single-storey, 3-bay rubble building. Now disused.

Smithy, Midlem, NT527274, early 19th century. A single-storey, 3-bay rubble building. Still in use.

Bridge, Toftbarns, NT539262, late 18th or early 19th century. A 2-span rubble bridge, with a segmental main arch and a semicircular arch over the lade to a nearby mill (now ruined).

CASTLETON

Bridge, Newcastleton, NY482869, probably built in the 1790s. A graceful 2-span bridge with flat-segmental arches. The arch rings are of dressed stone, with rubble spandrels. Above the centre pier is an arched recess.

CRAILING

Farm chimney, East Nisbet Farm, NT677260, mid 19th century. A circular-section brick chimney on a square stone base, with small single-storey rubble engine and boiler houses.

Bridge, Nisbet, NT675254, late 19th century. A 3-span bridge, with riveted bowed trusses, probably steel, on masonry piers with rounded cutwaters.

Smithy, Nisbet, NT675258, mid 19th century. An unusually well-built 1-storey, 6-bay rubble building. There is a bending machine outside. Still in use.

DENHOLM

Smithy, Cauldmill, NT531153, early 19th century. A single-storey, 3-bay rubble building with a roof ventilator. Still in use.

Mill, Denholm, NT567184, early 19th century. A large 3-storey rubble building, with a 1-and 2-storey outbuildings. Now gutted and used in part as a garage.

Stocking mill, Denholm, NT567183, late 18th century. A 3-storey, 2-by-6-bay rubble building with small windows for individual stocking frames in the upper floors. Later converted to a warehouse by the insertion of a door and wall crane at first-floor level.

Bridge, Trow Mill, NT533168, late 18th to early 19th century. A single-segmental arch, with dressed-stone arch ring and rubble spandrels and wing walls. The carriageway is slightly humped.

ECKFORD

Bridge, Caverton Mill, NT749357, built 1842. A pleasing small 2-span, dressed-stone bridge, with elliptical arches.

Mill, Caverton Mill, NT750258, late 18th to early 19th century. A 2-storey building on an L plan, with a small square kiln vent. Now gutted and used as a store.

Windmill stump, Caverton Mill, NT750258, late 18th century. The rubble-built, cylindrical base of a tower windmill, now used as a granary.

Bridge, nr Eckford, NT718270, early 19th century. A very attractive elliptical-arched, single-span bridge with dressed-stone arch ring and rubble spandrels and curved wing walls. There is a dentilated string course.

Suspension bridge, Kalemouth, NT709274, probably *c* 1820–30 (plate 56). A most interesting early suspension bridge, with a wooden-truss span supported by iron link chains and iron-rod suspenders. The ashlar pylons are of pyramidal form.

Mill, Ormiston, NT705277, early 19th century. A 2-storey range on an L plan, now part of a farm steading.

EDNAM

Smithy, Ednam, NT739372, early 19th century. A single-storey, 3-bay rubble building, with a 2-bay extension. Still in use.

Ednam Bridge, NT736371, early to mid 19th century. A most attractive 3-span bridge with elliptical arches, built of dressed stone. There are rounded cutwaters and a dentilated string course. Has inscription 'to Henry Francis Lyte, the hymn writer'.

Ednam West Mill (flour), NT736371, early 19th century. A large 3-storey, 5-bay rubble building, with a kiln at one end. Now gutted and wheel removed.

HAWICK

HAWICK

Albert Bridge, NT501145, built 1865. A 3-span masonry bridge, with elliptical arches.

Braemar Hosiery Co, NT498147, main block built 1875 and extended 1908. A large complex with a 4-storey, 2-by-13-bay front

56 Suspension bridge, Kalemouth.

block apparently extended from 2 storeys. To the east is a 2-storey, 8-bay building with a corner tower with an ogival cap.

Dangerfield Mill, NT502150, part probably early 19th century. There are 2 main ranges in this mill, one 2 storey, with a centre gablet, and the other 3 storey and attic 5 bay, both rubble-built.

Eastfield Mills, NT507153, built 1882 by Blenkhorn, Richardson & Co. A 2-storey and attic, 9-bay, French Renaissance block, with round-headed windows on the ground floor, with matching single-storey wings. At the rear are single-storey weaving sheds, and there is a large octagonal-section brick chimney.

Glebe Mills, NT509152, late 19th century. A long range of 1- and 2-storey buildings. The older part of the river frontage is a 2-storey, 7-bay, flat-roofed block.

Hawick Mill (corn), NT503143, built c 1805. A large 3-storey and attic, 7-bay rubble building, with a kiln at one end. Now modernized and still operating as a corn mill.

Hawick Station, NT505152, opened in its present form by the Border Union Railway in 1862. Formerly a 2-platform through station on an embankment. The platforms are on a curve, with the main offices on the southbound platform. These are in a 2-storey, 5-bay, coursed-rubble building. There is a coursed-rubble, single-storey building on the other platform, and there are substantial glazed awnings on both sides. The platforms are linked by a subway, and by a covered luggage bridge, with a hoist at each end. Surviving fittings include a cast-iron water tank on a stone base, 2 water columns, and cast-iron lamp posts, one with 'NBR' on the cross-piece. At the south end of the station there is a 6-span viaduct, on a curve over the Teviot, with dressed-stone arch rings and brick spandrels and piers. The large 2-road goods shed, with a wood-truss roof, has 2 whip cranes by JAMES TOD, Edinburgh. In the yard is a post crane by MEIKLEJOHN AND PURSELL, Dalkeith.

Hogg's Hosiery Works, NT504143, built 1887. An attractive 3-storey and attic, 1-by-5-bay block (1887) the main entrance at first-floor level, a range of 3-storey buildings, one 5-bay, one 6-bay, and some 1- and 2-storey outbuildings.

Mansfield Mills, NT506153, built 1880–1929 by James Renwick & Co. Three 3-storey and attic front blocks, the oldest 6-bay, a 4-bay building, and a 7-bay structure, all rubble-built, the two later with mansard roofs. At the rear are single-storey weaving sheds.

Melrose's Foundry and Engineering Works, NT502150, founded c 1875. An interesting group of buildings, consisting of a 3-storey,

9-bay rubble block, cut down from an early 4-storey spinning mill with single-storey wooden extensions. The foundry is a 1-storey, corrugated-iron-clad wood and cast-iron building with a brick wall for the small cupola. The leading millwrights in Hawick in the late 19th century.

North Bridge, NT504152, built 1832, widened 1882. A 2-span bridge, with segmental arches. The older part, on the north side, has arches of lesser radius than the newer part. The cutwater is circular.

Tower Mill, NT502144, early 19th century. A substantial 3-storey and attic rubble building, with the stump of a circular-section brick chimney on one corner. The mill is situated, in part, on a wide segmentally arched bridge over the Slitrig Water.

Turnbull's Dyeworks, NT498147, early 20th century. A 3-storey and attic, 9-bay modern steel-framed front block, with a mansard roof. At the rear are a 2-storey, 7-bay building and a 2-storey, 8-bay structure with a remarkable 'Modern Movement' tower (1911).

Victoria Steam Laundry, NT502149, late 19th to early 20th century. A 2-storey rubble building on a triangular site, with a 9-bay street frontage. At the rear is a boiler house with a circular-section brick chimney.

Weensland Mills, NT514154, mid to late 19th century. An extensive complex of buildings of various dates, incorporating Teviot Mills. The main range consists of a 4-storey, 4-by-16-bay rubble block forming an L with a more modern 4-storey, 4-by-10-bay building with octagonal bellcote. The other particularly interesting part is a 2-storey and attic, 9-bay building, with a central entrance, and at one end, a curious wooden gatehouse.

Wilton Mills, NT502152, early 19th century and later (see plate 5). A large complex, now in multiple ownership. At the front are 3-storey and attic, 3-by-8-bay, with a clock tower, and 3-storey, 15-by-9-bay, blocks with a castellated stair tower. There is a 2-storey, 7-by-2-bay French Renaissance office block and an older, plainer, 2-storey, 3-by-9-bay building. At the rear are 3-storey, and 4-storey, 8-bay blocks, one 5-storey, 6-by-6-bay building on an L plan, and the monumental pedimented stone base of a large chimney.

Bridge, nr Tower Mill, NT502144, 18th century or earlier. A 2-span bridge, with 2 segmental rubble arches, and triangular cutwaters. Footpaths, with cast-iron railings, have been bracketted out over the cutwaters.

Joinery, NT503153, early to mid 19th century. A neat 2-storey and attic, 5-by-2-bay rubble building with a short circular brick chimney.

HOBKIRK

Bonchester Bridge, NT586120, early 19th century. A single segmental-rubble arch, widened in concrete and refaced in the original manner.

JEDBURGH

New Mill, Bonjedward, NT658229, early 19th century. A large 3-storey and attic rubble building on an L plan, now gutted and part of a farm steading.

Waulk Mill, The Whinney, Bonjedward, NT658229, late 18th or early 19th century. A 2-storey rubble building on an X plan, with one arm of the X a wheelhouse and the opposite arm containing a kiln. Now gutted and used as a store.

JEDBURGH

Abbey bridge and tollhouse, NT651203, early to mid 19th century. A 3-span bridge, built of dressed stone, with segmental arches. The central arch is wider than the other 2. There is an attractive Tudor tollhouse, with a large mullioned bay window, now used as an antique shop.

Allars Mill (Laidlaw's), NT650199, early 19th century. The main block here is a 3-storey, 7-by-2-bay structure with a 6-by-3 bay wing, forming an L. There is a small bellcote on the gable. There are also some single-storey weaving sheds. Now used as a fertilizer depot, with part of the interior of the main building removed.

Barrass Tannery, NT652211, early 19th century. A 3-storey and attic, 4-by-8-bay building, with a projecting gabled stair tower surmounted by a bellcote. There are various single-storey outbuildings and an octagonal red-and-white-brick chimney.

Bongate Mill, NT656213, late 19th century. An irregular group of 1- and 2-storey snecked rubble buildings, including a 4-bay block of weaving sheds, and an attractive 2-storey, 5-by-6-bay block with dentilated cornice and central gable with bellcote (1878). There is an older 2-storey, 3-bay dwellinghouse, probably the mill house for the corn mill which preceded the woollen mill on this site. Part is now used as a pottery, the rest is disused.

Canongate Bridge, NT653205, 16th century. A 3-span, dressed-stone bridge, with approximately elliptical 4 ribbed arches of unequal size. The triangular cutwaters are carried up to form semihexagonal refuges. A particularly fine example of a 16th-century bridge.

Tannery, NT652209, early 19th century and later (see plate 8). A group of 1-, 2- and 3-storey buildings. Those at the rear are wood and brick, and there are two 3-storey rubble blocks, one 6-bay, with louvred ventilators in the top floor, and the other 4 bay with a bowed front. Now disused.

KELSO

KELSO

Kelso Bridge and tollhouse, NT728336, built 1800–3, engineer JOHN RENNIE (see plate 10). One of Rennie's finest bridges, precursor of London's Waterloo Bridge. A 5-span bridge, with elliptical arches. The rounded cutwaters support pairs of Doric columns which also appear on the abutments. There is a dentilated string course. The carriageway is level, a feature (unusual for the time) of Rennie's bridges. The tollhouse is a delightful single-storey, 3-bay building in the same architectural style as the bridge.

Kelso Mills, NT727338, early 19th century and later. A group of 2-, 3- and 4-storey rubble and brick buildings, modernized internally.

Kelso Racing Stables, NT728341, mid to late 19th century. A group of single-storey rubble buildings round a small courtyard, with awnings supported on cast-iron columns. Now used as a garage, it retains much of the atmosphere of its days as a stable.

Kelso Station, NT731331, opened 1851 by the North British Railway. Formerly a 3-platform through station, with the main offices on the down platform. The main building survives, a 2-storey rubble building on an L plan, with wooden offices filling the angle of the L. There is a goods shed with iron columns, wooden walls, and brick offices. The engine shed is a 2-road, 4-bay building with a long louvred roof-ridge ventilator. An unusual feature is the lime depot, with staithes.

Maxwellhaugh Mill, NT724338, late 18th to early 19th century. A 2-storey harled rubble building, on an L plan, with a kiln at one end. The kiln vent is of the circular type with a movable head.

Teviot Bridge, NT720336, early 19th century. A 3-span bridge, with a large segmental arch flanked by single, slightly smaller, segmental arches with carriageways sloping up to the centre of the bridge. There are pointed cutwaters supporting pairs of pilasters which in turn carry pedestrian refuges.

Mill (granary), Kelso Station, NT732332, mid 19th century and later. A group of buildings incorporating a rubble-built granary, reinforced-concrete silos and corrugated-iron sheds.

Wooden Mill, NT738342, early 19th century. Now largely ruinous,

with an intact pyramidal-roofed kiln. Was a woollen mill in 1859.
Suspension footbridge, Wooden, NT735338, early 19th century.
A small private bridge, with iron link chains, solid suspender rods,
and an ordinary link-chain railing. The pylons are of steel, set in
concrete bases, and the footway is made of wooden planks.

MAXTON

Mertoun Bridge and tollhouse, NT610321, built 1837, engineer
JAMES SLIGHT, Edinburgh. A 5-span bridge, built entirely of dressed
stone, with flat segmental arches on slender piers with rounded cutwaters. The tollhouse is a 2-storey building set into the embanked
approach to the bridge, with the toll door and bay window at first-
floor level.

MELROSE

Railway bridge, Darnick, NT534340, opened 1849 by the North
British Railway. A good example of a North British Railway type
of underbridge, with cast-iron arched side girders and steel or
wrought-iron trough main members both supported on rubble
abutments. Originally the main members were probably also cast-
iron.
Bridge and tollhouse, Darnlee, NT528348, mid 19th century. A
large 2-span bridge with segmental arches and a triangular cutwater.
The tollhouse is a single-storey rubble building with 2 bow windows,
projecting eaves and a gabled porch.
Leaderfoot Viaduct, NT563347, opened 1865 by the Berwickshire
Railway. A strikingly tall 19-span viaduct, with semicircular arches
on slender stone piers.
Drygrange Bridge, Leaderfoot, NT576347, built 1776–80. A 4-span
rubble bridge, with a large central segmental span flanked by 2
semicircular arches. At the south end is a small semicircular arch,
possibly designed as an accommodation arch. From the line of the
dentilated string course it appears that the bridge has been raised at
the ends to make the carriageway more nearly level.
Melrose Station, NT547339, opened 1849 by the North British
Railway. A very remarkable 2-platform through station, with the
main offices on the down side. These are contained in a 2-storey
building in Flemish style with the entrance from the street at ground-
floor level and from the platform at first-floor level. The remarkable
features are the platform awnings, which are of wooden construction,
and slope up at an angle of about 30 degrees towards the track. They

are supported on cast-iron columns, with lotus capitals, and there are curved wooden brackets to take the weight of the overhang. There is a cast-iron-framed wooden goods shed with a common wall with the up-platform awning. On the up platform is a cast-iron urinal in a remarkably good state of preservation.

Abbey Mill, Melrose, NT548343, early 19th century and later. A 2-storey, 4-bay rubble building with a kiln on one end, and a more recent 4-bay addition on 1 side. Now a small factory.

Suspension bridge, NT545346, built 1826. A footbridge, with iron-link suspension chains, a wooden deck and Gothic stone pylons. The vertical suspenders are iron rods, and there are light iron railings.

Mill, Newstead, NT560342, early 19th century. A 2-storey rubble building, with flaking harling, with the ruins of a large kiln. Now gutted and becoming ruinous.

Granary, St Boswells Station, NT578315, probably *c* 1849. The passenger station here has been demolished, but the railway granary, a 3-storey, 3-by-6-bay building with 2 hoists, survives as a store.

Langlands Mill (spinning), Newtown St Boswells, NT577320, built 1889 and later. The original building is a 6-bay block of single-storey, north-light sheds, with a 2-storey, 6-bay front block. Subsequently, 4 bays of north-light sheds have been added.

MINTO

Hassendean Station, NT548203, opened 1849 by the North British Railway. Formerly a 2-platform through station. The main offices are on the up platform, in a small 2-storey stone building, with the platform entrance at first-floor level. On the down platform there is a wooden shelter with an awning. Linking the platforms is a wooden footbridge, braced with iron. At the south end is a brick underbridge with a masonry arch ring.

MOREBATTLE

Joinery, Morebattle, NT773249, early to mid 19th century. A striking 2-storey and attic, 2-by-3-bay rubble building, with flat brick arches over the windows and doors. There is a Palladian window in the gable. Adjacent to the workshop is a 2-storey and attic, 2-bay dwellinghouse in similar style. Now disused.

Bridge, Primsidemill, NT813265, early 19th century. An attractive small 2-span rubble bridge with segmental arches.

Bridge, nr Morebattle, NT777253, built 1855. A single-segmental arch with dressed-stone arch ring and rubble spandrels and curved wing walls.

Bridge, nr Morebattle, NT783253, mid 19th century. A single-segmental arch with dressed-stone arch ring and rubble spandrels and wing walls.

ROXBURGH

Roxburgh Station, NT697306, opened 1850 by the North British Railway. The surviving building here is a 2-storey building with overhanging eaves, now used as a dwellinghouse but formerly the main offices.

Railway bridges, Roxburgh Station, NT697306, built *c* 1850 and *c* 1856 by the North British and Jedburgh Railways. Two similar, but not identical, segmental arched underbridges, with dressed-stone arch rings and rubble spandrels and curved wing walls. The eastern is the older.

Roxburgh Viaduct, NT702304, opened 1850 by the North British Railway (plate 57). A very fine curved viaduct. There are 6 main segmental arch spans of ashlar construction, flanked on each side by 4 shorter coursed-rubble semicircular arches. The 3 river piers of the

57   Roxburgh Viaduct.

larger spans on the downstream side are extended at a low level to carry a footbridge, with wrought-iron lenticular trusses with cast-iron compression members and a wooden deck.

Railway Cottages, Roxburgh Viaduct, NT703303, built 1868. A block of two 2-roomed, square-dressed rubble cottages, now used as cow sheds.

SOUTHDEAN

Southdean Mill, NT634104, early 19th century. A 2- and 3-storey rubble building with a wooden sawmill extension. A 6-spoke, single-ring, low-breast wood and iron paddle wheel drove 2 pairs of 4ft (1·22m) stones. Disused as a mill for many years and the stones dismantled.

Bridge, Camptown, NT679135, probably mid 19th century. A 3-span bridge, with semicircular arches on tall piers, similar in style to a railway viaduct.

SPROUSTON

Limekiln, Carham Station, NT791370, probably mid 19th century. A handsome single-shaft kiln, with 3 draw holes approached from parallel semicircular draw arches. In good condition.

Sprouston Station, NT759353, opened 1851 by the York, Newcastle & Berwick Railway. Formerly a 2-platform through station, with the offices on the down platform. The main building, which survives as a dwellinghouse, is a 1- and 2-storey rubble structure, with overhanging eaves. Nearby are 2 blocks of 2-storey railwaymen's cottages. The only surviving Scottish station built by an English company.

STICHILL

Farm chimney, Ballieknowe, NT712381, mid 19th century. A handsome, square-section chimney with neat single-storey engine and boiler houses.

Smithy, Stichill, NT714385, early 19th century. A single-storey, 4-bay rubble building, still in use.

YETHOLM

Bridge, Town Yetholm, NT823281, mid 19th century. A handsome 3-span bridge, with elliptical arches with dressed-stone arch rings and rubble spandrels and wing walls. There are a dentilated string course and modern steel railings.

Yetholm Mill, Kirk Yetholm, NT825281, early 19th century. A 2-storey and attic harled rubble building on an L plan. Now gutted and used in part as a garage.

Selkirkshire

Selkirkshire is primarily rural in nature, but its main towns, Galashiels and Selkirk, are the most important seats of the Scottish woollen industry.

ASHKIRK

Ashkirk Mill, NT473223, early 19th century. A small rectangular 2-storey rubble building, with a lean-to wheelhouse. Now gutted, there were 3 pairs of stones, 1 pair still in position. Two were 4ft 6in (1·37m) diameter, 1 was 4ft (1·22m).

ETTRICK

Bridge, Tibbie Shiels Inn, NT239205, late 18th to early 19th century. A single-segmental rubble arch, with curved wing walls.
Bridge, Tushielaw, NT303176, late 18th to early 19th century. A 2-span rubble bridge on an incline, with segmental arches of unequal size. The central pier has a rounded cutwater.

GALASHIELS

Lindean Mill, NT482313, early to mid 19th century. A 3-storey, 4-bay rubble building, with a kiln at one end, and a 2-storey store block forming an L. Adjacent to the main mill building is a single-storey rubble sawmill, with a wooden extension. There are two 6-spoke internal wheels, both all wood, except for the axles and fastenings. Both are of the low-breast paddle type 4ft wide by 14ft diameter (1·22 by 4·27m), but the sawmill wheel has 36 paddles, while the corn-mill wheel has 30 paddles. The corn mill, with conventional axle drive, has 3 pairs of 4ft 6in (1·37m) diameter stones. Drive to the sawmill is by an internal gear ring with 180 teeth and a spur wheel with 30 teeth.
Bridge, Lindean, NT488322, mid 19th century. A handsome 3-span bridge, with dressed-stone arch rings and rubble spandrels and wing walls. The 2 main spans are elliptical-arched, and there is a smaller semi-circular flood arch.
Smithy and cottages, Lindean, NT484313, mid 19th century. A range of 3 cottages and a smithy on a U plan, with the smithy in 1

limb of the U. Construction is of rubble, with crow-stepped gables. The smithy is still in use.

GALASHIELS

Buckholm Mill, NT481373, built 1846 for Henry Sanderson. A fine 5-storey, 4-by-20-bay whinstone rubble building with a bellcote on the south wall. On the opposite bank of the river is a large block of weaving sheds added in 1883 by Brown Bros. Lit by electricity in 1884. The tunnel lade and sluices can still be seen.

Comelybank Mill, NT486367, built 1852 by A. & R. Watson. Two large blocks of single-storey sheds, with a fine octagonal red-and-white-brick chimney.

Gala Dyeworks, NT483371, built 1883 for Kemp & Walker, dyers. The main part consists of 2 wide single-storey bays with roof ventilators at 2 levels.

Huddersfield Mill, NT498356, built 1818, for 4 local manufacturers. A 3-storey, 5-by-2-bay rubble building with 1- and 2-storey buildings at the rear. There is a large circular-section, glazed-red-brick chimney. Now disused.

London Shrinking Works, NT495362, mid 19th century. Two 2-storey blocks, one 7 bays long, with a 3-by-1-bay office block at one end, with round-headed windows, entered at first-floor level, and the other, lower, 2-by-11-bay.

Mid Mill, NT494359, founded 1793 by 5 local manufacturers. The present main block was added in the mid 19th century by Cochrane & Co, and is a handsome 4-storey, 15-bay building with a projecting central stair block surmounted by a pedimented bellcote. Adjacent is a fine beam-engine house (1866) with tall round-headed windows and a cast-iron roof tank.

Nether Mill, NT506353, built 1805 (plate 58). A 3-storey and attic, 2-by-8-bay whinstone rubble building, with a 4-by-6-bay, 3-storey addition dating from 1866, a beam-engine house, and a block of weaving sheds. There is a fine octagonal brick chimney at the rear.

Netherdale Mill, NT494360, built from 1857 for J. & W. Cochrane. The first block, 4-storey, 2-by-19-bay with a detached engine shed, cost £10,400 (1857). The second 4-storey, 2-by-19-bay block was added in 1873. Both have projecting stair towers, the older one having decorative corner turrets. There is a 14-bay block of single-storey weaving sheds built at various dates to 1893. Behind the weaving-shed block is a handsome classical engine house, and in front is a single-storey, 10-bay office block (1893).

Tweed Mill, NT483369, built 1852 for P. & R. Sanderson. The first steam mill in Galashiels, with a 3-storey and attic main block with 2 projecting stair towers (High Tweed Mill) and a 3-storey, 10-by-2-bay building (West Mill).

Victoria Dyeworks, NT495359, established by James Brownlee in part of the old Galashiels Gas Works. A long 2-storey rubble building. The roof has a full-length louvred ventilator, alternate slating and full-length roof lights. There is a 2-storey, 3-bay office block.

Waverley Ironworks, NT497358, founded before 1744 by the Aimers family. The old offices are in a 2- and 3-storey and attic, 4-bay rubble building. At the rear are single-storey machine and erecting shops, and a foundry, now disused, with two solid-bottom cupolas. In the yard is a hand-operated, rail-mounted crane, with cast-iron frame and wooden jib, said to have come with Mr MacLean from the Forth Railway Bridge contract *c* 1890.

Wilderbank Mill, NT487366, built 1862–90 for William Brown & Sons. An irregular group of buildings, the largest being a 5-storey, 4-by-7-bay block. The 2-storey office block was built in 1883.

58 Nether Mill, Galashiels.

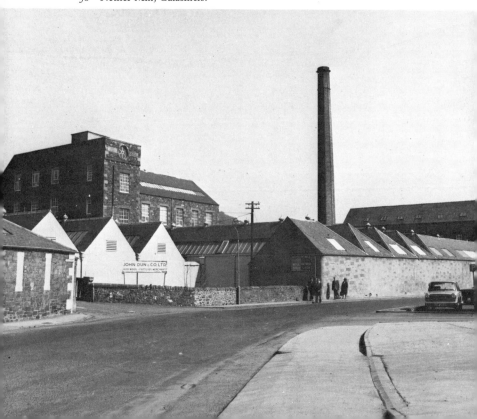

Brewery, NT493360, late 19th century. A 3-storey rubble building, with a pyramidal-roofed kiln.

Refuse destructor, NT503353, late 19th to early 20th century. A single-storey rubble building with a very fine and large red-brick chimney.

Skinworks, NT488367, established on this site c 1856 by Sanderson & Murray, fellmongers and woolbrokers. The main block is a 3-storey, 9-by-12-bay building, with the top floor largely roof-lit.

KIRKHOPE

Ettrick Bridge, Ettrickbridge End, NT390243, built 1780. A single-segmental rubble arch, with 1 end butting on to solid rock.

Suspension footbridge, Ettrickbridge End, NT393247, early 20th century. A small bridge, with wire-rope cables, wooden deck and wooden pylons.

Bridge, Singlie, NT368213, mid 19th century. A 3-span rubble bridge, with segmental arches and rounded cutwaters. One arch is a flood arch, smaller than the other 2.

SELKIRK

Bridge, Broadmeadows, NT417248, early 19th century. A 3-span rubble bridge, with large elliptical arch flanked by small semicircular access/flood arches. There is a dentilated string course.

Bridge, Broadmeadows, NT413300, early 19th century. A single-segmental rubble arch.

Bridge and tollhouse, Carterhaugh, NT430267, early 19th century. A single-segmental arch bridge, slightly humped. The tollhouse is a 1-storey building on an L plan, with overhanging eaves and 2 bay windows, 1 facing along the bridge and the other along the approach road.

Yair Bridge, Fairnielee, NT458325, mid 18th century. A handsome 3-span rubble bridge with segmental arches and triangular cutwaters extended upward to form pedestrian refuges.

Bridge, Philiphaugh, NT433281, early 19th century. A single-segmental rubble arch, with dentilated string course.

SELKIRK

Bannerfield Mill, NT467290, built c 1880. A block of single-storey weaving sheds, with a fine engine- and boiler-house group, with round-headed windows (1881). There is a sectional cast-iron water tank on the roof of the enginehouse, and the boiler house has a circular-section, red-brick chimney of medium height.

Mill housing, Bannerfield, NT467290, *c* 1880. A 2-storey range of 14 houses, with a range of 2-storey and attic houses, forming an L.

Ettrick Mill, NT473293, built 1836–50, (main block) and later. A large group with 2 principal blocks and associated weaving sheds. The older and finer of the main buildings is a 5-storey, 27-bay structure, with 8-bay wings at each end. The central 3 bays of the frontage are gabled, the middle bay having Palladian windows. The other is a 4-by-11-bay building with a projecting machicolated tower. The single-storey engine house has a cast-iron roof tank, and the boiler house is served by a tall octagonal brick chimney. There are interesting 8-, 4- and 8-bay blocks of weaving sheds, with the gable walls extended almost to the apex of the gables.

Forrest Mill, NT467288, built 1838 and 1868. The main blocks here are 4 storey and 2 attic, 6-by-2 bay and 3 storey and attic, 20 bay. The former has an attractive bellcote.

Linglie Mill, NT474295, mid 19th century. A large complex, with a 3-storey, 4-by-16-bay main building. This has a central projecting stair bay with a circular window. The other principal buildings are

59   Steam engine, Philiphaugh Mill, Selkirk.

2-storey, 17- and 18-bay blocks. There are several ranges of single-storey weaving sheds.

Philiphaugh Mill, NT457282 (plate 59). Two ranges of 1-storey buildings, the older dating from 1876 with a bellcote. The main power for the mills is supplied by 2 water turbines by JOHN MAC-DONALD & CO, Glasgow (1922), and there is a 250 hp twin tandem-compound mill engine by Petrie of Rochdale (1912) which was used as a standby until 1972. The single Lancashire boiler is still used for heating and process steam. The engine house is a particularly neat rubble structure with round-headed windows.

Philiphaugh Sawmill, NT450278, late 19th century. A group of single-storey wood and brick buildings, with an older 2-storey rubble block. The most interesting features are the operating low-breast, all-iron wheel, 12ft wide by 15ft diameter (3·7 by 4·6m) which drives through a gear ring a sawbench by D. M. WALLACE & SONS, engineers and millwrights, Kelso.

St Mary's Mill, NT473296, built 1894. A group of single-storey weaving sheds, with a single-storey, L-plan front building with

60   Yarrow Mill, Selkirk.

round-headed openings and a corner turret.

Selkirk Bridge, NT462285, 18th century and later. A 4-span bridge, with segmental arches of rubble widened by flatter segmental arches with dressed-stone arch rings and rubble spandrels. The first arch on the Selkirk side is a flood arch, smaller than the other 3.

Yarrow Mill, NT470292, built 1867–92 (plate 60). A handsome 4-storey, 4-by-16-bay rubble building, with a tall single-storey engine house and a 3-bay boiler house, with round-headed doorways having glazed fanlights. The office block, is a 1 storey and attic 11-bay building with a baronial centre feature.

Engineering works, NT467287, mid to late 19th century. A 2-storey, 3-by-5-bay rubble building, with a central hoist.

Tannery, NT464286, mid 19th century and later. A group of buildings of mixed date, on a sloping site, with a 2-storey, 8-bay drying shed with louvred ventilators.

Weaving sheds, NT467290, mid to late 19th century. A large group of single-storey rubble weaving sheds, the biggest being 6- and 9-bay

61 Ashiestiel Bridge, Yarrow.

ranges, of similar construction. There is a neat engine-house with round-headed windows.

Weaving sheds/ NT466288, built 1871. Two long single-storey bays of weaving sheds, with a 2-storey, 5-bay block and a tall circular-section, red-brick chimney.

YARROW

Ashiestiel Bridge, NT439351, built 1847, J. & T. SMITH, Darnick, engineers (plate 61). A remarkable single-segmental-arched rubble span. The spandrels have been reinforced by tie bars. Its span of 131ft 6in (40·1m) was the largest for a rubble arch when built.

Bridge, Mountbenger, NT309248, 19th century. A single-segmental rubble arch.

Yarrow Bridge, NT358276, early 19th century. A long flat elliptical rubble arch. Nearby is a good example of a contemporary bridge over a small stream.

Stirlingshire

Stirlingshire is a varied county, agricultural in the north and west, and industrial in the south and east. Its major manufacturing centres – Falkirk, Bonnybridge, Larbert and Denny – dominate the light end of the Scottish ironfounding industry. The Stirling area was notable for woollen manufacture, now extinct. Stirling itself is one of the natural centres for communications between the central belt and the north, and the county also embraces important east–west links. The artificial port of Grangemouth is of growing importance.

Edinburgh & Glasgow Union Canal, NS967758 to 865794, built 1818–22, engineer HUGH BAIRD. The part of this barge canal in Stirlingshire begins on the 12-arched Avon Aqueduct, with cast-iron trough supported on masonry piers, and contains several interesting features, including the Slamannan Railway basin, NS962762, a small drydock at NS965785, and Scotland's only surviving canal tunnel, NS881790–884784. The standard overbridges, which vary in detail, are segmental-arched, with the bridge number on the keystone. The locks linking the canal with the Forth and Clyde Canal were filled in in 1933, but part of the top lock entrance can still be seen (NS870794). The present terminal basin, Port Maxwell (NS865794) dates from 1823.

Forth & Clyde Canal, NS785785–973825, built 1768–73, engineer JOHN SMEATON. The Stirlingshire section include locks 4–19 of which the most interesting are locks 9–11 and 12–16 at Camelon (NS878805–868801). Beside lock 16, where the Union Canal joined the Forth and Clyde, is the Union Inn. All the original bascule bridges on this section have been replaced, and the part of the canal within the Grangemouth boundary has been filled in. There are original minor aqueducts at Carmuirs (NS847803), Bonnybridge (NS824801) and Underwood (NS808791) and an aqueduct over the Scottish Central Railway (1848) at Camelon (NS852803). The Townhead Reservoir (NS7378) and most of the feeders to Craigmarloch are also in Stirlingshire, as are the ruins of a stable block at NS737775.

AIRTH

Airth Mill (corn), NS903868, early 19th century. A 2-storey and attic rubble building, now gutted and used as a store.

Horse-gin houses, late 18th to early 19th century. There are hexagonal pantile-roofed structures at Powside (NS864868), Bridge End (NS871868) and North Greens (NS897879), a heptagonal pantile-roof specimen at NS907851 and a heptagonal slate-roofed building at South Doll (NS874875).

Ferry Pier, South Alloa, NS879919, probably early 19th century. A rubble and timber ramped ferry pier, becoming ruinous.

BALDERNOCK

Baldernock Mill, NS574748, mid 19th century. A rectangular 2-storey rubble building, with a restored suspended pitch-back wheel about 20ft (6·10m) diameter driving a sawmill. Converted to a dwellinghouse.

BALFRON

Balfron Station, NS952893, opened 1856 by the Forth & Clyde Junction Railway. Formerly a 2-platform through station, with the main offices on the down (Stirling) platform, in a 1- and 2-storey rubble building on a T plan, incorporating a dwellinghouse with an awning in angle of the T. The corrugated-iron goods shed also survives. Buchlyvie (NS563941) (plate 62), and Kippen (NS664957) are similar.

BUCHANAN

Buchanan Mill, NS444903, early 19th century. A rectangular 1-storey and attic rubble building, with the skeleton of an iron over-shot wheel with wooden buckets. A gear ring on the 'off-side' drove a sawmill in a wooden shed. Disused.

Buchanan Smithy, NS463895, early 19th century. A single-storey, 3-bay building, with an iron silhouette of a horse on a post projecting from one of the chimneys.

CAMPSIE

Limekilns, Balgrochan, NS627790, early 19th century. A range of 5 large clamp kilns, with 4 smaller ones at right angles to the main range. Now overgrown, but clearly defined.

Milton Printworks, Milton of Campsie, NS649767, founded 1786. A group of mainly single-storey brick buildings, with a red-brick clock tower, dated 1897. Now a wood-pulp container factory.

DENNY

Bankier Distillery, NS778789, founded 1828 by Daniel Macfarlane. A complex of buildings of various dates, dominated by 2 pyramidal-roofed kilns, serving a 2-storey range of malting floors. The distillery was served by a horse tramway to a wharf on the Forth & Clyde Canal, which still survives.

Bridge, near Carron Bridge, NS748838, 18th or early 19th century. A single segmental-arched span, with dressed-stone arch ring, and rubble spandrels and wing walls. There is a dentilated string course.

Duncarron Ironworks, NS817825, early 20th century. A group of steel-framed brick- and corrugated-iron-clad workshops and stores, typical of early 20th-century foundry design. The overhead cranes in the engineering shop are, most unusually, run on 2-phase alternating current.

Denny Iron Works, NS813822, founded 1870 by Cruickshanks and Co. A large complex of buildings, mainly modern. The machining and fitting shops and the 2-storey pattern store are 19th century. The office with its decorative cast-iron lettering dates from the 1920s.

62 Buchlyvie Station.

DRYMEN

Cast-iron bridge, Kelty Water, NS535963, mid 19th century. A curious bridge, with 'cast-iron truss' sides, with circular section top and bottom members. Cross members are fastened to the sides by wrought iron or steel ties. Now strengthened by a steel support on concrete piers, at the midpoint of the span.

DUNIPACE

Bridge, NS834817, early 19th century. A 3-span bridge, built of dressed stone, with segmental arches and rounded cutwaters. The voussoirs are rusticated. The central arch is larger than the other 2.
Paper mill, NS797830, mid 19th century. The bulk of this large complex is modern, but there is a neat single-storey Gothic lodge with decorative slating and cast-iron, roof-ridge ornament.

FALKIRK

Bonny Mill, Bonnybridge, NS824802, early 19th century. A 2-storey rubble building on a rectangular plan, with a kiln at one end. Now modernized internally and the wheel removed. The lade ran under the Forth & Clyde Canal.
Caledonian Stove and Iron Works, Bonnybridge, NS822798, late 19th century. A very typical light foundry of its period, with low single-storey moulding shops. These have brick walls and wooden roof trusses supported on cast-iron columns. There are 2 old cupolas, out of use, made in Grangemouth.
Columbian Foundry, Bonnybridge, NS824800, founded *c* 1870 by Smith and Wellstood. A large complex of 1- and 2-storey buildings. The 'old foundry', now mechanized, includes a 2-storey, 5-by-23-bay rubble block and a 2-storey, 3-by-12-bay range with round-headed windows, facing the canal. The 'new foundry' is mainly single-storey, with roof lighting.
Castlecary Viaduct, NS787783, opened 1842 by the Edinburgh & Glasgow Railway, engineer JOHN MILLER. An 8-span bridge, of dressed stone, with segmental arches, strengthened with old rails.
Firebrick works, High Bonnybridge, NS839796, late 19th to early 20th century (plate 63). A compact site consisting of a 2-vent firebrick kiln and a single-storey, red-brick moulding shop with heated drying floor. One of the last small firebrick works in the country.

FALKIRK

Abbots Ironworks, NS879815, founded 1856. A much-reduced group of single-storey rubble moulding shops. Now used as a garage.

Camelon Ironworks, NS881805, founded 1872. A much-reduced group of 1-storey, red-brick buildings, with corrugated-iron extensions. The main frontage is attractive, with a pedimented centre entrance surmounted by a belfry. There are, at the rear, 2 disused brick-topped cupolas.

Castlelaurie Ironworks, NS890813, founded 1875. A somewhat altered group of single-storey buildings, with 2 cupolas. There is a tall single-storey, red-and-white-brick building, presumably designed as a fitting shop. Now in multiple occupation.

Falkirk Ironworks, NS889811, founded 1819. A large group of single-storey buildings of various dates, including a tall red-and-white-brick building with round-headed windows, similar to that at Castlelaurie Ironworks.

Falkirk (Grahamston) Station, NS888803, opened c 1848 by the Stirlingshire Midland Junction Railway, rebuilt c 1880. A 2-platform through station, with the main offices on the down platform, in a 2 storey, red-and-white-brick block, with single-storey wings, incorporating a dwellinghouse. This building has awnings on both street

63 Firebrick works, Bonnybridge.

and platform sides, supported on cast-iron columns. The up-platform building is a single-storey brick structure, also with a substantial awning. The platforms are linked by a lattice-girder footbridge.

Falkirk (High) Station, NS883791, opened 1842, by the Edinburgh & Glasgow Railway. A 2-platform through station on a curve. The main offices are on the up platform, in a 1-storey and attic ashlar building, incorporating a dwellinghouse, with a platform awning added later, and subsequently modernized.

Falkirk Power Station, NS887794, late 19th to early 20th century. A 2-by-13-bay, single-storey, red-brick building, with round-headed windows, roof-ridge ventilators, and a scalloped wall-head. The main bay is wide, lit at 2 levels, and there is a subsidiary lean-to bay. Now used as a store.

Grahamston Iron Works, NS885805, founded 1868. An extensive complex, mainly modern. The most interesting feature is an ornamental cast-iron gateway, made for an exhibition.

Mungal Foundry, NS882818, built from 1897 by Carron Company. Two ranges of single-storey, red-brick shops, one a 3-bay fitting shop, and the other a 9-bay moulding shop.

Rosebank Distillery, NS876803, founded 1840, rebuilt 1864. A group of mainly 2-storey, red-brick buildings, some rubble-based, with 8-and-10-bay frontages to the Forth & Clyde Canal. There is a circular-section brick chimney. The 3 pot stills, of traditional pattern, but built in 1962, have worm condensers, the wooden tubs for which form a distinctive feature of the distillery's street facade. Diagonally opposite the main range is a 3-storey and attic bonded store, on a triangular site, with a rounded corner.

Springfield Goods Yard, NS890803, built by the North British Railway, c 1870. A fine example of a large late 19th-century goods yard, with 2 single-storey brick and wood transhipment sheds, with awnings for road vehicles, and a 2-storey brick office block. The former transit shed for iron castings, a steel-framed, corrugated-iron-clad structure, is now the headquarters of the Scottish Railway Preservation Society.

Springfield Sawmills, NS890804, late 19th century. A complex of 1- and 2-storey wood and steel-framed seasoning and storage sheds, served by a hand-operated, narrow-gauge railway. There is a 3-storey, 2-bay ashlar office block, incorporating a cart entrance, on Grahams Road.

Tannery, NS883800, late 18th to early 19th century. A group of 1- and 2-storey rubble buildings, round a courtyard, some with pantiled roofs. There is a typical 2-storey drying shed with louvred ventilators in the upper floor. Now a store.

FINTRY

Culcreuch Cotton Mill, NS615872, founded *c* 1795 by Peter Spiers. The surviving building is a 3-storey, 5-bay rubble structure with a wooden external stair. The wheelpit is some distance to the east of this block, and apparently contained a high-breast wheel about 11ft wide by 26ft diameter (3·35 by 7·93m). The dried-up mill pond, with wooden sluices, is still discernible.

Bridge, NS615868, built 1804. A 3-span structure of dressed-stone construction, with segmental arches and triangular cutwaters.

Low Bridge, Gonachan, NS633863, built 1750. A 2-span bridge, with segmental arches of unequal size and triangular cutwaters. The arch rings are of dressed stone and the spandrels are rubble.

GRANGEMOUTH

Grangemouth Docks, built from 1838 by the Forth & Clyde Canal and the Caledonian Railway. The first dock here was the Old Dock NS925825 (1838–43) entered from the river Carron, and linked with the canal by a short cut. This was widened to form the Junction Dock (completed 1859), and a much larger dock, the Carron Dock, also approached from the river, was added in 1883 (NS927825). The 2 river locks were reduced in importance by the completion in 1906 of the Grange Dock with its associated Western and Eastern Channels and new entrance lock (NS940827).

Shipyard, Grangemouth, NS920823, late 18th to early 19th century. Reputedly the birthplace of the *Charlotte Dundas*, first technically successful steamship in Britain. The present buildings are mainly of late 19th to early 20th-century date, but include a 3-storey and attic stone warehouse and quay built in the late 18th century by Carron Co.

KILLEARN

Glengoyne Distillery, NS528826, founded 1833. A group of much-altered 1- and 2-storey harled buildings.

Smithy, NS508852, early 19th century. A single-storey, 3-bay rubble building, still in use.

Tollhouse, NS523862, early 19th century. A single-storey, 3-bay ashlar cottage, with a projecting centre bay with side windows.

KILSYTH

Auchincloch Mill, Banknock, NS767788, early 19th century. A 2-

storey rubble building, on an L plan, with corrugated-iron additions. At the rear is a wood and iron, high-breast bucket wheel, about 3ft wide by 20ft diameter (0·91 by 6·10m). Now out of use. The wheel was fed from a mill dam, now silted, which also supplied a threshing mill, fragments of which survive.

Craigmarloch Paper Mill, NS738780, late 19th century, converted to this form 1936. A 1- and 2-storey brick building, now white-washed, containing a small board mill and ancillary machinery, and the ruins of a 2-storey brick block with a drying tower and square-section chimney.

Garrel Mill, NS720783, dated 1700 and 1774. A 2-storey and attic, 2-bay building, with 2 segmental-arched cart entries. Now gutted, and used as a builder's store. At the entrance to the adjoining yard is the stone weight of a cheese press. The mill house range opposite incorporates a granary, and dates in part from the 17th century.

KIPPEN

Smithies, Arnprior, NS613949 and 610947, early 19th century. A single-storey, 3-bay rubble building, with a cottage adjoining. Still in use. At the west end of the village is a neat detached single-storey building on an L plan, now part of a garage.

Cardross Bridge, NS598972, built 1872. A 3-span rubble bridge, with segmental arches and triangular cutwaters.

LARBERT

Carron Ironworks, NS880824, founded 1759. A large complex of buildings of various dates. Most of the older buildings and equipment have been demolished, but the main office block, a long 2-storey and attic range, built 1876, is still in use. On the other side of the road from the offices can be seen part of the canal which linked the works to the river Carron. One of the most interesting survivals is the water-supply system, with a long lade from the river Carron at NS856820 to reservoirs just west of the works. See R. H. Campbell, *Carron Company*, Edinburgh, 1961.

Mill, NS861819, early to mid 19th century. A neat 2-storey, 3-bay mill, with a kiln at one end. The front is of coursed rubble, the other walls of random rubble. Now modernized internally and extended.

Larbert Viaduct, NS859820, opened 1848 by the Scottish Central Railway. A 23-span viaduct, with dressed-stone arch rings and coursed-rubble spandrels and piers. The arches are strengthened by old rails.

LOGIE

BRIDGE OF ALLAN

Inverallan Mill, NS788977, 18th century. A 2-storey and attic rubble building on an L plan, with a peinded-roof kiln. The gables are crow-stepped, and surmounted by crosses. There is an 8-spoke, low-breast, wood and iron wheel 3ft 9½in wide by 14ft 9in diameter (1·15 by 4·50m). Converted to a shop, retaining 2 of the 3 pairs of stones.

Paper mill, NS787979, early 19th century. A large 1-storey and attic building on an L plan, now harled and used as a store. A 2-storey block of houses nearby was probably built in connection with the mill.

Smithy, NS788975, early 19th century. A single-storey, 6-bay rubble building with a roof-ridge ventilator, still in use.

Workers' housing, NS788974, mid 19th century. Four blocks of 2-storey rubble houses, with external stairs and open balconies giving access to the upper floors. The blocks are arranged in 2 rows, with the stairs facing each other, and wash and ashbin houses between the rows.

Bridge Mill, Causewayhead, NS798947, built c 1840. A 3-storey and 2 attic, 4-by-7-bay rubble building, now occupied as a garage.

Forthvale Mills, Causewayhead, NS799948, built in the 1860s by John Todd, woollen manufacturer, and subsequently extended. A complex of 1- and 2-storey brick buildings, of which the oldest appears to be a 6-by-7-bay block of weaving sheds. Since c 1900 a rubber factory.

Horse-gin house, Craigdownings, NS771981, early 19th century. A hexagonal rubble building, with a pantiled roof, beginning to decay. Inside, the central wooden post of the gin survives.

MUIRAVONSIDE

Avonbank Viaduct, NS967785, built c 1847 for the Slamannan & Borrowstounness Joint Railway. A 6-span masonry viaduct, with segmental arches, each of 50ft (15·24m) span.

Myrehead Windmill, NS965775, late 18th or early 19th century. A slender circular tower with a tapering central section, rubble-built.

Viaduct, Westfield, NS934727, built c 1850 for the Monkland Railways Co. A 16-span masonry viaduct, with 12 main spans, and a pair of smaller approach spans at each end, all semicircular. The main spans are strengthened with old rails. Now disused.

ST NINIANS

Royal George Mill, Bannockburn, NS810904, built c 1822. A 3-storey, attic and basement, 9-bay rubble building, part now used as a Masonic Lodge. The street entrance is at second-floor level, and has been modernized. The roof is now asbestos-tiled.

Bridge, Bannockburn, NS808904, built 1516, widened 1781. A small segmental-arched bridge, with dressed-stone arch ring, and part dressed-stone, part rubble spandrels.

Cambusbarron Limekilns, NS770930, built c 1850. An unusually long range of 6 limekilns, of which 4 are circular in plan, 3-draw, and the other 2 are oval in plan, 4-draw. Of the 15 draw arches, 10 give direct access to drawholes, the others are the entrances to tunnels from which pairs of draw arches open. Disused since 1909. There is a nearby mine at NS774927.

Carron Bridge, NS741835, built 1695, rebuilt 1715 and 1907. A 2-span bridge, with arches of unequal size, both with dressed-stone arch rings and rubble spandrels and wing walls. There are massive triangular cutwaters.

Bridge, Chartershall, NS793903, built 1696, rebuilt 1847. A small single-segmental rubble arch.

Corn mill, Chartershall, NS789901, late 18th to early 19th century. A small 1-storey and attic rubble building, on an L plan. Now gutted and used as a store.

Nailers' Cottages, Chartershall, NS793903, built 1782 and later. Two single-storey rubble cottages. One has a single-storey rubble building at the rear, with a chimney.

Craigforth Mill, NS779995. A 2-storey and attic rubble building on a rectangular plan, with a corrugated-iron roof. Now gutted and disused. A datestone of 1693 has been overcut with the date 1783, a likely date of the present structure. There are 2 small segmental wheel arches.

Sawmill, Cultenhove, NS785899, early 19th century. Two single-storey rubble buildings, at right angles, with the site of a waterwheel, formerly a sawmill. Nearby is a 2-storey and attic building of similar construction, also with a wheelpit, which was probably a threshing mill or farm corn mill.

Old Drip Bridge, NS770956, early 18th century. A handsome 5-span rubble bridge, with segmental arches increasing in size to the centre. There are triangular cutwaters extended up to form semi-hexagonal pedestrian refuges.

Hayford Mills, NS776928, founded *c* 1860 by Messrs Smith (plate 64). A very interesting complex of buildings, mainly red and white brick. The main block is 5 storeys high, 6-by-25-bay, and there is a striking 3-storey, 6-by-12-bay building with round-headed windows in the top floor, segmental-headed in the second floor, and flat-headed on the ground floor. There is a key-pattern motif below the dentilated cornice. The other sizeable structure is 2-storey, 2-by-24-bay, with round-headed windows in the upper floor. The complex is completed by a range of single-storey rubble weaving sheds and some minor ancillary buildings. There is a tall circular-section brick chimney. Now warehouses.

Horse-gin house, Hayford, NS774932, early 19th century. A circular rubble structure, with slate roof.

Mill, Howietoun, NS786883, 18th century. A long disused 1- and 2-storey rubble building, still recognizable as a mill. The 1-storey part was for a time a smithy.

Threshing mill, Milnholm, NS784877, mid 19th century (plate 65). A 2-storey rubble building, part of an L-plan steading range, with

64   Part of Hayford Mills.

stone steps to the first floor. Formerly housed a threshing mill. The Whitelaw-type reaction turbine which drove the mill is still in working order, being supplied with water by a cast-iron pipe from a large dam.

Milton Mill, St Ninians, NS802900, mid 19th century. A 2-storey and attic rubble building, with an internal breast wheel, 4ft 8in wide by 16ft diameter (1·42 by 4·88m), driving 3 pairs of stones.

Kerse Mill, NS813925, dated 1672, and 1754, rebuilt 1865. A complex block of 2- and 3-storey rubble buildings, some with pantiled roofs with a kiln at one end of the main range. Now gutted and falling into decay.

Weavers' cottages, Torbrex, NS788919, 18th to early 19th century. Several ranges of single-storey rubble cottages, mostly much altered, some with the distinctive double window.

Craigend Limekilns, NS762906, early 19th century. A range of three 3-draw limekilns, with the side draw holes approached by tunnels from the face of the range. Becoming ruinous.

Murrayshall Limekilns, NS774909, early 19th century. A long

65   Whitelaw-type turbine, Threshing Mill, Milnholm.

range of three 3-draw limekilns of similar construction to those at NS762906.

STIRLING

New Bridge, NS797944, built 1831, engineer ROBERT STEVENSON. A 5-span bridge, of rustic ashlar construction, with segmental arches and rounded cutwaters. The courses of the spandrels follow the lines of the voussoirs.

Old Bridge, NS797945, 15th or late 16th century, strengthened 1912–20. A particularly fine 4-span bridge, with semicircular arches and triangular cutwaters. The bases of the piers are now protected by massive rubble. The arch rings are ashlar, as is some of the masonry in the spandrels. Now a Guardianship Ancient Monument, and used as a footbridge only.

Stirling Station, NS798936, rebuilt 1912 by the Caledonian Railway, architect JAMES MILLER. A 9-platform, through and terminal station, with 2-island platforms, 1 with 2 bays at each end. The main offices are on the principal down platform, in a single-storey ashlar building with 3 crow-stepped gables. Inside this is a circular booking office with radial steel roof trusses, forming a roughly circular circulating area. Access to the main island platform is by a covered footbridge, and to the subsidiary island by an open footbridge. The main island building is a substantial stone structure, with extensive awnings, and the smaller island has wooden shelters.

Cotton mill, NS805939, late 18th to early 19th century. A 2-storey and attic, 10-bay rubble building, apparently cut down from a taller building. Now in multiple occupation.

Grain store, NS802928, late 19th century. A 3-storey and attic, 3-by-6-bay, red-and-yellow-brick building with 2 covered hoists on each side. The interior is steel-framed.

STRATHBLANE

Workers' housing, Blanefield, NS555796, early 19th century. Two 2-storey ranges of houses, forming an L, with external open stairs, and a single-storey range, all harled. Probably built in connection with the nearby (now demolished) printworks.

West Lothian

West Lothian owes its industrial importance mainly to its mineral resources. Apart from coal, iron and fireclay, it contained major oil-shale deposits which were the basis for a significant industry. Bo'ness, its only port, had sporadic importance as a manufacturing and trading centre. The main routes by canal, road and rail between Edinburgh and Glasgow pass through the county.

Edinburgh & Glasgow Union Canal, NT105706–NS967758, built 1818–22, engineer HUGH BAIRD. The West Lothian section of this canal begins on the Almond Aqueduct, a 5-span structure (see plate 11), and ends on the Avon Aqueduct, with 12 spans, the longest and tallest Scottish canal aqueduct. There are numerous overbridges of the standard segmental-arched type (plate 66), 1 at NT071765 being unusually ornamental. At NT049768, NT012770, NT006770 and NS992762, there are small single-arched aqueducts. Interesting features are the maintenance depot at Powflats (NT083712), where there are 2 old barges, and a range of 2-storey canal stables at Woodcockdale (NS975759).

Shale bings The most spectacular remains of the once important Scottish shale-oil industry are in this county, with particularly large bings at Addiewell (NT005628), Broxburn (NT0873), Pumpherston (NT0769), and Winchburgh (NT097747), all the flat-topped type, and, at West Calder (NT010640), conical. These pinkish heaps of spent shale, left after distillation of oil, are prominent landmarks, but are being eroded as a result of their value as bottoming for roadbuilding. No substantial remains of retorts or refineries survive.

BATHGATE

Atlas & Etna Brickworks, Bathville, NS944680, late 19th century. A large group of Hoffman kilns, with unusually tall chimneys. Some of the kilns have rounded ends.

Ballencrieff Limekilns, Bathgate, NS978702. An unusual range, with a 2-draw kiln between 2 single-draw kilns, served by 2 draw arches. Maintained in good condition in the garden of a private house.

BO'NESS & CARRIDEN

Pump, Blackness, NT052800, installed 1875. An elegant classical hand-pump, given by Alexander McLeod to the inhabitants of Blackness.

BO'NESS

Bo'ness Harbour, NT000819, opened after rebuilding 1881. A roughly rectangular wet dock, protected by a timber west pier. Disused and decaying.

Dock foundry, NT001817, founded 1900 by Stewart and Moir. A rectangular complex, with some older buildings. The single cupola appears to be the original, with solid bottom and uncased brick top.

Kinniel House, NS983806. Here James Watt carried out some of the development of his steam engine. The workshop he used is now a roofless ruin, but beside it is the cylinder of an engine used to drain the Schoolyard Pit, Bo'ness, preserved in Watt's memory.

New Grange Foundry, NT004815, founded 1856 by A. Ballantine & Sons. Some mid 19th-century, 1- and 2-storey buildings survive,

66   Union Canal at Ratho.

though the red-brick offices and pattern shop have recently been harled.

Warehouse, Scotland's Close, NS998817, built 1779 (plate 67). A 4-storey, 5-by-3-bay rubble block, with a stair tower on the west side, and a segmental-arched doorway on the south side. The interior has been reconstructed with hollow-tile floors on cast-iron columns.

Windmill stump, Bridgeness, NT013815, built 1750. A circular tower, modified by the addition of a corbelled brick parapet and an external circular staircase. Reputedly used for mine drainage. Now disused.

DALMENY

Dalmeny Station, NT139779, opened 1890 by the Forth Bridge Railway. A 2-platform through station, with wooden buildings with awnings supported on cast-iron columns. The stone offices of the bridge company are nearby.

Forth Railway Bridge, NT1379, built 1882–90, engineers SIR JOHN FOWLER and BENJAMIN BAKER. Probably best-known bridge in Scot-

67 Warehouse, Scotland's Close, Bo'ness.

land, with its 3 double cantilevers, and dramatically high approach spans. Its total length is 8,295ft 9½in (2,528·6m) and the 2 main spans are each 1,700ft long (518·2m).

Harbour, Queensferry, NT120788, rebuilt 1809–18, engineer JOHN RENNIE. A narrow rectangular basin formed by an L plan and a straight pier, both rubble-built.

Ferry pier, Queensferry, NT137784, built c 1812, engineer JOHN RENNIE. A ramped masonry ferry pier with a central wall. At the landward end is a hexagonal lighthouse.

Workers' housing, Dalmeny, NT140779, probably c 1871. Three blocks of red-brick houses, 1 single storey, the others 2 storey, built for employees of the nearby Dalmeny Shale Oil Works, opened 1871. The large bing of spent shale has been landscaped.

KIRKLISTON

Almond Viaduct, NT113722, opened 1842 by the Edinburgh & Glasgow Railway, engineer JOHN MILLER. A 'stupendous' 36-span masonry viaduct, with segmental arches of 50ft (15·2m) span. The

68   Workers' housing, Winchburgh.

piers and arches were originally hollow, but were filled with concrete in the 1950s to allow higher speeds. The spandrels are also braced with old rails.

Birdsmill Viaduct, NT109713, opened 1849 by the Edinburgh & Bathgate Railway. An 8-span masonry viaduct, with segmental arches.

Breast Mill, NT123737, early 19th century. A 3-storey rubble mill on an L plan, with a pantiled roof, now converted to a dwellinghouse.

Kirkliston Distillery, NT123743, founded late 18th century. A complex group of rubble and brick buildings of various dates, some apparently of mid to late 19th-century construction.

Bridge, NT123738, early 19th century. A 3-span rustic ashlar bridge, with segmental arches and rounded cutwaters.

Winchburgh Village, NT0874, built from 1901 by the Winchburgh Oil Co (plate 68). A group of single-storey, red-brick rows of cottages, mostly 3-roomed but some 2-roomed, perhaps the most complete mining village surviving in Scotland.

LINLITHGOW

Avon Viaduct, NS982770, opened 1842 by the Edinburgh & Glasgow Railway, engineer JOHN MILLER. A very fine 23-arch viaduct, with 20 main segmental spans and 3 approach spans, semicircular arched, at the east end. The viaduct is constructed of dressed stone, and has been strengthened with old rails.

Linlithgow Station, NT004771, opened 1842 by the Edinburgh & Glasgow Railway. A 2-platform through station, with the main offices on the up platform in a 2-storey ashlar building with the platform at first-floor level. This has been extended to the east by a 2-bay structure. An awning, supported on cast-iron columns, has also been added. There is a small wooden shelter on the down platform. The platforms are linked by a stone-vaulted subway.

Mains Maltings, NS989767, mid to late 19th century. A complex consisting of 2 main parts: an older 3-storey block on an L plan with a large pyramidal-roofed kiln, and a 4-storey, 2-by-8-bay building, with a double kiln.

Regent Works, NT006772, built 1900–2, and later by Nobel's Explosives Co Ltd, to make safety fuse. A large complex of brick buildings, 1 with 6 small towers, with a circular-section brick chimney. Now in multiple occupation.

St Magdalene Distillery, NT008771, founded late 18th century by Sebastian Henderson. A group of buildings of various dates; mostly rubble-built, including a 5-storey, 4-by-13-bay block of malting floors with a double kiln and a 3-storey block with a single kiln. **Railway bridge,** NT007771, opened 1842 by the Edinburgh & Glasgow Railway, engineer JOHN MILLER. A handsome skew segmental arch. The arch ring is of dressed stone and the spandrels are rubble.

Wairdlaw Limekilns, NS996730, early 19th century. A remarkably complete range of 2 single-draw kilns, with semicircular arched draw holes. To the north are the undisturbed remains of the quarry and mine. At Craigmailing (NS994721) is a much less complete pair of kilns with a large disused quarry.

TORPHICHEN

Bowdenhill Limekilns, NS977747. A range of 3 single-draw kilns, much overgrown, with 3 clamp kilns nearby.

Wigtonshire

Wigtonshire is almost exclusively agricultural, its few manufacturing industries relating to that base. Its harbours, trading with Ireland, Cumberland and the Isle of Man, are of interest, as is the supporting road system.

KIRKCOLM

Corsewall Point Lighthouse, NW981727, built 1815. An interesting tapering circular-section tower, on a castellated cylindrical base, with 3 projecting string courses. The keepers' houses are 2 storeys high.

KIRKCOWAN

Shennanton Bridge, NX343633, probably late 18th century. A 2-span, segmental-arched rubble bridge, now bypassed and decaying.
Waulk Mill, NX333603, built 1821 by R. W. T. Milroy and enlarged by W. T., 1835. A 2-storey and attic, 8-bay rubble main range, with a corrugated-iron roof. At the rear are single-storey brick weaving sheds, added in the 1880s, with an octagonal red-and-white-brick chimney. Disused and decaying. The nearby Tarf Mills (NX331603) are now completely ruinous, though the octagonal chimney survives, and the remains of a water-turbine installation can be seen.

KIRKINNER

Malzie Smithy, NX371541, late 18th to early 19th century (plate 69). A single-storey, 3-bay rubble building, with corrugated asbestos roof. There is a 6-spoke, low-breast bucket wheel fabricated from steel with galvanised buckets, 1ft 9in wide by 8ft diameter (0·53 by 2·44m), which drove tools and the bellows. The smithy is still used, but the wheel is derelict.
Windmill, Barwhanny, NX411493, late 18th or early 19th century. A small tapering rubble tower, 25ft (7·6m) high, probably designed to power a threshing mill.
Milldriggan Mill, NX421523, on an old site, but rebuilt in the early 19th century by William Routledge. A 3-storey and attic, 8-bay

rubble building on a rectangular plan, with an internal high-breast wheel, 3ft 10in wide by 20ft diameter (1·16 by 6·10m), by J. and R. Wallace, Castle Douglas Foundry.

Smithy, South Clutag, NX377521, early 19th century. A pleasing single-storey, 6-bay building, with 2 rectangular-section stone chimney stacks, now used as a garage.

KIRKMAIDEN

Wyllie's Mill, Drummore, NX136367, mid 19th century. A 3-storey, 4-by-8-bay, cement-rendered brick building, with a 24-spoke suspended all-iron, high-breast wheel, 2ft wide by 8ft diameter (0·61 by 2·44m), at the side. Still in use. Opposite the mill is an older 2-storey, attic and basement, 3-bay grain store.

Harbour, Drummore, NX138368, early 19th century. A natural haven, with a rubble pier with protective wood piles.

Logan Windmill, NX116438, late 17th century (plate 70). An interesting example of a vaulted-tower mill, with a circular rubble tower, now crenellated, and a vaulted chamber projecting to the

69 Malzie Smithy, Kirkinner.

70   Logan Windmill, relieving arch on right.

north. A relieving arch is built into the tower above the vault, which has collapsed at the junction.

Sawmill, Logan, NX116436, probably early 19th century. A 2-storey and basement rubble building on a rectangular plan, with an all-iron, 8-spoke suspended overshot wheel, 4ft wide by 20ft diameter (1·22 by 6·10m), with external gear ring. Gutted internally. Nearby is a 2-storey meal mill, now completely gutted.

Mull of Galloway Lighthouse, NX157303, built 1828. A tall tapering circular rubble tower on a semicircular base, with a corbelled parapet, and a triangular-paned lantern, with a domed top. The keepers' houses are of the usual flat-roofed type, 1 range having rather coarse classical features. The light is now given by a revolving bank of car headlights. Nearby at East Tarbet (NX144309) is a small harbour with a rubble pier, probably used for landing supplies.

Port Logan Harbour, NX094405, built 1818, largely at the expense of Col Andrew McDowall (see plate 12). The remains of a substantial pier of coursed rubble, protecting a natural harbour. The most distinctive feature of the harbour is the fine granite and sandstone lighttower, which is well preserved.

Terally Tile Works, NX120407, opened *c* 1840. Well-preserved double kiln, formerly with 8 vents per kiln, the stump of a square-section chimney, and a rectangular brick building which probably housed the extruding machinery. Nearby are extensive flooded clay-pits. The existing structures are probably 20th century in construction.

MOCHRUM

Bone and meal mills, Elrig, NX323473, late 18th and early 19th centuries. A large group of ruinous rubble buildings.

Port William Harbour, NX337437, built *c* 1800. The quayed mouth of the Killantrae Burn, with a small basin at the landward end. The quaying is on the south side, terminating in a short pier, and the work is executed mainly in coursed rubble. There are some 1- and 2-storey stores on the quay of 19th-century origin, and stone walls and gate-posts at the entrance.

Port William Mill, NX339436, late 18th or early 19th century. A substantial 3-storey rubble building on a T plan, with a kiln in 1 arm of the T and lower wings on the opposite side. Still used as a mill, but now electrified.

Barr Mill, West Barr, NX318462. The roofless remains of a wool-carding and spinning mill, consisting of a 2-storey rubble structure on a rectangular plan. Though marked as early as 1654, the present building is probably late 18th or early 19th century.

NEWTON STEWART

Gas works, NX412652, late 19th century. A beautifully kept horizontal-retort works, with 2 settings of 6, 1 of 7 and 1 of 8 retorts. There are purifiers by D. M. NEILSON & CO, Glasgow (1897), HENRY BALFOUR & CO, Leven (1913 and 1924), and a steam-driven Walker exhauster. Of the 2 holders, the older has a cast-iron tank and 4 cast-iron columns, linked at the top by lattice girders.

OLD LUCE

Bridge of Park, Glenluce, NX192573, late 18th century. A 2-span bridge, with 1 segmental and 1 semicircular arch, both with dressed-stone arch rings and rubble spandrels. There are triangular cut-waters.

Viaduct, Glenluce, NX192573, opened 1861 by the Portpatrick Railway. An 8-span masonry viaduct, with segmental arches. The arch rings and the quoins of the piers are of dressed stone, and the rest rubble, extensively repaired in brick.

Harbour, Stairhaven, NX208537, early 19th century. The much decayed remains of a substantial L-plan rubble pier, with the landward end intact. About 100 yd (90m) east of the harbour is a 2-storey, 3-bay store with a central hoist.

PENNINGHAME

Carty Tile Works, NX431625, 19th century and later. A typical small agricultural tile works, with a single 12-chamber kiln and an L-plan range of drying sheds. There are a square-section brick chimney, and a steel pipe conducting the flue gases to the drying sheds. Nearby are the wood-piled remains of a small early 19th-century quay operated in connection with the works and with local agriculture.

Tollhouse, Low Knockbrex, NX395643, built c 1802. A neat single-storey building on an X plan, with gabled wing facing the carriage-way. At NX353633 is a similar, though somewhat modified structure.

Bridge of Cree and tollhouse, Newton Stewart, NX412657, built 1813, engineer JOHN RENNIE. A 5-span masonry bridge, with flat segmental arches and rounded cutwaters extended up to form semi-hexagonal pedestrian refuges. At the east end is a single-storey toll-house, with a projecting semi-octagonal bay, now a shop.

PORTPATRICK

Killantringan Lighthouse, NW981564, built 1900, engineer D. A. STEVENSON. A slightly tapering circular tower of medium height, with a lantern of normal type. The keepers' houses are, unusually, 2 storeys high, with a neat gabled porch.

Portpatrick Harbour, NW998542, dates in its present form largely from 1820–36, engineer JOHN RENNIE. The harbour was designed to have 2 massive protecting piers, but only the south pier, with a circular brick lighthouse, was completed. Behind the remains of the north pier, and a natural rock barrier, is a rectangular basin, improved 1857–63. An interesting minor feature is a navigation light fixed to an ordinary cast-iron lamp standard on the east side of the harbour.

Tollhouse, NX000543, early 19th century. A single-storey rubble building with a rounded end.

SORBIE

Harbour, Garlieston, NX480462, built in the late 18th century, and rebuilt 1838. A natural haven improved by the construction of a rubble pier and quay with wood-piled face, protected by a breakwater. There are two 2-storey granaries on the pier, and a modern grain mill.

Sorbie Station, NX436475, rebuilt after a fire in 1880 by the Wigtownshire Railway. Now dominated by a recently enlarged creamery, the up platform and its single-storey building still survive.

Smithy, NX437469, early to mid 19th century. A single-storey, 4-bay rubble building, with an asbestos roof. At the back are 3 square brick chimney stacks. No longer in use.

STONEYKIRK

Windmill, NX095522. A short tapering rubble tower. Donnachie suggests that it was the base of a turret post mill, which seems reasonable.

STRANRAER

Gas works, NX061610, early 20th century. A good example of a steel-framed, brick vertical-retort house, now disused. From an earlier phase of operation, a 2-storey, 3-bay house/office block and a small gasholder survive.

Lochans Mill, NX072565, 19th century. A 2-storey, rubble range, with the skeleton of a 6-spoke, wood and iron, high-breast wheel, 4ft 6in wide by 12ft diameter (1·37 by 3·66m), with drive from a gear ring. Probably a threshing mill in its present form, though a meal mill in the 18th century. Now gutted and disused.

Meal mill, NX054612, late 19th and early 20th century. A 3-storey and attic rubble and brick complex, with a castellated brick water-tower.

WHITHORN

Harbour, Isle of Whithorn, NX478363, formed in the 16th century, but substantially rebuilt in 1790 and later. An L-plan pier, of rubble construction, with 1- and 2-storey stores. At the landward end of the pier is a slipway with a wooden single-storey building, formerly a boatbuilding yard.

Brewery, NX447403, possibly 18th century. A 2-storey, 3-bay rubble building, now with a corrugated-iron roof, in poor condition.

Railway Station, NX447409, opened 1877 by the Wigtownshire Railway. The passenger station here has been demolished, but the large 2-storey, 6-bay, cement-rendered goods shed survives.

WIGTOWN

Bladnoch Bridge, NX421542, early 19th century. An attractive 2-span masonry bridge, mainly of dressed-stone construction. The arches are elliptical and the cutwaters triangular.

Bladnoch Distillery, NX421543, founded 1817 by John and Thomas McClelland, and rebuilt 1878. The complex consists of 1-, 2- and 3-storey rubble buildings, with a single kiln, substantially 19th century in construction.

Wigtown Harbour, NX438547, built 1818. A stretch of rubble and wood quay on the river Bladnoch, with a small rectangular basin of similar construction. Now disused.

Tollhouse, NX431548, early 19th century. A neat single-storey rubble building with a rounded end, now disused.

Bibliography

The books mentioned here are all either recent publications or standard works which should be available in larger libraries. The articles included are those which refer to a number of sites listed; more specific articles are alluded to in the gazetteer. Most of the books referred to contain bibliographies.

GENERAL WORKS

Groome, F., *Ordnance Gazetteer of Scotland*, William Mackenzie, London, 2nd edn, 1893.
Third Statistical Account of Scotland, various publishers and editors.

GENERAL INDUSTRIAL ARCHAEOLOGY

Bracegirdle, B., *The Archaeology of the Industrial Revolution*, Heinemann Educational Books, 1973.
Buchanan, R. A., *Industrial Archaeology in Britain*, Penguin Books, 1972.
Butt, J., *Industrial Archaeology of Scotland*, David & Charles, 1967.
Butt, J., Donnachie, Ian L. and Hume, J. R., *Industrial History in Pictures: Scotland*, David & Charles, 1968.
Cossons, N., *The BP Book of Industrial Archaeology*, David & Charles, 1974 (gazetteer somewhat out of date as regards Scotland).
Donnachie, I. L., *The Industrial Archaeology of Galloway*, David & Charles, 1971.
Hume, J. R., *The Industrial Archaeology of Glasgow*, Blackie, 1974.

ARCHITECTURE AND HISTORICAL MONUMENTS

Dunbar, J. G., *The Historic Architecture of Scotland*, B. T. Batsford, 1966.
The Royal Commission on the Ancient and Historical Monuments of Scotland, *Peeblesshire: an Inventory of the Ancient Monuments Vol 2*, HMSO, 1967.
The Royal Commission on the Ancient and Historical Monuments of Scotland, *Stirlingshire: an Inventory of the Ancient Monuments Vol 2*, HMSO, 1963.

BIOGRAPHIES

Boucher, C. T. G., *John Rennie, 1761–1821*, Manchester University Press, 1963.

Bracegirdle, B. and Miles, P. H., *Thomas Telford*, David & Charles, 1973.

Gibb, Sir A., *The Story of Telford*, Alexander MacLehose & Co, 1935.

ECONOMIC BACKGROUND

Campbell, R. H., *Scotland since 1707*, Basil Blackwell, 1965.

Hamilton, H., *The Industrial Revolution in Scotland*, Oxford, 1932, reprinted Frank Cass, 1966.

Lythe, S. G. E. and Butt, J., *An Economic History of Scotland 1100–1939*, Blackie, 1975.

MANUFACTURING, PROCESSING AND EXTRACTIVE INDUSTRIES

Barnard, A., 'The Whisky Distilleries of the United Kingdom', *Harper's Weekly Gazette*, London 1887, reprinted David & Charles, 1969.

Donnachie, I. L. and Stewart, N. K., 'Scottish Windmills: an Outline Inventory', *Proceedings of the Society of Antiquaries in Scotland (PSAS)*, 1964–6, *98*, 276–9.

Jespersen, A., 'Watermills on the River Eden', *PSAS*, 1963–4, *97*.

Lenman, B., Lythe, C. and Gauldie, E., *Dundee and its Textile Industry, 1850–1914*, Abertay Historical Society, Dundee, 1969.

McDowall, R. J. S., *The Whiskies of Scotland*, John Murray, 2nd edn, 1971.

Shorter, A. H., *Paper Making in the British Isles*, David & Charles, 1971.

Skinner, B. C., *The Lime Industry in the Lothians*, University of Edinburgh, 1969.

Thomson, A. G., *The Paper Industry in Scotland*, Scottish Academic Press, 1975.

TRANSPORT: *Canals*

Cameron, A. D., *The Caledonian Canal*, Terence Dalton Ltd, Lavenham, 1972.

Graham, A., 'Two Canals in Aberdeenshire', *PSAS*, 1967–8, *100*, 170.

Lindsay, J., *The Canals of Scotland*, David & Charles, 1968.

TRANSPORT: *Harbours*
Graham, A., 'Archaeological Notes on some Harbours in Eastern Scotland', *PSAS*, 1968–9, *101*, 200.
Lenman, B., *From Esk to Tweed*, Blackie, 1975.

TRANSPORT: *Roads and Bridges*
British Bridges, Public Works, Road and Transport Congress, 1933.
Haldane, A. R. B., *New Ways Through the Glens*, Nelson, 1962.
Stephen, W. M., 'Tollhouses of the Greater Fife Area', *Industrial Archaeology*, 1967, *4*, 248.

TRANSPORT: *Street Tramways*
Hunter, D. L. G., *Edinburgh's Transport*, The Advertiser Press, Huddersfield, 1964.

TRANSPORT: *Wagonways and Railways*
Baxter, B., *Stone Blocks and Iron Rails*, David & Charles, 1966.
Ellis, C. H., *The North British Railway*, Ian Allan, 1955.
Nock, O. S., *The Caledonian Railway*, Ian Allan, 1961.
Nock, O. S., *The Highland Railway*, Ian Allan, 1965.
The Stephenson Locomotive Society, *The Glasgow and South Western Railway*, 1950.
The Stephenson Locomotive Society, *The Highland Railway Company and its Constituents and successors, 1855–1955*, 1955.
Thomas, J., *The Callander and Oban Railway*, David & Charles, 1968.
Thomas, J., *The North British Railway, Vol 1*, David & Charles, 1969.
Thomas, J., *A Regional History of the Railways of Great Britain: Vol 6 Scotland the Lowland and the Borders*, David & Charles, 1971.
Thomas, J., *The West Highland Railway*, David & Charles, 1965.
Vallance, H. A., *The Great North of Scotland Railway*, David & Charles and Macdonald, 1965.
Vallance, H. A., *The Highland Railway*, David & Charles and Macdonald, 2nd edn, 1963.
Whishaw, F., *The Railways of Great Britain and Ireland*, London, 1842, reprinted David & Charles, 1969.

Index of Place Names

General Index